Chronicles from the Environmental Justice Frontline

This book provides a rare look into the environmental justice movement as it plays out in four landmark struggles at the turn of the twenty-first century. Roberts and Toffolon-Weiss chronicle the stories of everyday people who decide to battle what they perceive as injustice when their minority neighborhoods are disproportionately threatened by industrial pollution. The four cases detailed here are epic struggles: conflicts between U.S. environmental and civil rights agencies over the siting of a chemical plant and a nuclear facility in ex-slave communities; a class-action lawsuit by 300 Cajun and Houma Indian residents over a huge oilfield waste dump built next to their tiny town; and an uphill political and legal battle for relocation by a middle-class African-American neighborhood built with federal assistance atop a reclaimed landfill.

The authors place these struggles into the historical context of inequality and race relations in the U.S. South and apply social science theory to reveal how situations of environmental injustice are created, how they are resolved, and what accounts for their success or failure. While the cases featured here take place in Louisiana, America's "pollution haven" and the "frontline" in the battle over environmental justice, a major portion of these battles are fought in Washington, D.C. These cases have set precedents and created quandries for government agencies as they handle conflicts occurring across the nation. The struggles have left behind subtle and profound changes in the individuals, firms, and communities involved.

Chronicles from the Environmental Justice Frontline is intended for general readers, policymakers, businesspeople, and scholars wishing to learn about these landmark cases and about environmental justice politics more broadly. It will also benefit environmental and social justice activists and students in environmental studies, law, planning, administration, communications, business ethics, sociology, geography, and political science.

J. Timmons Roberts is Professor of Sociology and Director of the Mellon Foundation Program in Environmental Studies at The College of William and Mary. Until mid-2001 he was Associate Professor of Sociology and Latin American Studies at Tulane University, where he served as Director of the undergraduate Environmental Studies Program and conducted research for this book. He co-edited *From Modernization to Globalization: Perspectives on Development and Social Change* (2000), and he is completing a book on environmental struggles in Latin America. His articles have appeared in such journals as *Social Problems, World Development, Sociological Inquiry,* and *Economic Development and Cultural Change.*

Melissa M. Toffolon-Weiss is a Visiting Assistant Professor of Sociology at the University of Alaska, Anchorage. She has published in the journals *Evaluation Review* and *Organization and Environment.* She recently completed her Ph.D. at Tulane University, examining corporate and social movement strategies and shifts in community power relations in two major environmental justice struggles involving the Shintech Corporation.

Chronicles

FROM THE

Environmental
Justice Frontline

J. Timmons Roberts
The College of William and Mary

Melissa M. Toffolon-Weiss
University of Alaska, Anchorage

CAMBRIDGE
UNIVERSITY PRESS

PUBLISHED BY THE PRESS SYNDICATE OF THE UNIVERSITY OF CAMBRIDGE
The Pitt Building, Trumpington Street, Cambridge, United Kingdom

CAMBRIDGE UNIVERSITY PRESS
The Edinburgh Building, Cambridge CB2 2RU, UK
40 West 20th Street, New York, NY 10011-4211, USA
10 Stamford Road, Oakleigh, VIC 3166, Australia
Ruiz de Alarcón 13, 28014 Madrid, Spain
Dock House, The Waterfront, Cape Town 8001, South Africa

http://www.cambridge.org

First published 2001

Printed in the United States of America

Typeface Fairfield 10.5/13   *System* QuarkXPress 4.04 [AG]

A catalog record for this book is available from the British Library.

Library of Congress Cataloging in Publication Data
Roberts, J. Timmons.
Chronicles from the environmental justice frontline / J. Timmons Roberts,
Melissa M. Toffolon-Weiss.
p. cm.
Includes bibliographical references and index.
ISBN 0-521-66062-9 – ISBN 0-521-66900-6 (pb.)
1. Environmental justice – Louisiana – case studies. 2. Environmental
policy – Louisiana – Case studies. I. Toffolon-Weiss, Melissa M. II. Title.
GE185.L8R63 2001
363.7'056'09763–dc21   00-067450

ISBN 0 521 66062 9 hardback
ISBN 0 521 66900 6 paperback

Contents

v

CONTENTS

Preface

Chronicles from the Environmental Justice Frontline examines how local movements have succeeded and failed in Louisiana – a state that has been called a "pollution haven": a place where companies come to exploit natural resources, cheap energy, nonunion labor, tax breaks, and lax environmental enforcement. We believe that the Louisiana cases chronicled in this book are particularly illustrative of processes at work *everywhere;* and the stakes in these cases were enormous and national. These cases have pushed politicians and policy at the Environmental Protection Agency, the Nuclear Regulatory Commission, the U.S. Commission on Civil Rights, the Department of Energy, and the Agency for Toxic Substances and Disease Registry. The combatants have brought their battles to these agencies in Washington, D.C., and to the UN Commission on Human Rights in Geneva, Switzerland.

The cause of protecting these tiny Louisiana communities has been taken up by rock stars, celebrities, politicians, international and national environmental organizations, and networks of environmental justice activists and lawyers. Their efforts have been resisted by powerful business lobbying groups in Washington and Baton Rouge, chambers of commerce across the state and nation, probusiness politicians, and highly placed government agency leaders. The cases are illuminating partly because so much of the coordination between business and government in advancing economic development over the complaints of citizens groups is publicly expressed in Louisiana. To give some idea of the imbalance between corporations and civil society in the state, legislative sessions have more than one hundred registered professional lobbyists working for polluting firms, whereas three part-time lobbyists and a dozen volunteers work for the cause of environmental justice.

How can any victories be expected in this context? Surprisingly in a state known for its disempowered citizens, Louisiana's environmental coalition has been described as "exemplary" by Washington specialists.

The shifting coalitions of labor, civil rights, and mainstream environmental groups have fought some epic battles over polluting facilities and legislation and have accumulated several landmark victories cited nationally as precedent setting. Some say it is because there are so many truly devastating environmental disasters occurring here; others see the roots in organizations born of civil rights and labor battles. Both are probably correct.

In this bleak setting, new forms of grassroots organizing and a landmark 1994 Executive Order by then-president Clinton on environmental justice have provided environmentalists and communities with leverage to sometimes tip the balance of power. That order required every department of the federal government to "make achieving environmental justice part of its mission." Still, exactly what environmental justice *means* for this executive order remains contested. Former Environmental Protection Agency head Carol Browner and her staff were charged with leading the effort; the struggles described in this book persistently forced her and the EPA to decide if they constitute cases of environmental injustice. The EPA's position has slowly been emerging, pushed in part by the need for clarification in the LES and Shintech cases, described in Chapters 4 and 5. The agency's retreat under pressure from business and state governments is chronicled in Chapter 7, leading to the official June 2000 release of its *Guidance* on how to proceed in cases where environmental injustice is charged under Title VI of the Civil Rights Act.

The examination of the cases in this book allows a test of the arguments put forward by Christopher H. Foreman, Jr., in a Brookings Institution book entitled *The Promise and Peril of Environmental Justice*. Foreman portrays the environmental justice movement as irrational and misguided because it draws the attention of minorities and the poor away from important community issues like crime, drugs, and lifestyle habits that are undermining their health (e.g., smoking, drinking, or eating poorly). We acknowledge that there are problems in the movement while we attempt to understand and reveal the logic of the communities facing hazards and how they have driven real, national change in environmental protection. One of our central goals is to uncover the deciding elements that led to a community's choice of strategies and what determined their level of success or failure. And we attempt to chronicle some of the impacts the battle itself has had on the individuals who fought it and on their communities.

This volume is written for general lay readers, policymakers, and scholars wishing to get quickly up to speed on these cases and on environmental justice politics more broadly. It is also intended for environmental and social justice activists and for students in environmental studies, planning/administration, communications, sociology, geography, and political science. Our goal therefore has been to make the case studies as engaging as possible, keeping the academic jargon to a minimum while addressing some important broader issues in the book's introduction and conclusion. We hope that the book will be useful as a companion to core texts in undergraduate or graduate courses on environmental issues, including environmental communications, community planning, environmental sociology, environmental politics, environmental law, and courses on social movements, race and ethnicity, or regional studies.

The four case study chapters include recent and current struggles of chemical plants, uranium processors, landfills, and oilfield waste dumps. Chapters 1 and 2 place these cases into larger contexts of the national struggle over environmental justice, national and state environmental politics, the growing discussion of "contaminated communities," and changes in the environmental movement in the new millennium. Chapter 2 attempts to provide a brief history of race and development in Louisiana and of how its toxics and environmental justice movements have evolved. The backlash to these cases is chronicled and discussed in Chapter 7.

We acknowledge the limitations of this work, but we propose that our chronicling of these cases provides a unique window into what are among the most dynamic popular struggles at the turn of the millennium. We write in the old tradition of scholar-activists, as insiders in communication with communities and assisting them as we can. However we must acknowledge the important ways in which we are outsiders, as academics and as white, European-origin Americans whose ancestors were not brought here in chains and kept down by laws and practices for centuries. Certainly our perspective is colored by the experience we have been afforded due to the color of our skin. We acknowledge the difficulty of writing across ethnic and racial lines in this polarized nation, but we optimistically believe in the value of efforts at understanding and the critical need for mutual support. We also are outsiders because we are middle class and we have only lived in Louisiana a decade, our fathers did not work in manufacturing plants or cutting sugar cane, and we have not had to live in close proximity to toxic facilities. So our goal here has been to give voice to those who are fighting these battles as best we can: We have made a special effort to include their own words. They are the only ones who can truly understand and tell what has happened to them. To advance, social sciences need insider and outsider perspectives; sometimes astute outsiders provide new directions for thought and action on long-standing problems.

As social scientists with an interest in racial justice, social movements, and environmental issues, we have been collecting data for this book for the past eight years. We have conducted numerous interviews with activists, industry representatives, and government officials on each case and many others we couldn't fit here. We have attended numerous meetings, protest events, and hearings as participant observers. We have assembled more than seven hundred newspaper and magazine accounts on these local toxic struggles, the industries they battle, and the environmental justice movement in general. In these cases, these are some of the only written records. We have collected hundreds of social movement organization pamphlets and reports, company materials, and government documents. We have sought to publicize and clarify the important and sometimes bewildering human struggles we saw around us. No social science research is value-free, and we have been taught to be skeptical of anyone who claims theirs is. We admit some bias in that we are now convinced there is a problem of unequal burden of pollution by race and class, but we have sought to present a complete portrayal of the battles we chronicle. We believe our work's validity is as strong as the care with which it was researched and composed.

We would like to thank the dozens of people whose generous help made this book possible. None but the authors themselves are responsible for the accuracy of the material in this book. Amanda Leiker conducted tireless background participant research on the Agriculture Street Landfill case for two years and organized a mountain of clippings, pamphets, and memos. Seth Willey conducted the background research and assisted in interviewing on the LES case. The Environmental Studies program and the Center for Bioenvironmental Research at Tulane (directed by John McLachlan) provided summer funding for both of them, and the Department of Sociology (chaired by Joel Devine) provided office space during the summer of 1999. Doctoral student Nicole Youngman did mountainous editorial work, including preparing the bibiography, the footnotes, and editing the document. Tulane's Dean of Liberal Arts and Sciences provided financial support for some of that final work. We would like to thank Tom Rudel, David Pellow, Barbara Vincent, Mike Meuser, Jerry Speir, Jim Elliot, and especially Willie Fontenot for thoughtful comments on earlier drafts of the manuscript.

Numerous universities, government agencies, businesses, organizations, and individuals provided us with interviews and access to their files, and we sincerely want to thank them all. Among them were the Louisiana Chemical Association, the Louisiana Department of Environmental Quality, Citizens Against Nuclear Trash, Earthjustice Legal Defense Fund, Senator J. Bennett Johnston, the Tulane Environmental Law Clinic, St. James Citizens for Jobs and the Environment, St. James Citizens Coalition, PROTEST, Save Our Selves, Inc., Shintech Louisiana LLC, the Labor Neighbor project of the PACE Union, Louisiana Communities United, AWARE, Sierra Club Delta Chapter, the Louisiana Office of Public Health, the Louisiana Environmental Action Network, the State of Louisiana Department of Justice, the Concerned Citizens of the Agriculture Street Landfill, and many others listed in the notes and bibliography and several who preferred to remain anonymous.

At Cambridge University Press we would like to thank Mary Child, Mike Green, Cathy Felgar, Ernie Haim, Wendy Bolton, and the staff of Agnew's, Inc. We would like to express our deep gratitude to our families for their unwavering support and encouragement. Many thanks to Jeffrey Weiss for always being there for support and to discuss and review chapter drafts. Holly Flood and Jim and Gann Roberts helped make this work possible in many ways. Quinn, we wish you health and joy.

Finally, we believe that people on all sides of this issue agree with the goals of the movement: to improve human health and environmental conditions for all people. We know that the disagreement is over how to get there. We humbly hope that these chronicles and the insights they afford can provide some measure of understanding and progress in that direction.

I

Environmental Justice Struggles in Perspective

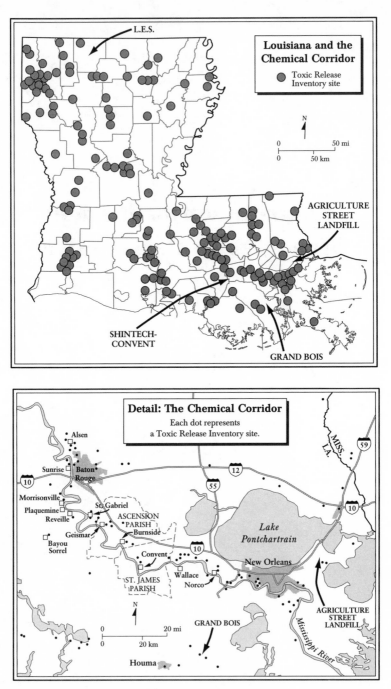

Top: Map: Louisiana and the four case studies.

Bottom: Map: detail map of the Chemical Corridor with conflicts mentioned in Chapters 1 and 2.

SILENT BATTLEFIELDS IN A FRAGILE LANDSCAPE

Driving along Interstate 10 from east New Orleans to Baton Rouge, the traveler first climbs steeply over the Industrial Canal between the Mississippi River and the Intracoastal Waterway and then drops just as precipitously, rumbling past dingy railroads and industrial land before passing signs for the French Quarter. The Industrial Canal has barges backed up waiting their turn to go through a century-old shipping lock. Today it is the site of a bitter struggle between the U.S. Army Corps of Engineers who want to spend twelve years expanding the lock and residents of the neighborhood who fear it would release toxics from contaminated soils, block traffic, and rattle their homes for over a decade. The predominantly African-American neighborhood claims that choosing to expand the lock rather than siting it in wetlands to the south constitutes environmental racism and has sued the Corps and placed a restraining order to prevent the beginning of the project.[1]

Just past the Canal, off to the left of the highway, is the Agriculture Street Landfill neighborhood, where a middle-class black subdivision was built directly on top of the old city dump in the late 1970s with Federal Housing Authority money. Noxious odors, illnesses, and sinking houses alerted neighbors to the risk, and the Environmental Protection Agency (EPA) put the site on the Superfund "National Priority List" for cleanup in 1994 after conducting soil tests that uncovered 150 toxins in the dirt. They are afraid of toxic materials found in their yards atop the landfill, and the homes they've been paying on their entire adult lives are now nearly worthless. In protests, vigils, and trips to Washington and the UN Commission on Civil Rights in Geneva, Switzerland, the neighbors have clamored for the EPA to move them out, but they have consistently been denied the relocation they seek. Their fear and endless frustration in gaining relocation from the EPA is analyzed in Chapter 6.

Just past this point, billowing flames engulfed the Interstate itself on September 9, 1987, as a CSX railway car holding butadiene, a petroleum byproduct, exploded just under the raised expressway. Almost two hundred city blocks of residents were evacuated in the middle of the night.[2] Many people reported breathing difficulty, rashes, and other problems; others claimed damage to their homes and mental anguish. This community took a private, class action approach with a team of lawyers, including a few locally famous trial lawyers. Their lawsuit focused on psychological stress and illnesses, as residents struggled to rebuild their lives after the explosion. Still, no one suffered permanent physical illness. Citing the carelessness of the rail and tank car companies in endangering people's lives, the jury of the original suit levied one of the world's largest penalties on the five defendant companies, $3.4 billion. Upon appeal, the amount was reduced to less than $1 billion, and several of the firms negotiated lower settlements. The legal battle of suits, appeals, motions, and countermotions has waged for thirteen years, and residents have yet to receive any compensation.

Then, on the left, skyscrapers loom for a moment with the names of internationally owned hotels and oil companies in the background; three-story brick buildings that look like army barracks – the Iberville public housing project – are nearer the road. Beautiful but falling-down old Creole cottages and storefronts stand just feet from the road on the right, the remains of the Treme neighborhood. This highway was originally planned to pass straight through the heart of the French Quarter, between historic Jackson Square and the Mississippi River it fronted.[3] In a struggle noted by many locally as the beginning of the environmental movement, preservationists fought to save the French Quarter. By rerouting the highway they were among the first in the nation able to force an interstate highway to change. But in winning, the white preservationists dealt a devastating blow to oak-lined North Claiborne Avenue and Treme, an historic Creole neighborhood, long the cultural and business centers of New Orleans' black community.[4] The expressway helped destroy the famed Storyville district – the city's zone for legalized prostitution from 1897 to 1917 – said to be the birthplace of Jazz and one of the most racially integrated places in the South during the Jim Crow era.[5] The courtesy of public hearings about the highway was never given to Treme, nor were studies of the impact on the black neighborhoods ever conducted.[6]

Moving through Gert Town, a working-class black neighborhood, the I-10 passes a few blocks from the old Thompson-Hayward Chemical Company, where Agent Orange defoliant for use against the Viet Cong and other toxic pesticides were carelessly mixed in open vats in the 1960s and 1970s. The soil under the asphalt around the boarded-up plant is so toxic that no dump in the country could accept it. No signs mark the monitoring wells around the boarded-up factory, put on EPA's Superfund list in 1994. Residents sued the current Dutch firm that owns the plant; lawyers received the bulk of the out-of-court settlement, and locals are infighting about how to spend a small community trust fund that was left over.

Crossing a levee and a wide drainage canal into the suburbs of Metairie and Kenner, one might spot on one of the unpretentious brick square bungalows a Confederate flag, or a "Duke Country" sign, for the ex–Ku Klux Klan leader and perennial political candidate David Duke, who represented this district in the legislature. Just past the bungalows and suburban apartment buildings that stretch nearly to the airport is a levee, where suddenly the road lifts off the earth to a raised bridge that goes on for miles, over cypress and willow swamps and open marshes bordering Lake Pontchartrain. What drivers don't see here is an exit for the 50-mile outer loop "Dixie Expressway," a huge project blocked by environmentalists.[7]

The next thirty miles are punctuated by little more than a few pickup trucks pulled over on the side of the highway, where hunters and fishers have ducked into the thick willows by foot or flatboat. A watchful passenger might notice dozens of egrets and ducks, while motor boaters fish right under the elevated highway. Only driving the road at night do most people notice the flares from a distant refinery. Chemical plant construction along the Mississippi River took off in the 1930s when it was dredged to make Baton Rouge reachable by ocean-going ships. There are now over one hundred petrochemical plants along the river between the two cities, but from the highway, one sees only one refinery, the flares of the Shell-Motiva NORCO plant next to the Bonne Carre Spillway. On the fenceline of the Shell Chemical plant next door, the Black Diamond community, descendents of ex-slaves, is demanding that Shell pay for their relocation, saying they're too close to the chemical plant that has steadily grown larger and closer since the 1950s.

Much of the air, land, and bayous around these facilities are laced with heavy metals and other toxic chemicals that have been leaked and dumped over the decades. Some plants still simply pump millions of

5

pounds of toxics deep into the earth's crust and hope it doesn't resurface into the drinking water.[8] Many use the mighty Mississippi as their source for water and their sewer, and since the river here contains the effluent of a million square miles over half of a continent, it is difficult for EPA officials and environmentalists to pin particular spills on individual firms. One commentator in a *National Geographic* special issue on water called the river a "chemical soup," saying, "This river is our drinking water here in New Orleans. . . . It's just as if you put your child's mouth up against the tailpipe of a car."[9]

About halfway between New Orleans and Baton Rouge, exit signs alert the driver to the towns of Grammercy, Gonzalez, and Sorrento – chemical industry towns near Convent, a tiny community that for two intense years battled over whether a Japanese chemical company named Shintech could build a $750 million polyvinyl chloride (PVC) plastics factory. Shintech became the test case upon which the EPA was developing its federal policy on environmental justice. Here, if you get off the highway and travel along the Mississippi River Road, you will see bucolic, green pastures peppered with the vestiges of plantation houses, overseers cottages, and falling-down slave quarters. In places, sugar cane fields spread back from the road as far as the eye can see. Nestled amid the southern country landscape, huge smokestacks rise up from fertilizer, chemical, and metals plants, the hundred-year-old Colonial sugar refinery, tall grain elevators, and the enormous Motiva Enterprises petroleum refinery. Trucks lumber down the highway transporting their tanks of oil, trains pull away from the mighty plants loaded down with vats of chemicals, and large pipes cross the road overhead to deliver sugar, grain, and petrochemicals to barges and huge tankers waiting patiently on the other side of the big green levee in the Mississippi River.

Back on the interstate, it is not too long before the new suburban malls of sprawling Baton Rouge interrupt the reverie as the traffic snarls. Just past downtown the road rises to the river bridge and looking to the right one can see paddlewheelers and casino boats in the foreground, the state capital in the middle distance, and the huge Exxon refinery looming just behind it. The construction of that refinery in 1909 anchored the development of the petrochemical pole here, and some critics argue that the blue state flag featuring a mother pelican feeding her young, which flies over the capital, should be replaced by a flag with the Exxon tiger or the Texaco star. Around the capital, another series of struggles over "environmental justice" is raging. Just beyond the Exxon refinery is the historically black Southern University, where students in 1998 protested the burning of leftover Vietnam-era Napalm at the Rhodia plant near the school.[10] Off to the north is Alsen, where Rollins dumped and incinerated waste for a generation over the protests of locals and where a company named Petro Processors polluted a now aptly named place called Devil's Swamp.[11]

In driving just ninety minutes, a motorist on I-10 has passed 156 facilities, which are the sources of 129.3 million pounds of toxic releases each year, as reported by the petrochemical firms themselves.[12] This equals over one-sixteenth of the entire emissions in the United States of America.[13] How did this "Chemical Corridor" (as the industry calls it) or "Cancer Alley" (as environmental justice activists call it) get to be this way? One explanation is that the proximity to rich gas and oilfields and the ability of the river to handle ocean-going tankers made industry keenly interested in the area. Another is that, due to their poverty and lack of political power, the poor rural communities along this Delta floodplain have had to welcome any firm wishing to utilize the long plantation lots that stretched back into the fields and marshes from the river's levees. Some observers point out that people simply didn't know what was coming into their communities, and, when they did come, they were simply unaware or misinformed of the potential health effects. Another common explanation is that a majority of Louisiana politicians, like those in most places dependent on oil, have always been more attentive to the needs of industry than those of average residents and corrupted by the concentrated wealth oil brings.[14] Currently, a majority of state politicians are heavily dependent on donations from the oil and chemical industries to pay their campaign bills.

But life along the corridor is no longer so simple, if it ever was: many residents have grown skeptical of industry and government promises of jobs, tax money for schools and roads, and safe production if they accept the plants. The economy is shifting away from oil toward tourism, health care, and transportation,[15] and a new coalition of activists is arguing that the focus on heavy manufacturing and attracting firms with lax environmental enforcement and tax breaks is backfiring for the state.

No one knows that the political climate in Louisiana is shifting better than the Japanese plastics maker Shintech, who wanted to build the plastics plant in Convent. After initially getting support from the governor and permission from the Louisiana Department of Environmental Quality (DEQ), they ran into strong opposition from local black and white residents who had support from Greenpeace and legal representation from law clinic students at nearby Tulane University. The struggle has had huge local and national repercussions and is the subject of Chapter 4 and much of Chapter 7. After years of suits and protests, the firm decided to move upriver and build a much smaller plant next to a large Dow Chemical facility. Shintech faces opposition there, but they have hired effective public relations firms and have used Dow's long-standing community presence to help counter discontented residents and environmentalists.

The struggles over the environment and racial justice are so common along this river that another author might highlight an entirely different set of cases. The net result of all these struggles is a patchwork quilt of land despoiled and protected, of communities where people feel perfectly safe, and of communities where citizens are terrified of leaks, explosions, or contamination. From this patchwork, we selected four struggles to address some questions with broad implications not only for local residents but also for the formulation of sweeping new national environmental and civil rights policy and heated academic debates.

Our goal in this book is to avoid overwhelming nonspecialist readers with heavy doses of social theory. Several such theories underlaid the questions we asked and the way we designed our research and laid out this book (such as those on social movements, the political economy of space, and some social psychology of risk and coping). We do not provide a review of social theories on environmental justice here, nor even a substantial analysis of that debate. To do this would take this book in a different direction and reach a different audience. The aim of this book is to focus on four environmental justice struggles in one state and to understand how they came to be; how residents, state and local government officials, and company representatives felt about the struggles; and how they were contentiously resolved. To understand these powerful cases, we need to develop an historical understanding of the place. There are three core questions.

The obvious first question is, *What is environmental justice?* This term has been thrown around but continues to be misunderstood and its definition debated. The second question is, *Who are the players in these struggles over environmental justice, and what tools do they use to get their way?* It has been observed that citizens' groups might win some battles, but that the coalition of industry and government officials interested in growing the local economy – what some social scientists call "the growth machine" – inevitably win the wars. This is the one main conceptual tool we believe readers will benefit from in understanding why environmental injustice is created by the everyday decisions people make. Growth machine theory also clarifies why environmental justice is interpreted differently by different categories of people and helps to explain why these uncomfortable situations are resolved the way they are.

Third, we ask how people experience environmental injustice. That is, *What does it feel like to be consistently afraid of having your health endangered, especially when it seems to be related to the color of your skin, the amount of money you have, and your lack of political clout?* We argue that stress from hazards and social pressure – and how people cope with these – influence the form these struggles take and who wins in the long run. These questions frame the core of this book and help us understand why the battles start, why they end up the way they do, and what effects they are having on people and their communities. We begin with the first question.

WHAT IS ENVIRONMENTAL JUSTICE?

In 1982, during protests over dumping of highly toxic polychlorinated biphenyls (PCBs) in Warren County, North Carolina, Benjamin Chavez, the future director of the National Association for the Advancement of Colored People (NAACP), coined the term *environmental racism*. This racism can be conscious or unconscious, intended and unintended, and comes at two stages. It can be the "the great disparity in the siting of waste facilities, polluting industries, other facilities having a negative environmental effect."[16] It can also be the uneven "enforcement of environmental law between People of Color communities and White communities," as suggested by a 1992 study by the *National Law Journal*.[17] The study of 1177 Superfund toxic waste sites found that "White communities see faster action, better results and stiffer penalties than communities where blacks, Hispanics and other minorities live. This unequal protection often occurs whether the community is wealthy or poor."

Many critics misrepresent this most central point: environmental racism does not solely refer to actions that have a racist *intent*, but it also includes actions that have a racist *impact*, regardless of their intent.

9

As several authors have described it, environmental justice embraces the concept that every individual, regardless of race, ethnicity, or class has the right to be free from ecological destruction and deserves equal protection of his or her environment, health, employment, housing, and transportation.[18] In 1991, the landmark People of Color Environmental Leadership Summit drafted seventeen core Principles of Environmental Justice. Holistic and universalistic, these principles emphasized that the movement was not just about environmental issues.[19] The goals of the movement included broader social justice issues, such as economic and cultural liberation for all people of color.[20] The principles stress the importance of increased participation of people of color as equals at all levels of decision making. Finally, the movement made clear that although pollution and environmental degradation didn't belong in communities of color, it also didn't belong anywhere else.[21] The movement thus dedicated itself to reducing environmental hazards for all people, and, to do that, its focus was on protecting those least protected.

As illustrated by these principles, environmental justice is not a simple or unidimensional concept. It does not just concern the preservation or conservation of the environment. Robert Bullard, a sociologist at Clark University and a leading environmental justice advocate, describes the wide swath that the environmental justice movement encompasses. He states,

It basically says that the environment is everything: where we live, work, play, go to school, as well as the physical and natural world. And so we can't separate the physical environment from the cultural environment. We have to talk about making sure that justice is integrated throughout all of the stuff that we do. What the environmental justice movement is about is trying to address all siting and industrial development.[22]

The reason why the environmental justice movement did not focus only on the environment was because activists saw that the economic and social disparities that surround an individual's life are rooted in hundreds of years of economic and political inequalities. For example, in Louisiana there are numerous small, poor, black communities that have grown up on the outer edges of large plantations along the Mississippi River Road. African Americans in Louisiana, descendents of slaves, have never enjoyed the same level of political power as whites in their communities. In fact, in some parishes, the descendents of plantation owners still control the local government, and poor, uneducated black voters are often manipulated by promises of money or jobs or threats of violence.[23] By not sharing in political power, these black neighborhoods have little input into the decision making that affects land use near their homes. Wealthier, whiter, and more politically connected neighborhoods have been more successful at keeping hazardous facilities away.

To fully understand the term *environmental justice,* it is necessary to define the term *environmental injustice.* Florence Robinson, a longtime African-American activist from Alsen, Louisiana, and biology professor at Southern University, says that "an environmental injustice occurs whenever a person or persons . . . are impinged upon by an environmental burden for the alleged good of this society, that the rest of the society does not bear. An environmental injustice may impact a person of ANY race, class or income level as long as the environmental insult is through no fault of their own."[24]

Environmental injustice can apply to unequal impact to groups by race, class, or ethnicity; however, there is a specific term for the injustice that exclusively affects people of color – environmental racism. The struggles of all other oppressed groups fall under the umbrella of environmental justice. Bullard argues that poor whites in Appalachia, who have had little voice or control in the decisions relating to their communities, experience environmental injustice. However, he is careful not to lose focus on racism. He proposes that "A lot of people say it's class, but race and class are intertwined. Because the society is so racist and because racism touches every institution – employment, housing, education, facility siting, land use decisions – you can't really extract race out of decisions that are being made by persons who are in power and the power arrangements are unequal."[25] Based on much of the history that follows, we agree with Bullard that racism – both individual and systematic and intentional and unconscious – is driving much environmental injustice in America. We also believe that for mobilizing participants, social movements often have to make simple and powerful claims that resonate with their followers, and the feeling of having been done an injustice due to racism is an effective motivator of participants, both black and white. Even though claims of environmental racism have motivated and focused African-American community members, the term *environmental justice* succeeded in bringing other ethnic groups into a bigger tent.

All the struggles that we explore in this book involve grassroots, poor, and people-of-color groups who are fighting against environmental injustice. This is not surprising since the cultural, political, and economic history of Louisiana has created a situation in which the populations most affected by the negative effects of development are poor people of color. The proposed uranium (LES) and PVC (Shintech) plants would have had the greatest impact on the poor rural black communities closest to the facilities (Chapters 3 and 4). The massive oilfield waste pits in Grand Bois most endanger the poor people of Houma Indian and Cajun descent who live right next door (Chapter 5). The Agricultural Street Landfill's potential risk is to the low- and middle-income blacks whose homes were built directly atop it (Chapter 6).

WHO ARE THE PLAYERS?

Three groups typically face each other in grassroots struggles over environmental justice: residents, businesses, and the government. Each group has different strengths, divisions, and vulnerabilities, and each draws upon a changing set of allies and resources to try to shift the rules of the struggle to their advantage. This section seeks to provide the tools to understand the roots, direction, and outcomes of environmental justice disputes. Three core points will guide us. First, residents, businesses, and governments are three profoundly unequal players, and the evidence here shows that the balance is tipped even further because local government almost always comes down on the side of businesses over community groups.

Second, governments are actors with their own interests, seeking to build highways, incinerators, landfills, airports, drainage projects, and the like in neighborhoods that don't want them there. At the same time, the government is an "arena," where conflicts are worked out based on who plays the game most effectively. For governments the problem is keeping their constituents' trust while meeting the demands of industries, which often impinge on the lives of local people. Third, the communities involved in these struggles are often divided on whether there is an environmental injustice at all and, if there is one, how it should be resolved. Different groups of residents respond differently to news of pollution, depending not only on their race but also on the benefits they believe they might receive from the facility, their past work experiences, their gender and age and family connections, and the distance they live from the plant. This divisiveness can heighten the stress for residents fearing for their health, and weaken their ability to struggle against the other players, businesses, and government.

The job of the economic development arm of a state government is straightforward: to court new companies. The state environmental agency's job is to decide if the operation is polluting within the limits of the law or if an existing factory or waste pit presents a hazard to the neighbors or environment nearby. The Louisiana state constitution says, "The natural resources of the state, including air and water, and the healthful, scenic, historic, and esthetic quality of the environment shall be protected, conserved, and replenished insofar as possible and consistent with the health, safety and welfare of the people. The Legislature shall enact laws to implement this policy."[26] The state agencies' work becomes political because both of these "booster" and "protector" agencies have leaders who are appointed and serve at the pleasure of the same person: the governor. If the governor has stated that "everyone must be on board in the all-out push for jobs," then both the development and environment departments must play that game.[27] In aggressively supporting firms when they run into local resistance, as occurs in the following cases, the state agencies of development and environment are both seen as creating and perpetuating situations of environmental injustice.

Why do state governments have such a predominant focus on economic development? After all, this is what sometimes makes citizens wonder if elected officials and state agencies are really protecting *their* best interests, health, and safety. Government officials and lower-level employees dealing with environmental justice issues are caught in this dilemma. Even if they are not appointed directly by someone elected, chances are that one of their supervisors was. So, like politicians, they have two masters. One is the citizens, who if well organized and informed can hold them accountable at the ballot box. The "pluralist" view of the government that we were taught in junior high civics class is that these officials must, therefore, ensure that the social welfare needs of the people are met and that their civil rights are protected. However, to get elected in this age of multi-million-dollar election campaigns, big corporate donors are the ones who can make the difference.

Those who make large contributions to campaigns, of course, do so for a reason: to have access to politicians once they are in office, making decisions that affect their business. And even more immediately when in office, government officials need corporate tax payments to meet their payrolls and expand their programs to meet voter demands. Politicians like to claim credit for job creation. So to do these things, James O'Connor pointed out, they need to "grow the tax base." This makes decisions favoring development over protection essentially nondecisions: it's a matter of political survival.[28]

A coalition that works to foster development emerges in most communities and states. Sociologists Harvey Molotch and John Logan call this coalition of entrepreneurs who seek to make profits on property and local business "the growth machine."[29] The core of the coalition is made up of real estate developers, land speculators, and landlords. Many local business owners, government officials, local newspapers, TV stations, utility companies, museums, theaters, expositions, professional sports clubs, organized labor, and corporate CEOs and owners also see the growth of their enterprises tied to local urbanization and industrialization.[30] Political scientist Clarence Stone proposed that growth regimes develop because mayors and governors, in fact, have little power on their own, so they work with private businesses to promote development that will help to build their tax base; thus, giving them more money and power.[31] So the role of government in the growth machine is complex and sometimes can be contradictory because it is both an actor and an "arena" within which the struggles get battled out.

As everywhere, a growth machine exists in Louisiana at both the state and local levels, precisely as proposed by Stone, Logan, and Molotch. On the state level, governmental agencies, such as the Louisiana Department of Economic Development (LDED) and the Port Commission, work to attract development to the state by providing information and assistance on labor issues, potential sites, utilities, incentives, training, markets, environmental permitting, and transportation costs. Additionally, state-level incentive programs and tax breaks offer financial benefits to new businesses that locate there or existing businesses that expand within the state.

The LDED web site plainly states that expanding economic development is a major goal for the state.[32] There, the LDED outlines the "Top Ten Reasons" to locate in Louisiana. These reasons include a wealth of natural resources, productive workforce, proximity to markets, comprehensive transportation network, and low-cost energy. The LDED offers the assistance of location specialists to the new companies, along with advertising the private business support services that are available in the state. Incentives include a "10 year industrial tax exemption, inventory tax credits, job tax credits, Enterprise Zone benefits, tax credits/refund based on percentage of gross payroll, investment tax credit, and a tax exemption on goods in transit."[33] Many of these tax exemptions pertain to specific industries, such as a tax exemption for oil and gas exploration or a sales tax exemption for shipbuilders.[34] The 10-year tax exemption, which is available to manufacturing plants, waives property taxes for new facilities or expansions for ten years. The state's Ten-Year Property Tax Exemption program and the Enterprise Zone program have generated controversy among social justice and environmental activists in the state. They question whether these incentive programs are hurting the people of the state, rather than helping them. The nonprofit Louisiana Coalition for Tax Justice reported that the state's public schools are losing over $100 million each year due to the exemption. They report that, unlike many other southern states that have similar tax exemption programs (Alabama, Arkansas, Mississippi, Oklahoma, South Carolina, Texas), Louisiana is the only state that doesn't allow local governments to approve the exemption so that they can protect revenue for education programs.[35] Thus, the Ten-Year Property Tax Exemption program is a perfect example of the inherent contradiction that often exists within governmental policy that pits support for industry against support for human services for citizens.

Another important state incentive is the Enterprise Zone program. Throughout the state, areas where there is high unemployment, low income, and/or large numbers of residents who are receiving some form of public assistance are identified and labeled. The poorest 40 percent of the state are included in the program. If a company locates or expands in these zones and creates a minimum of five new jobs within the first two years, they qualify for certain incentives, such as a one-time tax credit of $2,500 for each new job that is filled by a Louisiana resident created in the first five years.[36] These companies are also eligible for a full rebate on state sales tax and the return of a portion of the local sales tax for material purchased during construction of their facility.[37]

The Enterprise Zone program is entirely consistent with the progrowth philosophy of the state, which espouses that impoverished areas need development to raise the standard of living of the residents.[38] This philosophy, however, does not reflect the views of many local environmental justice advocates. Rather, they believe that these zones actually create environmental injustice. In Louisiana, the individuals who are likely to live in qualifying zones are often black and poor. Additionally, the program does not delineate as to the *type* of industrial operations eligible to take advantage of the tax breaks. Combined with the fact that many parishes do not have zoning regulations for development, this creates a situation in which heavily polluting industry is effectively being encouraged to locate near poor communities of color who live in these depressed areas. Many African Americans note that the jobs created by these incentives are filled by commuters: firms take the tax breaks without hiring poor, minority locals.

So, who is watching out for the health of the people and the environment? The mission of the Louisiana Department of Environmental Quality (LDEQ) is to "maintain a healthful and safe environment for the people of Louisiana."[39] However, many activists feel that the state agency that is charged with protecting the environment is just another cog in the growth machine. Governor Foster has stated that LDEQ's job is to "make it as easy as they can within the law" for companies to obtain permits.[40] The person he chose to head the agency, Dale Givens, was quoted as saying, "My job is to write permits." Gustave Von Bodungen, assistant secretary of Department of Environmental Quality, explained the role of LDEQ, stating,

We're accused, I guess, of conspiring with industry, because we always give them permits. But it's kind of like getting a driver's license. If you come in and you have all the information that meets the rules – we have to give you a permit. We can't just arbitrarily and capriciously say "well, we're going to give you one, but we won't give *you* one."[41]

As will become apparent in the following cases, a significant amount of controversy has surrounded the activities of the LDEQ. Many citizens do not feel that the agency is doing enough to protect their health and safety. Although the 1998 levels of reported Toxic Release Inventory (TRI) emissions have decreased 76 percent from the first year that TRI data were available (1987), the state still has the second highest level of non-mining emissions in the country (186.6 million pounds per year).[42] Additionally, the state's industrialization has left a lasting legacy of pollution that has not been fully regulated. It was not until 1980 that the state began to monitor hazardous waste pits and industrial injection wells – before that, industry could dispose of waste as they saw fit. This has left much of the marsh, lake, and river water in the Mississippi River Delta Basin contaminated.

Environmental justice advocates claim that the Louisiana Department of Environmental Quality is not adequately enforcing environmental regulations throughout the state. In 1997, the EPA charged that the state agency did not sufficiently enforce financial penalties in compliance with the Clean Air Act, and they did not adequately enforce the handling of hazardous waste in accordance with the federal Resource Conservation and Recovery Act.[43] Additionally, in 1998 the EPA criticized the state agency for an inadequate penalty policy, poor record keeping, and informal resolution of violations.[44] A 1998 study by the Louisiana Environmental Action Network (LEAN) found that the enforcement activities of LDEQ were at an all-time low. The study examined the level of enforcement activity from 1988 to 1997. In 1997, the agency assessed only forty-two enforcement actions. The number of enforcement actions had steadily decreased since 1991, when the number of actions was at an all-time high of 162.[45] Finally, a seven-month investigation by three local *New York Times*–affiliated newspapers found that even fined companies rarely pay their penalties.[46]

Federal politics also create environmental injustice. A member of Congress might be courted by industry and given campaign contributions so that when legislative issues, such as deciding to classify oil-field waste as "nonhazardous," are before them, they will vote favorably for the oil industry. This political move has a direct impact on the local communities that have to live next to and breathe the fumes from this "nonhazardous" waste. The resolution of many of these local struggles is decided in the arena of national politics. Grassroots activists, whose homes are being contaminated or who want to prevent a chemical plant from locating next to them, complain and ask for help from federal agencies like the Environmental Protection Agency. The EPA, which is under intensive pressure from legislators who are in support of wealthy national and transnational companies, is caught in the middle of a contentious political fight. Likewise, elected officials put pressure on state agencies, whereas protest groups, lobbyists, and corporate dollars try to sway opinions and influence decisions from the outside. What is seen first as a local struggle over land use becomes a political tug-of-war with contestants pulling from locations across the map.

Helping communities through these battles hundreds of times, Willie Fontenot from the Louisiana Attorney General's Office has the most useful description we've found anywhere of the way local pollution issues become political games. He told us:

What we are doing here is playing a game. The problem is we don't know whether or not the game is being played on this table or in another room and we don't know who the players are necessarily and we don't know what game we are playing. We think we are playing soccer, but the real game is baseball, because it may be some decision being made by a bunch of people sitting up in Washington, D.C. Or it may be some deal being cut on something that we are not even aware of – that is where the game is. It might involve players, maybe organized crime is involved in it and they don't use public records necessarily. You go in and check the file and you don't see the stuff you are looking for and is relevant to you being able to succeed because there are no records.

Fontenot's words ring true through the twisting tales of environmental justice struggles that make up the core of this book. It does not mean that the game is unplayable, but it does mean that the game is always shifting and that creative, multiple strategies are needed to play it, along with a complex network of coalition partners. Likewise, the concept of Logan, Molotch, and Stone does not mean that the "growth machine" uniformly gets its way. These coalitions are sometimes held back in their plans by people interested in *using* the land, not just making money by selling or renting it. Those people are often interested in keeping it in the condition that they knew it before it was so heavily "developed."[47]

Politics is even involved when it comes to science – a discipline usually perceived as being based on concrete, unalterable facts. Most people would agree that it is important to acquire a scientific understanding of the level of exposure to pollutants and the effects of exposure on human health. However, this has proven to be a major point of contention between governmental officials and community residents. Once industrial plants or waste dumps have polluted their neighborhoods, if there is a scientific investigation, the process is controlled by experts, and the findings are often so technical that the residents feel excluded from the political process. Bob Kuehn, former director of the Tulane Environmental Law Clinic in New Orleans, described the effect of scientific risk assessment, stating, "Quantitative risk assessment . . . transforms disputes over values and politics into scientific disputes that are inaccessible to many citizens and may be particularly inaccessible for communities of color and lower incomes. . . " His main concern is this: "Taking the struggle for environmental justice out of the community and into the domain of scientists plays into the domain of risk producers because they have re-sources and access to scientists."[48] As Jurgen Habermas said three decades ago, by focusing on "rational" questions that experts can an-swer, government officials have excluded vast issues that concern cit-izens, and this can cause a profoundly "irrational" outcome.[49]

Here's a striking example of what science can look like from the per-spective of an outsider. In Mossville, Louisiana, residents living near huge chemical plants have been found to have abnormally high levels of persistent and toxic dioxin in their bodies.[50] Experts have been called in to evaluate the situation. In a press release, a scientist cri-tiqued an analysis of the blood work, writing in the technical language of biostatistics. "What you should have compared is the national mean to the mean of the samples from Mossville – maybe a single-tailed test of means at a 95 or 99 percent significance level." The coordinator of the local environmental justice group, Mossville Environmental Ac-tion Now (MEAN), expressed her frustration in an e-mail message posted to the scientist and the statewide environmental listserver.

I, as an average citizen, do not know what half the words in the below sen-tence from your e-mail means. I do know that many people in Mossville are ill. I personally invite you to come to Mossville, meet the people, and discuss it with those who are affected. Then, perhaps you could go back and find a way to help us instead of playing with words. We are sick. We need help. We need medicine, doctors, tests, etc. Not a play with words. If you want to come, we have an open meeting every Monday night. E-mail me and I will give you directions on how to get here and certainly will let you ask questions. Then, perhaps, you will understand that we don't know what you are talking about. We know that our children are sick, our young women are sick, our insurance companies are canceling insurance policies, many of our friends and relatives are dying of Cancer. Do I need to say more?[51]

Often officials at the Department of Environmental Quality and other governmental agencies do not take these symptoms seriously. They have publicly attributed the poor health of these communities to unhealthy lifestyles (e.g., eating fatty foods, smoking, drinking alco-hol, and doing drugs). Evidence to support the officials' or activists' claims is difficult to obtain, due to a lack of "baseline data" on the community's health prior to the advent of industry. And much has changed in the world since those days. Additionally, doing compre-hensive health assessments is expensive and lengthy, and the state health agency has few funds and staff to do them. Even if there are re-sources to pay for these investigations, environmental justice advo-cates sometimes have such a strong mistrust of government officials that they refuse to participate in government-led health studies (see Chapter 5).

Under our current system, the resolution of many of these cases rests on identifying pollution levels and determining the physiological effects of exposure to contaminants. However, this will continue to be a contentious issue until accurate methods of data collection and de-finitive scientific findings that are acceptable to both sides in disputes (if that is even possible) are available. If citizens do not trust the pro-fessionals who are conducting these investigations, even the most ac-curate scientific findings will have little impact on resolving these dis-putes. Politics will.

An important final aspect of this core issue of power and the growth machine is determining who speaks for the community. The word *com-munity* is often used to describe a group of people who have shared in-terests, live in the same place, share an ethnicity, and so on. However, it is often used to sweepingly describe a group of people as if they were a unit – a unit that shares the same point of view. This usage is partic-ularly problematic when one is discussing struggles over development. Should community decisions be made by the elected leaders in the parish seat or the state capitol or by a referendum voted on by all com-munity members? Should those who will live closest to the proposed industrial site have the last word? If so, how big a radius should be in-cluded? This is a pivotal point of contention in most environmental jus-tice struggles because communities are often split on whether to wel-come or resist a facility. These divisions can be along lines of economic class, race, gender, distance from the plant, and many other factors. Sometimes they rip old friendships and even families apart.

Many parishes in Louisiana do not have zoning regulations, and de-velopment issues are handled by the parish government.[52] The presi-dent of one rural parish told us that it was the responsibility of elected officials to make development decisions, and if the residents don't like the decisions, then they should vote them out. In the same parish, the director of economic development said that she listens to the com-munity residents when it comes to development decisions. However, when asked if a formal mechanism exists to determine their opinion, she said, "No." Because poor people are usually short of money to finance campaigns and of power to play the game more generally, this ad hoc system for deciding land use issues has the potential to exploit poor and minority groups.

The visions of the elected officials on what the area's future should look like may not be shared by the residents whose health and land values may decline if industry becomes their neighbor. A dramatic example of this can be seen in the town of Alsen, the predominantly African-American town just north of Baton Rouge. Environmental justice activist Florence Robinson first became aware of institutional racism through learning of how development decisions were made for her town. She described it this way:

The first plant came about 1955. As a matter of a fact, it was in 1955 that the Louisiana legislature passed a resolution and in that resolution they designated industrial zones around the state. For East Baton Rouge Parish they designated five industrial zones. Four of those zones were in Alsen or contiguous with Alsen. What is really significant about that is in 1955 we [African Americans] couldn't vote. We were systematically denied the right to vote. So, that was taxation without representation. . . . Alsen is a classic example of what the 1969 civil rights commission called "institutionalized racism." So this place was zoned without the permission of the people who lived here, without the support of the people who live here – it was zoned industrial.

For Alsen residents, this had meant the transformation of their town into one of the most contaminated places in the country.

Environmental justice advocates complain that poor individuals and people of color have always been effectively shut out of political decision making about development in their communities. One of the Principles of Environmental Justice "affirms the right to participate as equal partners at every level of decision making including needs assessment, planning, implementation, enforcement and evaluation." Although this principle sounds ideal, there is not currently a mechanism for ensuring that it is carried out. Even if hearings and public comment sessions are held, residents' views are commonly dismissed at decision time, and how can a resolution be reached if citizens have differing opinions? In both the Shintech and LES facility siting struggles described later, the local officials and a group of residents wanted the plant to locate in the parish, whereas another group of citizens opposed the plant. Each citizen group claimed that they spoke for the community. Even conclusions from a poll of parish residents differed depending on the resident's proximity to the plants, so there is no easy answer to this question. In the following cases, we will see how residents and elected officials have wrestled over who speaks for their communities.

THE LASTING IMPACT OF STRUGGLES ON THE PEOPLE
AT THE FRONTLINES

One of the most striking observations that we kept seeing when we spoke to the individuals involved in environmental justice struggles is that they can leave lasting scars. Local residents bear the brunt of the disputes. Their daily lives are plagued by worry over their own and their children's health, worry about the plummeting value of the homes that they have spent their lives paying for, and worry about losing the land and neighborhoods where generations of their family have grown up. There is the uncertainty of not knowing if their risk of cancer is increasing, or if there will be an explosion in the middle of the night or a chemical spill from a train derailment or pipeline leak. One local said that it is just a matter of course to make sure you are prepared – like making sure before you go to bed that there is a half tank of gas so that if there is an evacuation in the middle of the night you will be able to get your family out.[53] People also worry about what their friends and family will think of them if they raise questions or protest a facility that the community relies upon for employment.

The stress of living with constant fear and worry wears people down and can actually affect their health, probably as much as the toxins they fear. Compounding their emotions is the extra effort it takes to try to fight for their neighborhood. How people cope with fear of exposures is a critical question for the environmental justice movement. Studies of coping suggest that people's attitudes about technological risks depend upon their familiarity with them, and their power to *control* the dangers.[54] This, for example, is why many people fear nuclear plants but will readily drive cars, when statistically, driving is far more dangerous. Control over risk depends on one's economic class. For example, if you are the mayor or in the local police department, you probably at least know and might be friends with the person who is managing the chemical plant or hazardous waste landfill. People who can't get a job at the plant for class or race reasons are less likely to have these connections, and they might perceive the plant as an alien presence in the community. Unable to control the risks around them, people are more likely to experience the world in a negative way, as sinister and out of their control. Some studies have shown that this feeling leads to depression, anxiety, and even risky health choices like smoking and drinking.[55]

Overwhelmingly, activists in these grassroots community groups are women. The female activist role often stems from the traditional woman's socialization to be the caretaker of the family. Those women who do not work outside the home may also have more adaptable work schedules, allowing them to attend daytime hearings and protest events. Even if they do work outside the home, unlike their husbands, they are less likely to work for the offending company or industry. Thus, fear of retribution for their protest activities does not affect them as much as it affects their husbands.[56]

The effort and time required to attend public hearings, launch letter writing campaigns, research environmental permits, and track down elected officials is unpredictable, and sometimes it is unimaginably high. These women often have to work at a job and feed and care for the kids, while waging a time-intensive battle with both the company and the state agencies that are supposed to protect them. During these struggles, there is often just a small core of activists who do most of the work. Many men and women drop out of the battle because they just can't juggle their job and family responsibilities and attend protest events. Many of these women have told us that, if it were not for understanding and supportive husbands, they never could have carried on with the battle.

One thing that helps many environmental justice activists cope with the constant worry, fear, and anxiety is their unwavering devotion to their religion. Many protest meetings are opened and closed with prayers and gospel hymns ring out during workshops and conferences. If you ask any one of these activists what is the most important thing that keeps them going during their long, exhausting struggles, many will answer that they are doing the Lord's work – that the Lord is guiding them. After one of the struggles chronicled in this book, a black activist and a white activist stood together and told us very earnestly "I'm saying this in all sincerity: God led us. We had divine guidance. We tell that to everyone who interviews us, but it never ends up in print."[57]

Although many of the struggles can cause divisions within a community, women and men in these protest groups often find a surprising unity and camaraderie with their fellow activists that they have never experienced before. Shared hard work, triumphs, and defeats create long-lasting friendships and bonds. Some women drop out of the movement after their community's conflict has been resolved and return to their families and resume their old lives. Others continue the fight and come to the aid of other communities that are facing similar threats.

The people on the other side of the struggles, who work for growth machine businesses and government agencies, are also men and women with families and lives. They also experience stress, sometimes intensively. The major difference between them and the activists is that they are in the struggle because it is their *job*. They can go home at night to a place they don't fear is killing them. They are paid to write environmental permits, to grow a business, to lobby, or to be a politician. The state and federal agency employees may be working in disorganized, understaffed offices where unintentional oversights and misplaced files serve to inflame the actual injustice issues. The private businesspeople are fighting for their professional careers and the anticipated windfalls that the new development will bring. Politicians are constantly calculating how their actions will impact their chances for reelection and the promises they have made to their powerful constituents. For many, they are just trying to earn a living and to promote economic development, which they view as bringing jobs and tax dollars to their communities. For many, their beliefs about the right way to address the problems of poverty, development, and even racial inequality are as fervently held as those of the activists they face at public hearings. So, when it comes right down to it, these are all individuals trying to do their jobs – as protectors of their children or as government workers or businessmen.

The core of this book is the four chapters where we describe the struggles of communities fighting long and fascinating battles against environmental injustice. Our goal in presenting these cases is to provide readers with a sense of what it is like to endure these fears and the battles and how they are being resolved. They each reflect on the three themes posed: of politics and who gets their way, of who gets to speak for communities, and of the impact of the hazards and battles on the residents. We return to those questions in Chapter 7, where we also recount the fierce backlash from these cases and other environmental justice battles around the country. It becomes clear there that the ripples from these four cases go on and on and on. But to understand them, we first need to provide the context in which they grew: a state with an important history, policies, and social movements.

WHY LOUISIANA? WHY THESE CASES?

Readers might be wondering about limiting the cases in this book to Louisiana. Many readers in other parts of the United States or Europe where environmental protections are stronger, and enforcement not so subject to governmental corruption, might say the place is merely a unique "outlier," and that these things couldn't happen in their communities. A closer look suggests they do all the time; virtually no community is exempt. But Louisiana is important because the state serves as something of a haven for polluting industries, and so the struggles are more common, the social and political scene is more polarized, and the debate is right on the surface. We believe that Louisiana is illustrative of typical interactions in our nation's economic and political system, especially of the alliance between industry and the local government. Since inequality is so extreme here and civil society is so weak, politicians and business leaders say openly what is often said only in private elsewhere: if industry doesn't want something, then it doesn't happen.[58] If Louisiana is not typical in this regard, it provides a cautionary tale to the rest of the nation because, in many ways, such as extreme inequality, the nation has been growing more similar to Louisiana.[59]

Louisiana is also part of a national movement toward "flexible" environmental protection. Firms have been strongly pressuring local and state governments across the country to weaken environmental enforcement and provide tax breaks to create a "good business climate." Louisiana's governor has been advertising it as a state that "bends over backwards for business," as his 1995 *Wall Street Journal* advertisement read. Some critics argue that Louisiana has been battling with Mississippi and Texas in a "race to the bottom" of environmental protection, which in turn may pressure other states whose industries are threatening to relocate.

Some local critics call Louisiana an "American Banana Republic" because it has an economy like that of those Central American countries that are dependent on a few commodities extracted from nature and where the political system is based on disempowerment of the masses and rule with a relatively "iron fist."[60] We do not use the term lightly. As U.S. District Judge Tucker Melancon said from his bench to Dale Givens, the state's lead environmental enforcement official:

I used to get upset when big newspapers referred to Louisiana as a banana republic or Third World country. Regrettably . . . I have to conclude that [Louisiana's] enforcement actions when violations of federal and state laws, permits or regulations are known to have occurred on a repeated basis for an extended period of time, resembles more closely what one would find in a Third World country rather than in the richest and, by most standards, the most health conscious country in the world.[61]

Serving at the pleasure of the governor's office, the state's environmental agency DEQ has been repeatedly blasted by citizens and environmentalists for not protecting their health and environment, for leading the race to the bottom.[62]

The claims of ruling with an iron fist may seem like exaggeration, but Chapter 7 describes a series of ways in which industrial lobbying groups in Louisiana curtailed the means for civic groups to fight polluters, especially by limiting the lawsuits they could file and curtailing their access to legal aid. The pointed question at stake in the struggles chronicled in this book is precisely this: whether the rest of the nation will feel the need to join this race to the bottom, or whether popular movements within the state, combined with pressure from without, will pull this "pollution haven" up to the levels of the "developed world."

Many books written on the environmental justice movement tell the story of struggles that occur across the country. We have chosen to focus on struggles that have occurred within a single state for two important reasons. First, Louisiana is situated in the Deep South – a region that continues to be a central battleground in the environmental justice movement.[63] This is because it combines a legacy of racism, inequality, and political exclusion with polluting industries that have grown explosively since World War Two. With its huge petrochemical industry on old plantation lots, Louisiana is the epicenter of this explosive conflict. Second, to understand fully how environmental injustice comes to be and how it is negotiated in a society, it is important to understand its context well. To understand what is happening in one struggle, we need to appreciate how local history and other recent struggles in the state set and changed that context. In Chapter 2, we briefly describe how the unique history of the state has contributed to creating cases of environmental injustice and how the environmental justice movement has developed over the last twenty-some years. Each struggle builds on the others, as people learn of a victory on the news, the reaction to one class-action lawsuit changes the rules for the next, local activists gain battle experience, and so on. We see this lack of local context as a major deficit in the literature.

That said, it was still very difficult to select the cases for this book; there were dozens to choose from. The first two cases, the LES and Shintech siting struggles, were selected because they represent watershed cases that changed the landscape for all future environmental justice cases. The LES case (Chapter 3), in which a community group blocked the siting of a uranium-enrichment facility, represents the first actual victory for environmental justice activists using an important Executive Order issued by President Clinton in 1994. The Shintech case, where a coalition of local residents and state and national groups prevented the siting of a multi-million-dollar chemical plant (Chapter 4), is considered a path-breaking victory for environmental justice forces. However, this landmark case caused a major backlash at the state and national level that has limited the opportunities available to future grassroots protest groups (Chapter 7).

The other two cases describe conflicts over existing contamination. We wanted to include ongoing contamination cases because they present substantially different challenges for protestors as compared to the siting of a new facility. Due to the notorious history of poorly regulated dumping of toxic waste in the state, we had to select from literally hundreds of contamination cases. We chose the Agriculture Street landfill case (Chapter 6) because, similar to the Love Canal struggle, the toxic waste threat could not be more direct or personal – it seems to be seeping up from the ground and invading these residents' homes, the very place most people go to feel safe and secure. Similarly, in the Grand Bois case wafting fumes from nearby oilfield waste pools caused illness and fear in local residents (Chapter 5). As this book goes to press, these two cases remain unresolved, and it appears extremely unlikely that the communities' demands for relocation (at Agriculture Street) and closure of the waste pits (at Grand Bois) will be granted. All these cases provide observers with accounts of how environmental injustice is experienced, endured, challenged, and sometimes re-solved. We examine the state and national political repercussions from these cases that have sent shock waves through the activist commu-nity in Chapter 7, where we attempt to draw some conclusions and dis-cuss the future of the movement.

2

Roots of Environmental
Injustice in Louisiana

Top: Former slaves and their children stand outside their homes near a sugar plantation in Ascension Parish, circa 1890. [Photo courtesy of Historic New Orleans Collection]

Bottom: The Great Louisiana Toxics March of 1988. [Photo courtesy of the *Baton Rouge Advocate*]

RACE AND DEVELOPMENT IN LOUISIANA

In Louisiana, race and economics have always been intricately inter-twined. Struggling to occupy and profit from its vast territory along the Mississippi, the French Crown in 1717 granted a monopoly called the Company of the West to a Scot named John Law.[1] His company parceled out land along the river and financial support to those who would develop tobacco and rice farms there. Two years later the first major shipment of enslaved Africans arrived, and over the next decade their population grew sevenfold, going from half the population of white Europeans to over twice their numbers.[2]

Where slaves outnumbered owners by a large margin, repression was intense. Slaves were brutally treated upon their capture, in tran-sit, and upon their arrival in Louisiana, many dying each year from maltreatment and disease. Slave ship captains sailed with orders to bring rice from Africa and slaves with experience in growing it and the dye plant indigo.[3] For these reasons slaves from the Senegambia region of West Africa were prized in Louisiana.[4]

After France ceded control of Louisiana to Spain in 1763, the Spaniards poured energy and resources into its new colony. In the next quarter century, the numbers of slaves grew fourfold.[5] This was the period in which the Acadians (later dubbed the derogatory "Cajun"), French speakers who had been exiled from Canada, began to arrive. During this time, Spain and France went to war, and revolution swept over the British colonies nearby and, more importantly for Louisiana, over France. In 1795, buoyed by stories of a slave revolt in Haiti and a belief that the Spanish unlawfully kept them in bondage after French revolutionaries had freed slaves in all their colonies, slaves and a few white supporters planned a revolt along the Mississippi River. Fifty-four slaves were arrested at Point Coupee near Baton Rouge, of which twenty-three were hanged.[6] Their heads were marched through the towns and plantations along the river and posted on poles all the way to New Orleans. Historian Gwendolyn Midlo Hall ties that rebellion and the experience of escaped slave colonies in the swamps around New Orleans to the particularly brutal repression of slaves and distrustful racism that comes with American rule after the Louisiana Purchase just seven years later.[7]

The appetite of the American planters for slaves was voracious, as sugar took off as the region's new crop. Even though the import of slaves ended in 1807, their numbers skyrocketed (by purchase from other states) to 331,726; a third of a million people were doing the backbreaking work of hacking cane, running the sugar mills, cutting firewood, digging levees and canals, and building the glamorous plantation houses now visited by thousands of tourists each day.[8]

With few options after slavery was abolished, many exslaves continued to work on the plantations as wage laborers or sharecroppers.[9] Very few managed to secure their own farms, so for many, the period after the Civil War was scarcely better than the time before it. Sharecroppers were advanced provisions at rates set by the landowner, and, once they were in debt to him, state law prohibited them from moving.[10] Wage laborers couldn't even get one dollar a day, and generally their wages were withheld until the harvest came in. Either way, most lived on in what is called debt peonage, essentially a form of semi-slavery. Living hand to mouth, many exslaves were able to secure a small lot for a house and garden on the margin of the giant plantation tracts. They built small communities along a dirt lane off the river road, stretching from the levee to the "back marsh" behind the dry land along the river.

With freed and disgruntled blacks nominally given the right to vote after the Civil War, however, new innovations in their repression were needed. To blatantly keep blacks off the voting rolls might draw interference from the North, so whites simply terrorized them. Henry J. Heogey, the editor of the New Orleans *Daily States* newspaper wrote bluntly in 1899: "We bulldozed the negroes [flogged them, threatened to kill them to keep them from voting]; we killed the worst of them; we killed carpetbaggers [Northern meddlers]; we patrolled the roads at midnight; we established in many localities a reign of terror."[11] The statistics bear him out: between 1882 and 1952 at least 335 blacks were lynched in Louisiana.[12] His description described the modus operandi for decades to come as the Klu Klux Klan boomed through the 1920s when its official membership reached 25,000 in the state.

In 1896 Louisiana's policy of strict racial segregation in schools, restaurants, and trains was given national legal basis by a 7:1 vote of the U.S. Supreme Court in the landmark *Plessy vs. Fergeson* case.[13] Homer Adolf Plessy, one-eighth black, was excluded because of his race from riding in a white-only East Louisiana Railroad carriage out of New Orleans. The "separate-but-equal" standard would be the law of the land for another sixty years. And by 1898 when a new state constitution was passed, the fear of Northern interference was gone. Blacks were more directly excluded from voting with a poll tax and a literacy test and by parish registers, officials who were empowered to exclude anyone they wished.[14] Black registration plummeted from 128,150 in 1888 to just 1,342 in 1904.

At the beginning of the 1900s, a new boom economy took off; oil was being drilled all over the south of the state for the exploding demand of industry. The building of the Standard Oil refinery in Baton Rouge in 1909 launched the state on a transition from agriculture and fishing to petrochemicals. The Mississippi River provided easy transportation for oil production operations and a high-capacity sewer for disposal of chemical waste.

Bettsie Baker-Miller, of the Louisiana Chemical Association, described the oil refinery as the "anchor" for bringing in chemical plants. She stated, "Once you have an anchor, and Standard Oil was at the time, you develop. Other people see opportunities for processing and the feed stock chain falls into place." Between 1909 and the early thirties, ten to twenty chemical plants located in Louisiana. Then, in the forties when Indochina cut off exports of natural rubber, local companies worked to develop synthetic rubber.[15]

During this era, the state government set out to actively encourage more industrial development.[16] To attract more industry to the state, in 1936, the legislature exempted new manufacturing industries from paying property taxes for their first ten years of operation. The program, still in effect today, set the state on a path toward heavy industrialization. By the 1970s, the previously agricultural parishes between Baton Rouge and New Orleans were producing a significant portion of the country's chlorine, nitrogen fertilizer, and vinyl chloride.[17] By 1995, the state was producing 25% of the nation's chemicals,[18] and 16.9 billion gallons of gasoline a year.[19]

As the state was industrializing, the agricultural sector was declining. Once the "king," cotton production fell from two million acres in the 1930s to 352,000 acres in 1966. In the two decades after 1940, the total number of farms in the state was cut in half, with the number of black-owned farms dropping by two thirds. In 1940, one in four of the state's workers was tilling the land. By 1960 it was one in thirty. Due to mechanization, there were sometimes precipitous drops in the number of agricultural jobs.

When large chemical plants and oil refineries searched for land to develop, they were delighted to see large plots of plantation land available for the taking. It was much easier to buy out a single plantation landholder than to negotiate with many owners of smaller plots. This conversion of plantations to industrial facilities has contributed to a pattern in which poor, black communities are located close to large industrial plants. The communities founded by freed slaves who had settled on the edges of the plantations have thus become the reluctant neighbors of large industrial operations. Often the chemical plants start at the center of the plantation lots far from the communities, but they slowly add on and get closer and closer.

As this development was occurring, Jim Crow laws were still in effect in Louisiana, and most of the African American population was disenfranchised. Although these African Americans were nominally free, these laws limited their capability to participate in the political arena, obtain adequate healthcare and education, and earn a living. It was not until 1942 that white-only primaries were outlawed in the South, and voter registration was opened up. For example, in 1940 only 400 blacks in New Orleans were registered to vote.[20]

In the changing economy, blacks were consistently on the bottom rung of the economic ladder. As opportunities decreased in agriculture, industrial employers only hired blacks for low-wage, unskilled jobs. When there were layoffs, blacks were the first to go. Additionally, white-dominated unions often encouraged discriminatory practices at the workplace and often excluded black workers as members. Blacks composed almost half of the population in New Orleans in 1950, but they constituted only 0.015 percent of utility workers, 0.054 percent of city government employees, and 0.015 percent of phone workers.[21]

The major areas of employment growth for blacks occurred in the post office and the schools. In Baton Rouge in 1960, 60 percent of blacks worked in manual jobs, one quarter more than whites. The percentage of blacks living below the poverty level in the state at that time was 50 percent, as compared to only 11 percent of whites.[22] Thus, the pattern of blacks receiving little benefit from economic development continued a hundred years after the abolition of slavery. In spite of all the economic growth, the situation in the 1990s was no better. In Louisiana's metropolitan areas, 11 percent of whites lived in poverty, whereas 43 percent of blacks did. Rural areas were worse: 18 percent of whites and 53 percent of blacks lived in poverty. That is, in 1995 nearly half of urban and rural blacks in Louisiana were living on less than $7,763 for individuals, and less than $15,569 for a family of four.[23] For families, that's less than $3,892 per person per year, or just under $75 a week for everything. In 1996, Louisiana was the state with the second-highest proportion of African Americans (32 percent), so one in six Louisianans today is black *and* poor.[24] To understand the environmental justice struggles that follow, one needs to appreciate this chasm between the life experiences of whites and blacks in the state.

This brief history of the intersection between race and development in Louisiana provides a compelling backdrop for the development of a protest movement by the state's poor and people of color who had enough of widespread societal inequality and political corruption. To truly understand the cases that we present in this book, one must have a basic knowledge of the events that led up to these conflicts, the precedents that had already been set, and the organizations that had been established to support local groups. This chapter seeks to paint, using broad brush strokes, a picture of the development of the toxic and environmental justice movements in the state. This overview will also highlight key national events that have had an impact on the statewide movement. Although it is impossible to include all the events and actors that have contributed to the creation of the vital and energetic movement that exists today, we have hopefully included some of the most important.

In response to the abysmal environmental record of the state of Louisiana, combined with a long brutal history of slavery and oppressive civil rights violations, it is not surprising that a strong, energetic environmental justice movement flourished in the state. This movement has been intricately intertwined with the antitoxics movement. In fact, the environmental justice movement was active in the form of the antitoxics movement before the label "environmental justice" came into use. Activist Florence Robinson explains, "You have to be very careful about these problems – talking about environmental justice. Environmental justice is a relatively new word. But, there had been people fighting for environmental justice before the term was coined. And these people were not always black – I think that point gets lost."

One must realize that even though labels are very important to a social movement because they create a sense of identity, attract participants, and convey a message to the general public, different people may not use them in a similar manner. In Louisiana, events that one person considers to be part of the antitoxics movement may, to another, be considered a crucial part of the foundation of the environment justice movement. However, to the local residents who comprise the grassroots protest groups, the label that is used to describe their struggles is not foremost in their minds. Rather, their main concern is to protect their families and communities from environmental hazards.

THE BIRTH OF A MOVEMENT

One of the first incidents to draw Louisiana's attention to the human cost of prioritizing economic development over the environment occurred in 1978, the same year as the Love Canal struggle. Nineteen-year-old Kirtley Jackson died of inhalation of fumes as he emptied his eighteen-wheeler truckload of toxic waste into a hazardous waste pit owned by Environmental Purification Advancement, Inc., near Bayou Sorrel. The fumes from the pit, combined with Jackson's load of high-sulfur-content waste, formed a deadly vapor of hydrogen sulfide that left the young worker dead in the cab of his truck (see Chapter 5). News of the incident and the slow response of state officials to regulate such waste pits set off protests from angry residents from the nearby community. They burned a wooden bridge that had to be traversed to get to the waste pits.[25] Although residents in the state had been complaining about toxic dumping for years, this highly visible incident galvanized their efforts, and the media and public officials were forced to take notice.[26]

The very next year, 1979, the state government opened the Office of Environmental Affairs (OEA) which was quickly placed under the Department of Natural Resources (DNR). In 1980, state government officials also formed the Environmental Control Commission (ECC) by merging the Stream Control Commission and the Air Control Commission. The OEA served as staff support for the ECC. Initially, the environmental agencies were primarily concerned with developing regulations for hazardous waste. By 1984, the Louisiana Department of Environmental Quality was established and became a freestanding cabinet-level agency.[27]

In 1978, an official in another arm of the state government was also interested in protecting the environment. At that time, Attorney General William Guste created a small office to serve as a place where citizens could be put in touch with the proper authorities if they faced problems in the areas of health, toxic substances, transportation of hazardous materials, and coastal resources and wetlands.[28] Guste said that he created this office because the state was doing nothing to protect the environment.[29] He stated that, to his knowledge, there had never been a single legal action in the history of Louisiana against anybody for desecrating the environment. In 1980, the office collected the first major environmental fine ($350,000) against Good Hope Refinery near Norco, Louisiana.[30]

Ironically, the environmental agency and the attorney general's office should have been working together on the same issues; however, they were continuously at odds. Guste states, "There is no question at all, in fact, the state agencies considered us [the attorney general's office] the enemy. That was because the state agencies had the view that they were the protector of industry, more than the environment."[31] The office that Guste created employed one of the most valuable, longstanding protectors of Louisiana citizens and the environment – Willie Fontenot. He has been with the attorney general's office since 1978 and has assisted literally hundreds of grassroots community groups fighting environmental threats across the state. Fontenot provides support and guidance to groups on how to negotiate through the state's bureaucratic environmental maze; he will accompany groups to the Department of Environmental Quality to access the permit files or help them set up a meeting with department officials. He stated that the most important part of his job is "to help people understand how to organize, how to hook up with other groups and how to work with their local officials, the media, and other groups."[32]

As state government officials were arguing over how to regulate and protect the environment, a struggle that is considered by many to be the start of the environmental justice movement was occurring in Warren, North Carolina. In 1982, a poor, African-American community was protesting the dumping of PCB-contaminated soil in a landfill in their community. This protest, although unsuccessful, promoted an awareness throughout the nation that race and environmental degradation are intricately linked in our society.[33]

That same year in Louisiana, one of the key organizations for environmental justice was formed – the Gulf Coast Tenants Organization. The organization, which was created to improve federal, state, and local policies affecting public housing tenants, quickly expanded its focus to work with communities poisoned by environmental polluters. Its executive director, Pat Bryant, was a son of a Baptist minister and grew up in public housing himself, coming to New Orleans as something of a civil rights missionary for the Southern Organizing Committee.[34] Bryant and several other local activists took part in the 1983 Urban Environmental Conference, entitled, "Taking Back our Health," which was held in New Orleans. Sociologist and activist Robert Bullard identified this conference as one of the first events in which people of color and progressive whites came together to discuss environmental justice and coalition building.[35]

The next year, Bryant and a white activist, Darryl Malek-Wiley, organized a busload of like-minded activists to attend a Sierra Club conference in Atlanta. The conference, which was held on an election year Super Tuesday, took place at the same hotel as a series of presidential debates. Malek-Wiley remembers that an "ad hoc" minority caucus formed at the conference. He stated,

Reverend [Benjamin] Chavis [future NAACP head] was there, along with Charles Lee [of the United Church of Christ's commission on environmental justice] and Joseph Lowry of the Southern Christian Leadership Coalition – who was the closing speaker. When he closed the conference he said that he was going to walk over to see those Republicans because they didn't come to the conference. Basically, there was an en masse march through the conference center to where the Republicans were going to come through. So, actually the Republicans had to come through us to get to the reception area. It was intense.[36]

This experience gave birth to the idea for the First Great Toxics March, which came to life four years later.

As the statewide infrastructure for an environmental justice movement was evolving, several community groups throughout Louisiana were waging intense battles against polluters and proposed industrial facilities. One of the most dramatic and most visible was the African-American community of Alsen, which began organizing against Rollins Hazardous Waste Treatment and Disposal Facility and several other polluters in 1980. Willie Fontenot from the office of the attorney general worked with a coalition of farmers, residents, and workers who were being affected by noxious chemical fumes. Workers at the nearby Allied Signal Chemical Plant scrambled to don gas masks every time the wind blew toxic fumes from the Rollins facility in their direction. A local farmer, Katherine Ewell, who lived just north of Rollins, kept a diary in which she recorded noxious fumes and cattle deaths that she believed were related to Rollins and two Petro Processor waste sites in the area.[37] The Alsen area had numerous polluting facilities, including two Superfund sites and a large concentration of petrochemical industries.

Residents complained of sinus problems, headaches, asthma, rashes, chronic fatigue, cancer, and spontaneous nosebleeds. In 1980, the resident's group attended a monthly meeting of the Environmental Control Commission and for the first time in the state demonstrated that workers, farmers, and residents could come together to protest environmentally related health problems. The next month the environmental affairs office presented the first-ever state report on toxic waste, which showed that the Rollins site was an environmental mess and that the company was guilty of countless violations of state law.[38]

In 1981, residents filed a class-action suit against Rollins that resulted in a $3,000 settlement awarded to each plaintiff in exchange for releasing the company from all future liability of health-related problems.[39] In the mid-1980s, residents from the area and neighboring Baton Rouge successfully prevented the same company from burning PCBs. In the mid-1990s, residents successfully protested Rollin's request for a ten-year industrial tax exemption from the state. In 1998, residents protested the expansion of the Exxon Polyolefins Plant. Currently, a group in the community is waging a war against the proposed siting of an industrial landfill operation.[40]

On a tour of the heavily industrialized community of Alsen, activist Florence Robinson described an example of the lack of concern for public safety on the part of industry in the early years when the state did little to regulate hazardous waste disposal. She pointed out a waste pit on the side of the road saying, "Some guy from Texas came over and said 'you got a hole in the ground – you got a gold mine here.' He told them [the owners] to start dumping chemicals in the pit. That became the first waste pit here." Walking a little farther, she pointed at a house:

See that light through the trees? There was a family of people. The man brought his family down here from Mississippi. He has seven or eight or more kids and those kids used to come over here and swim in this pit. Then, when they started dumping those chemicals in, they didn't put a fence around it or a sign that said that you shouldn't come and swim. They [the children] would still come and swim in this pit. They would get these black balls – these tar-like balls and they would throw them and play with each other. One of them says 'you used to go in there and swim and when you came out you were dirtier than when you went in.' There's a lot of neurological problems in that family.[41]

The state is peppered with similar hazardous waste pits and other toxic dump sites. An eleven-parish area at the lower end of the Mississippi River has approximately 2,000 oilfield waste pits, hazardous waste sites, injection wells, and surface impoundments. Other waterways in the state are severely polluted; this includes the Devil's Swamp area in North Baton Rouge, the aquifer that supplies Calcasieu Parish with drinking water, and the Amite River and Lake Maurepas Northwest of New Orleans. Low-income individuals who supplement their diets through fishing are at high risk for exposure to pollution if they fish in these contaminated waterways. Over a dozen waterways were recently listed as containing hazardous levels of mercury, a dangerous neurotoxin.[42]

NEW COALITIONS: LABOR, ENVIRONMENTALISTS, AND NEIGHBORS

When the world's second-largest chemical manufacturing firm decided to begin a union-busting campaign and lock out its own workers at a plant in Geismar, Louisiana, they got more than they bargained for. What began as a labor issue between BASF Wyandotte, a German chemical producer, and its workers ended up strengthening the state's environmental activist network. Rather than quietly sitting by the plant gate holding signs, after a year of being locked out of their jobs, the union took an about-face in strategy. They pioneered a revolutionary and savage attack on their own firm, which the management would later refer to as a "scorched earth campaign."[43] The Oil, Chemical, and Atomic Workers union (OCAW, now called PACE for Paper Allied–Industrial, Chemical and Energy Workers International Union) built networks of new allies, nationally and internationally. These included members of the German parliament, victims of the Bhopal disaster in India, and environmentalists around the world. By one account, "the most important of the union's far-flung allies was Louisiana's grassroots environmentalist network, starting with environmental activists in Ascension Parish and spreading out to national groups like Greenpeace, the Sierra Club, and the National Toxics Campaign."[44]

Locked-out workers had time on their hands, and many took on the tasks of doing research about the plant's toxic emissions and safety lapses.[45] Many of the lapses were traced to the use of contract workers during the lockout. LA WATCH, Louisiana Workers Against Toxic Chemical Hazards, was formed and worked with Loyola University's Institute for Human Relations.[46] Working with the Sierra Club, they showed that fifteen plants in the Geismar area had dumped 76 million pounds of toxics into the Mississippi in just one year.[47] They highlighted the links between contaminated marshes, drinking water, and cancer and miscarriage rates in the parish. Huge billboards went up along Interstate 10 asking motorists, "Is BASF Chemicals the Gateway to Cancer Alley?" Another read: "BASF: Bhopal on the Bayou?" It continued: "Stop BASF before they stop you."

With time to do "outreach" to the community in which they worked, and realizing the importance of local support, the union helped in the creation of a group called the Ascension Parish Residents Against Toxic Pollution. Richard Miller, a union organizer sent in from the union's central office in Denver, described the difficulties of the work. "Organizing was frightening for many of the people, this industry is economically very powerful in Louisiana. The communities' needs are great, and their resources are few. Often it forces them to accept the companies' money and sing to their tune. When I got there, I looked around for allies. I thought, 'who are the other victims?' The residents of Geismar are the first ones I saw."[48]

A local protest group from Geismar, with the help of the chemical workers' union local and student lawyers from Tulane University's law school, filed a lawsuit in 1986 to make the state Department of Environmental Quality raise the fines assessed on BASF for releases of toxins. They won. In 1988 they pushed the DEQ to ban the unchecked injection of hazardous wastes underground, a surprisingly common practice in the state. This coalition has changed the face of environmentalism in the state: the beleaguered workers looked to environmentalists and forged a new alliance that makes the Louisiana environmental coalition one of the strongest and most unique in the nation.[49]

The OCAW also helped to create two initiatives that have provided extensive support for environmental justice struggles: Labor Neighbor and Louisiana Citizens for Tax Justice. Labor Neighbor is an OCAW program that provides support to community groups that want to address community issues and problems. They have assisted many community residents in the river parish area form groups and fight to protect the health of their families and environment. The Louisiana Citizens for Tax Justice is an advocacy group that analyzes and compiles statistics on the state's industrial tax incentive programs in an effort to inform citizens on the use of their tax dollars.

The weakness of the labor movement found strength in the environmental movement, as Richard Miller, Labor Neighbor's chief organizer said. "What we've discovered is that our strength here comes more from coalitions with the community rather than from the labor movement. We're trying to institutionalize these gains so that this local union will never again be left naked to a union-busting company."[50]

With the increasing information about the dangers these plants might pose, people began to draw new connections. Chris & Kay Gaudet, white pharmacists in St. Gabrielle, Louisiana, were startled by the number of women they saw coming in who had experienced a miscarriage. Kay started a list of miscarriages, which in the small town (population 2,100) grew to sixty-three in just a year.[51] She estimated that one third of all pregnancies resulted in the death of the fetus. Kay contacted the DEQ and Office of Public Health (OPH), requesting a systematic health study, but there was no response. Then the Sierra Club financed her travel to Washington, D.C., to talk to members of congress and hold a press conference. Nearly immediately the state agencies began to act.[52] The Louisiana Department of Health and Hospitals (DHH) contracted a study to be federally funded by the federal Agency for Toxic Substances and Disease Registry (ATSDR) and to be conducted by the Tulane University School of Public Health. The study found no higher miscarriage rates than national averages.[53] Community groups were angry that the study had not been designed to link environmental exposures to fetal loss.[54] Kay Gaudet railed that the study was inconclusive by its very design and expressed the widespread distrust of residents against such studies. "Beware of community health studies . . . no study has ever proven a link between adverse health effects and industrial emission. . . . Federal and state governments are not ready to take responsibility and admit what they've done to us."[55]

During their struggle, the Gaudets heard that chemical plant managers told their employees to avoid shopping at their pharmacy, and they were subsequently driven out of business. They later mused, "Why should they be afraid of us, we're ordinary citizens. I mean we're not eloquent. We know the facts, but I think that's what they're afraid of. It's that ordinary citizens are coming out and bringing up problems, highlighting them, raising up for everybody to see."[56]

In 1986, one of the missing links in the environmental justice and toxics movement came into being – an activist umbrella group called the Louisiana Environmental Action Network. LEAN's mission is "to foster cooperation and communication among individuals and organizations to address the environmental problems of Louisiana. Its goal is the creation, maintenance, and preservation, of a cleaner and healthier environment for all inhabitants of this state."[57] LEAN has been able to create an infrastructure to support community groups throughout the state by providing financial, technical, and organizational resources. Board member Florence Robinson described the activities of the organization, stating that LEAN's form of help is that of empowerment.

LEAN doesn't come into your community and say "I've got all the answers." LEAN comes to try to teach, to help you, to provide you with information, to help you develop your own skills, to support you so that you can go to workshops to develop your skills. LEAN does technical work for you – that kind of thing.[58]

LEAN's executive director was Mary Lee Orr, who feared her own children's health was being damaged by pollution. She said that she knew from the start that the people they were going to advocate for would be the disenfranchised people who didn't have a voice or the financial resources to fight for their communities. The organization is funded by foundations and individual member donations. Orr described her role as one of support for community groups and leaders. She stated, "People call here at the end of their rope and we try to help them." She stated that this work can be psychologically, financially, and emotionally draining and if LEAN staff can alleviate some of the stress for the people in the trenches – that is what they are there for. She stated, "It goes back again to respect. It goes back to seeing people's personal resources and commitment and respect, you know learning from one another. And I think what LEAN is really effective at is bringing together people who feel like that."[59] LEAN has been tremendously effective at bringing people together. Currently eighty-five groups throughout the state are members of LEAN. They have helped hundreds more. Their board of directors and membership reads like a Who's Who of toxic struggles in Louisiana.

In 1989, another important player entered the Louisiana environmental justice movement – the Tulane Environmental Law Clinic. As part of the Tulane Law School, the clinic's mission is primarily educational – to train environmental lawyers through a "hands-on" program where students serve as lawyers under the watchful eye of a supervising attorney. Since its founding, the clinic has provided over 170 groups – ranging from very small groups to groups affiliated with national organizations – with free legal assistance. And in 1991, Sierra Club Legal Defense Fund (SCLDF) set up its regional office in New Orleans. Though extremely selective in what cases they could take on, SCLDF played a major role in some of the landmark struggles in Louisiana, as we'll see later. Before the clinic and SCLDF were established, there was almost no place to turn for citizen groups who could not afford to pay for legal assistance. Now they have some of the best in the world.[60]

THE MOVEMENTS COME TOGETHER:
THE GREAT TOXICS MARCH AND THREE EXTOWNS

One of the defining events for the environmental justice movement in Louisiana came in 1988 with The First Great Toxics March. March organizers realized that there were many toxic struggles raging in communities from Baton Rouge to New Orleans.[61] The organizers wanted to have a march that would serve as an organizing tool to tie together different struggles in the industrial corridor. Darryl Malek-Wiley, a white Sierra Club organizer, and Pat Bryant, the African-American head of the tenants' organization, approached foundations to raise money for the march. Malek-Wiley stated, "Pat Bryant and I flew to New York to talk to foundations. It was one of the first times that they saw an African American and a white man come in talking about the environment in Louisiana – so we raised sixty to seventy thousand dollars."[62] The march was a pivotal event because it brought very diverse groups, such as labor, church, environmental, and tenants' rights groups, together against the same enemies. The main sponsors were the Oil, Chemical, and Atomic Workers Local 4-620, the Gulf Coast Tenants Leadership Development Project, the Sierra Club, Baton

Rouge Youth Group, and the Louisiana Environmental Action Network.[63]

The march coincided with the Louisiana leg of Greenpeace's six-month boat trek down the Mississippi River, which was aimed at drawing attention to the pollution problems in the Mississippi River Valley. The march, which lasted ten days, covered 80 miles of the industrial corridor between Baton Rouge and New Orleans. March organizers let community groups in each parish dictate which industrial facilities would be protested during the march. These groups were charged with finding the marchers a place to stay (mostly at churches) and to cook for them as they passed through their parish.

The march had some similarities to the civil rights marches that had covered some of the same southern roads. During the civil rights movement, Louisiana parishes tried to deter marches by requiring participants to purchase permits to march. Several parishes that the toxics march went through still had these laws on the books. In St. James parish the fee was $10,000 and in St. Charles it was $100,000. Officials in these parishes waived the fees. However, this did not occur in Jefferson Parish where the permit fee was $340. One of the most intense moments occurred in Jefferson Parish when Sheriff Harry Lee, considered extremely racist by many local African Americans, stopped the march. Malek-Wiley described what happened when they gathered in the parish to march on that cool Friday morning in December:

We had a brass band playing and the local community folks were there. These deputies were there and they said, "if you walk in Jefferson Parish, we are going to arrest you." So, the crowd kept growing because the music was going and the people saw all the police cars and wanted to find out what was going on. The television and radio was there. It was a real carnival atmosphere. The deputies kept saying that if you walk we are going to arrest you.

Finally, the deputies said that they would give the group a police escort to anywhere in the parish if they rode there on their bus. So, Pat Bryant, thinking quickly, rattled off the address of the Sheriff's department. He was planning to conduct a sit-in at the department. Instead, Sheriff Lee came down to talk with the organizers. Malek-Wiley described the scene:

So, Pat is talking to the Sheriff with Rev. Clifton McFarland, he is a leader of the Southern Christian Leadership Conference on the West Bank, and Rosemary Smith, who was President of the Gulf Coast Tenants Organization. Rev. McFarland, who was a good Southern Baptist preacher, decided it was time to

45

pray for Sheriff Lee. So, he grabbed Sheriff Lee's hand and put his other hand on his shoulder and proceeded to pray [out loud] for the man for twenty minutes. So, what happens when he starts praying is the whole crowd gathers around Sheriff Lee and puts out their hands [saying] "heal."

When the Reverend finished his prayer, the sheriff was asked if he would still arrest them and he responded, "yes." The group, however, didn't end up getting arrested in Jefferson Parish because they went to an area of the parish that didn't require a permit to march. Press photographers captured the dramatic prayer scene and the picture appeared in newspapers across the country.[64]

At the end of the march, the protestors met a similar obstacle in New Orleans. Although they had gotten a permit to march, they did not pay the required $370 per day for police protection. The New Orleans police allowed marchers to walk through the city to Louis Armstrong Park, where they arrested eight men whom they thought were the organizers. About 200 protesters showed up at the park for a rally, but they were instead met by police. When the arrests were made, the other marchers sat down on the stone pavement around the police paddy wagon and started chanting. The arrested marchers were eventually taken downtown to the central lock-up. State representative Reverend Avery Alexander, a veteran civil rights and environmental justice activist, got the protestors released without bond after about forty marchers conducted a rowdy demonstration in the lobby of the central lockup.[65]

The march, especially after the police standoff and the arrests in New Orleans, generated considerable statewide press coverage and successfully placed the toxics issue in people's minds. A public opinion survey sponsored by the Louisiana Chemical Association measured the impact of Greenpeace's activities and the Great Toxics March. The study found that most of the 450 respondents who were surveyed thought that the march was organized by Greenpeace. Almost 23 percent of the respondents reported that their level of concern for environmental problems had increased as a result of Greenpeace activities, as compared to less than 2 percent who said that it had decreased. Similarly, a third of the respondents reported that Greenpeace had increased public awareness of environmental problems.[66] In the executive summary of the report, the chemical association's consultants reported the grim findings: voters perceived environmental laws and regulations as inadequate, they blamed serious health and environmental problems on chemical plant pollution, and they felt that chemical companies only comply with regulations because they are forced to by environmental organizations and state agencies.[67]

Greenpeace released a study in the late 1980s that concluded that the death rate along the Mississippi River corridor was significantly higher than the national average. They reported that, between 1968 and 1983, 66,000 additional deaths above the national average occurred in river corridor parishes. "Deaths linked to cancer are increasing in the river counties at a rate that is twice that of the rest of the nation and that increase is especially high in those parishes below Baton Rouge."[68] Though the chemical industry and state agencies responded with their own studies, attitudes were shifting. People believed that chemical plants were poisoning the river and that their dangers must be thought of in terms of *cumulative* effect rather than in terms of individual chemicals. And the movement's term *Cancer Alley* was replacing the industry's *Chemical Corridor* in popular speech.

As the public was becoming more and more aware through statewide protest events of the environmental degradation that was endemic to Louisiana, the struggle was continuing at the local level. In three locals battles, communities actually *lost* their lives. These poor, primarily black communities had to be totally relocated because chemical companies had built too close to their borders and residents were complaining that they were inundated by pollution.

In 1971, Georgia Pacific, a producer of chemicals and plastics, located just 200 yards away from Revilletown, a small unincorporated exslave town on the west side of the Mississippi River. The town, which was composed of 150 black residents, had an average income below the poverty level; the majority of residents were not high school graduates. Many homes did not have indoor plumbing, and the area did not have adequate municipal services, such as fire and police protection, recreational facilities, or access to a sewage system. As a result of a lawsuit against the company alleging property damage and personal injury from plant emissions and separate agreements with landholders, the town was completely bought out by the company.[69] The company relocated twelve of the households that wanted to stay together to a subdivision called Revilletown Park. The company also built a new church in the subdivision to replace the 112-year-old church that the community had lost.[70] The company, however, did not move the town cemetery. If residents want to visit the graves of their relatives, they must traverse company grounds to do so.

In the same parish, the town of Morrisonville, founded in 1790 by freed slaves, was voluntarily relocated by the Louisiana Division of Dow Chemical, USA, which produces chemicals, plastics, pharmaceutical, and agricultural materials. The town, which was 60 percent black and composed of poor and working-class individuals, had six businesses, two cemeteries, two churches, eighty-seven landowners, and thirty tenants. Due to expansions that encroached on the community, Dow finally offered in 1989 to relocate the residents. In a manner to similar to Revilletown, the company established a subdivision called New Morrisonville for residents who desired to remain together. Almost all residents participated in the voluntary relocation. The community also lost its cemeteries to the confines of the company's property. Morrisonville residents were assisted by several nonprofit organizations – the Gulf Coast Tenants Organization, Louisiana Environmental Action Network, and Citizens for a Clean Environment.

The third community was the town of Sunshine located in West Baton Rouge Parish, which borders Iberville Parish. The town, which was 83 percent black, was founded by former slave Alexander Banes in 1874. The majority of the ninety households earned incomes below the federal poverty level. The Placid Refining Company, which refines and markets oil, was less than 50 yards away from the community. The company bought out 90 percent of the residents as a result of both a company-initiated buyout program and an out-of-court agreement from a lawsuit brought by residents that alleged that the company's pollution had caused health, economic, and psychological damages. The residents were assisted in their struggle by the Gulf Coast Tenants Organization and the nonprofit organization, Victims of a Toxic Environment United.[71]

What do these cases mean? Who won these battles? The Louisiana Advisory Committee to the U.S. Commission on Civil Rights reviewed the cases of Morrisonville, Revilletown, and Sunrise and released a report in September of 1993.[72] They concluded that "the impact of industrial development appears to fall on disproportionately or predominantly black areas of Louisiana." Interviews conducted with Dow buyout participants from Morrisonville/Cut Off found that their feelings were mixed – they got away from the noise, trucks, and odors but lost their ancestral land and the community's history.[73] Peter Wayman, Senior Vice President of the New York–based consulting firm that designed the Morrisonville buyout for Dow, bluntly said, "It is cheaper to buy the real estate than pay for litigation, and pay the settlement, than buy real estate."[74] He warned firms to be responsible to communities where they operate, "Otherwise, you're going to need more PR people and lawyers than you can shake a stick at."

A strong critic of the environmental justice movement, Christopher Foreman reviewed these cases in his 1998 Brookings Institute book.[75] He concluded that "at the very least these cases clearly portray communities far removed from the helpless victims of movement lore. . . . In no case did overwhelmed residents wind up with little or nothing to show for their interaction with the firms in question." We believe that there is a certain dishonesty in not acknowledging that these are the success stories; Foreman has not considered the hundreds of unorganized or unsuccessful communities in Louisiana alone. Finally, the destruction of these communities did nothing to change the state or federal guidelines governing plant siting or expansion: a decade later there is still no law on "buffer zones" between plants and communities, and dozens of other communities continue to fight for relocation.

THE NATIONAL AND STATE MOVEMENTS INTERSECT

As community/industry battles continued to rage in Louisiana, several landmark studies were being released at the national level that lent credence to the claims of environmental justice activists. In 1983, the U.S. General Accounting Office released a study of hazardous waste landfill siting in The South. The study's findings suggested that more than chance had put toxic landfills in predominantly African-American communities. Three out of the four communities in the region that had hazardous waste landfills also had majority black populations, with greater than 25 percent of the population living on incomes below the poverty level.[76]

A few years later, the United Church of Christ's Commission on Racial Justice released a now-famous study that examined the demographic patterns associated with commercial hazardous waste facilities and uncontrolled toxic waste sites. Their findings revealed a statistically significant relationship between race and the siting of commercial hazardous waste facilities: communities with the most facilities also had the highest percentage of nonwhite residents. When they controlled for socioeconomic status (income and education), race still played a role in the location of facilities – indicating that race is a more significant factor than class in terms of where facilities are located.[77] More studies followed.[78]

By the beginning of the decade of the nineties, two very active environmental justice groups, the Gulf Coast Tenants Leadership Development Project and the Southwest Organizing Project from Albuquerque, New Mexico, were growing impatient with the lack of response of mainstream environmental organizations to environmental racism and injustice. In 1990, the two organizations sent a letter to the "Big Ten" national environmental organizations expressing their frustrations and charging that the organizations' staff and advisory boards did not have adequate representation of people of color.[79]

The very next year, Pat Bryant, the director of the Gulf Coast Tenants Organization, served on a steering committee for the landmark People of Color Environmental Leadership Summit. Bryant and Malek-Wiley took the steering committee on one of their infamous toxic tours of Cancer Alley. Many activist groups and government officials have taken this tour to see firsthand the effects that industrialization and inequality have on people of color communities. It is in these poor, black communities scattered throughout the Mississippi River Valley that one sees the stark reality of poverty and environmental destruction.[80]

Thus, the voices and images of the people from poor Louisiana communities were able to influence and inform the landmark People of Color Environmental Leadership Summit. Soon after that conference, another large environmental gathering sponsored by the Gulf Coast Tenants Organization and the Southern Organizing Committee to discuss race was held at Xavier University in New Orleans, a traditionally black university.[81] This and collaborative grant making by academics and activists led to the founding of the Deep South Center for Environmental Justice, headed by Beverly Wright at Xavier University. Dr. Wright, a sociologist, has written extensively on environmental justice and is considered to be one of the leading national activists in the movement. The center works in several different arenas to fight environmental injustice in the state. They develop curricula to teach students of all ages about environmental justice and train workers on hazardous materials.[82] They conduct research in local communities to substantiate environmental injustice and have supported a community/university partnership that attempts to resolve injustice.

TWO PRECEDENT-SETTING STRUGGLES

During the 1980s and early 1990s, two precedent-setting struggles signaled that a change in the balance of power is possible and can enable small community groups to sometimes defeat large corporate giants. One battle was fought by a white environmental community group called Save Our Selves (SOS) in heavily industrialized but rural Ascension Parish, and the other battle was waged just down river in St. John the Baptist Parish by a multiracial coalition of black residents, plantation owners, historical preservationists, and environmentalists.

In Louisiana, every battle over the siting of a new industrial facility is influenced by a May 1984 Louisiana Supreme Court decision. The decision results from a ultimately successful battle led by two young white Ascension Parish housewives who did not want the world's largest hazardous waste treatment dump in their backyard. In 1980, when the two women, Teresa Robert and Ruby Cointment, walked into a room full of lawyers and officials they were opposing, they whispered to each other under their breath, "If we're going to pray we'd better start praying right now."[83] Robert attributed the endurance that was needed to pursue the battle and their ultimate success to the group's strong faith and confidence that they were doing the work of the Lord. She stated, "And that's what we did. We prayed our way through it for the next nine years, we worked harder than we'd ever worked on anything in our lives and we made up our minds we would never give up."

The court ruling was on a lawsuit filed by their environmental group, Save Our Selves, against DEQ's predecessor agency.[84] The company was International Technology Corporation, and the site was 1,100 acres in Burnside, Louisiana. The Louisiana Supreme Court forced the state environmental agency to review the company's permit and answer a series of tough questions about it, documenting whether alternative sites and solutions had been considered. These questions are now known as the IT Questions. They include such questions as: do the social and economic benefits of the plant outweigh the risks? And, have alternative sites and technologies been considered? [85] Every major pollution emitter in Louisiana must now answer these questions as part of their permit application process. The hazardous waste facility was never built in Burnside.

In March 1989, Taiwanese plastics company Formosa Chemicals and Fibres Corporation planned to build a $700 million rayon plant, which would have been the world's largest.[86] The company bought the 1,800-acre site of the Whitney Plantation antebellum home in the predominantly black town of Wallace, a community three parishes upriver from New Orleans. The plant would bring 1,000 jobs to the parish at a time when virtually no new industrial projects had been built since the oil bust of the 1980s. In 1990, parish officials voted to give local tax breaks to the plant and to rezone the site for industrial use.[87] To prevent the siting, a local group called River Area Planning (RAP) Group, Greenpeace, Sierra Club Legal Defense Fund, the Louisiana Coalition for Tax Justice, and Save Our Wetlands sued the parish over the zoning change.[88]

A key element in the oppositions' fight were two African-American members of RAP who owned small parcels of land that Formosa needed for building a dock on the river. These residents refused to sell their land to a company, they viewed as a health threat to their community. At a community meeting, one of the landowners, Wilfred Greene, reasoned with a man anticipating employment at the proposed plant. He said, "You don't need a job if you have to give every nickel you make to the doctor – or to the undertaker. You don't want that kind of job."[89]

In response to opponents' demands and due to a similar struggle that was taking place in Texas, the EPA required that the company do an extensive study of how the plant would affect the community.[90] Additionally, in May 1992, Matilda Gray Stream of New Orleans, who owned the Evergreen Plantation located next door to the proposed plant, sued the company, fearing noise and pollutants. Although the parish won the lawsuit against plant opponents, the firm announced in October 1992 that they were pulling out.[91] In canceling the plant, Formosa blamed the Evergreen Plantation suit and the EPA's extensive permitting demands, which caused the case to drag on and delay their entry into the global rayon market.[92] The plant was never built in another location.[93]

Looking forward to the Shintech case described in Chapter 4, the Formosa struggle brought together many of the same coalition members on both sides, and the battle broke the once total dominance of industry in the chemical corridor. Gail Martin from Greenpeace said it this way, "If we can beat a plant in the middle of Cancer Alley, we can beat a plant anywhere."[94] Natalie Walker of Sierra Club Legal Defense Fund said, "It is exactly what you are going to see more and more of." From another perspective, Jim Edmonson, director of the South

Central Planning and Development Commission agreed. He argued, "If this was the first chemical plant along the river, it wouldn't have run into the opposition it did. But it gets progressively harder with every new plant. And that's partly because people are more educated about the downside."[95]

STATE AND FEDERAL GOVERNMENT UNDER PRESSURE

As an infrastructure was developing in the state, and individual battles were being waged in many local communities, the state and federal governments were trying to figure out how to handle the red-hot political issue of environmental justice. As already mentioned, the U.S. Commission on Civil Rights conducted an investigation into the environmental problems in predominantly black communities in Louisiana. This marked the first time that the commission had reviewed race discrimination in terms of environmental policies and practices anywhere. They heard from state and federal officials, industry leaders, environmental and civil rights groups, elected officials, environmental experts, and individual residents, interviewing over fifty individuals during a six-month time period. The Advisory Committee concluded that "black communities located along the industrial corridor between Baton Rouge and New Orleans are disproportionately impacted by the present state and local government system for permitting and expansion of hazardous waste and chemical facilities." They reported that state and local governments have failed to regulate industrial operations in the region adequately in order to protect the residents from the risks associated with living close to these facilities. The commission's investigation revealed that black citizens and organizations do not trust Louisiana Department of Environmental Quality and other state agencies because they believe state officials are biased in support of industry.[96]

The commission recommended that state officials specify adequate set back distance around industrial facilities to protect nearby residents from the effects of emissions. They also recommended that the state legislature pass a bill that would address environmental justice issues. Additionally, they recommended that state health officials develop database and risk assessment methodologies that address pollution emissions and exposure in terms of race, ethnicity, and income. Finally, they recommended that the EPA assess the state's permit and siting practices in terms of civil rights issues and monitor the black communities identified in the report as disproportionately impacted by pollution. This final recommendation foreshadows the Title VI civil rights complaint filed by protesters in the Shintech facility siting battle three years later.

In response to the Civil Rights Commission investigation, the state legislature requested that the Louisiana Department of Environmental Quality hold four public hearings throughout the state to gather information on environmental justice. Residents, nonprofit organizations, industry representatives, and university faculty attended these hearings, which were held in Baton Rouge, New Orleans, Lake Charles, and Ruston.

Their report, presented to the legislature, revealed the people's anger even through the bureaucratese language:

Individuals living near industrial facilities expressed genuine concern about risk in the event of an industrial accident. They also indicated that they believed that they are unreasonably burdened by emissions emanating from their industrial neighbors, but are denied employment opportunities and other benefits that are generally considered available as a result of having an industrial facility in the community. Also, many of the individuals who testified believe that neither government nor industry takes their concerns seriously. They expressed their collective belief that there is virtually no environmental justice for low-income minority residents who live next to industrial facilities or hazardous waste sites and insisted on immediate action to remedy the perceived inequities.[97]

The LDEQ came up with several recommendations as a result of the hearings. These included drafting legislation to implement the mandates of the International Technology (IT) decision; strengthening state landuse planning requirements in relation to environmental justice issues; strengthening requirements on transportation of toxic materials; using tax incentives to reduce hazardous waste generation and disposal; and strengthening policies related to community emergency response. The report also included recommendations to increase LDEQ funding to create an Office of Environmental Justice and support programs to train local residents in emergency response and to encourage the employment of minorities at DEQ by supporting environmental sciences and engineering programs at historically black colleges and universities.[98]

The LDEQ report signaled the beginning of the state's Environmental Justice Program – the first state program in the country. The LDEQ received a $75,000 grant from the United States EPA, Region 6 Office. The program instituted three community "Environmental Justice Panels" in which elected community members met with industry representatives to resolve environmental justice issues. The program also conducted workshops with community members on technical issues, claims of governmental discrimination, and emergency response procedures. Janice Dickerson and Roger Ward, program representatives, reported that "the program strives to teach people how to solve their own problems, for they, better than anybody else, understand the needs and problems that exist within the community."[99]

In a 1995 report on the LDEQ Environmental Justice Program, Dickerson and Ward cited the accomplishments of the program that range from Cargill, Inc., providing a recreation area for the children of Lions, to having a community resident of Mossville placed on the Conoco community advisory panel, to industry supporting emergency response training for local residents. According to Dickerson and Ward, LDEQ is playing a peripheral facilitative role in helping communities and industry work together. The program representatives stated:

Once the [environmental justice] panels are firmly established and the benefits of participating on a panel are appreciated, it is hoped that the LDEQ can remove itself from the process and entrust the continuation of the panel to both the community and industry. Such a panel consisting of only industry and community meeting together as neighbors and partners, is the vision that the LDEQ Environmental Justice Group has for panels.[100]

Some of the notable groups that are excluded from these panels are environmental or social justice groups. Dickerson feels strongly that "outside" environmental groups can be detrimental to the best interest of poor communities. She complained that traditional environmental groups have a history of exploiting communities in Louisiana. She stated, "Environmental groups would descend upon these communities, express concern for the people and the state of the environmental quality, bring in the media, get press coverage, receive donations for their groups, and then depart – leaving the community in no better condition than it was prior to the group's advent."[101]

When Governor Mike Foster came into office in 1996, he changed the name of the Environmental Justice Program to the Community Industry Relations (CIR) Office. This name change may provide evidence as to why office activities and statements generate opposition from some environmental justice advocates. For example, in the Shintech siting case (Chapter 4), environmental justice activists accused the office of siding with industry and actively creating a supportive proindustry residents' group in the parish. The root of the conflict between the CIR office and certain environmental justice groups may stem from a differing opinion on how to handle environmental justice cases. The CIR office attempts to get industry and community residents to work together. Conversely, some environmental justice advocates feel that industry has unfairly exploited their communities and that there is no more room for negotiation or compromise. Furthermore, many activists believe that it is extremely difficult for residents and industry representative to meet on an equal playing field due to the dramatic difference in levels of resources and technical knowledge between the two groups.

At the same time that the state office of environmental justice was forming, President Clinton issued an executive order that helped to validate and invigorate the environmental justice movement nationwide. The executive order 12898 of 1994 decreed that "all communities and individuals, regardless of economic status or race are entitled to a safe and healthy environment."[102] This order was instrumental in providing a legal basis with which to pursue state and federal regulations to protect poor and minority communities. In the nineties, community groups throughout the country cited this order and filed complaints using Title VI of the 1964 Civil Rights Act with the EPA claiming that they, as minorities, were being disproportionately impacted by pollution.[103] Since the order was extremely broad and vague, it has taken the EPA over six years to issue regulations and instructions to state environmental agencies outlining how to handle environmental justice. In Chapter 7, we will explore the EPA's actions stemming from the executive order and the response of state and industry representatives.

RACIAL TENSION WITHIN THE MOVEMENT?

A discussion of the history of the environmental justice movement in Louisiana would be incomplete without an examination of how racial tension has influenced and shaped the movement. The antitoxics and environmental justice movements in the state were, at times, unwittingly pursuing conflicting goals. This occurred when white antitoxic

groups, also called NIMBY (not-in-my-backyard groups), would successfully oppose a proposed hazardous landuse for their neighborhood, only to have it successfully sited in a community of color that
did not have the resources, organization, or power to fight it successfully.

Another common complaint from people-of-color activists is that
white environmental organizations are racist, ignore the needs of
people-of-color communities, and do not hire or listen to African
Americans. This complaint has been heard repeatedly in Louisiana. In
fact, as we were writing this book, the DEQ coordinator of the CIR office said that she didn't think that white individuals could adequately
tell the story of environmental justice in Louisiana. She believed that
we would not mention in the book a meeting that environmentalists
had during the David Duke/Edwin Edward governor's race in which
they discussed who to endorse for governor. Although Governor Edwards did not have a favorable environmental record, the thought that
white environmentalists would even consider voting for avowed white
supremacist David Duke enraged black activists.

These accusations against white environmental groups are not new.
They hearken back to the 1990 letter written by environmental justice
activists to the "Big Ten" national environmental organizations accusing them of not truly representing the interests of communities of
color. Even now, ten years later, social justice activist Pat Bryant argued that environmental organizations are not employing people of
color. He stated,

Environmental groups still have a problem with race. There is no rush to make
sure that the people that represent them have racial balance and understand
racial politics, or are taught to be effective. I don't see any outreach to the His-
panic community up and down the river. I don't see the first Spanish speaking
person employed in the environmental community in the state.[104]

The demand for participation of people of color comes directly from
the Principles of Environmental Justice discussed at the October 1991
People of Color Leadership Summit. The seventh principle states,
"Environmental Justice demands the right to participate as equal partners at every level of decision-making including needs assessment,
planning, implementation, enforcement, and evaluation."[105] Planners
of the summit focused on bringing people of color together to discuss
their plight. Robert Bullard, a sociologist and national environmental
justice activist stated,

The planners of the Summit expected the obvious: that religious, government, and national environmental leaders would find fault in any process in which people of color put their heads together to break up the genocidal games all the major institutions play on them. Delegates to the summit demonstrated to themselves that African Americans, Native Americans, Latino Americans, and Asian Americans must plot a course together and ask other progressives to join their vision and struggle for a just world.[106]

In Bullard's writings, he expressed a certain hesitancy when he spoke of whites and people of color working together for environmental justice and viewed these coalitions with uneasiness. He stated,

Although these groups are beginning to formulate agendas for action, mistrust still persists as a limiting factor. These groups are often biracial with membership cutting across class and geographic boundaries. There is a downside to these types of coalition groups. For example, compositional factors may engender less group solidarity and sense of control among black members compared to indigenous social action and grassroots environmental groups where blacks are in the majority and make the decisions. The question of who is calling the shots is ever present.[107]

It is not surprising that there is great mistrust between blacks and whites in Louisiana. The state's history with slavery and civil rights has given blacks very little reason to trust whites. This attitude should not be surprising to people of either race. Additionally, the perceptions and interests of people of color and whites are often different, stemming from the fact that, due to racism and inequality, the two races have very different experiences in the same world.

One black environmental justice activist reported to us that he met resistance when he tried to promote activism on environmental issues in the black community and among state and local black social justice organizations. He said that ministers and other black leaders questioned his affiliations with environmental organizations and accused him of being an "Uncle Tom." They dismissed environmental issues as "white people's issues." Part of this is tied to the fact, seen in two of the cases presented in this book, that sometimes black social justice organizations side with development forces in environmental justice struggles because they feel that poor black communities will benefit more financially than they will suffer environmentally from economic development projects.

Environmental justice advocates throughout the state voiced different opinions on the existence of racial tension within the movement.

Florence Robinson, a black activist who began fighting polluters in her community of Alsen, believes that the movement can overcome racial tension. She stated,

I think that racial tension has cropped up in the movement over the last four or five years. I think that it has been generated by a few individuals who for some reason seem to thrive on racial tension. I don't think it does the movement any good at all. It's something I really hate to see. I use the word, "environmental racism," and I can use the word, "racist," with the best of them. When I do it, I have a real intention – you are not my target. The government is my target, the chemical company is my target.[108]

Bullard and many other environmental justice activists believe it is crucial to have people of color at the helm in the movement. Harold Green of the Southern Christian Leadership Conference agrees that it is important to have black leaders on board and in the front of the movement – a multiracial movement. He stated,

So, concerns of having more black people [leading the movement are real]. Yes, because the masses of uneducated with respect to the environment are people of color. Because the perpetrators are these big multinationals who [are exploiting] people of color. So, the people that are already in the communities – who have the credibility and that people respect – are the black leaders. So, we need them right there.

However, he warns against racial polarization in the movement. He states, "If we [racially] compartmentalize, then we are polarizing our own movement to our detriment. Even though I'm with the people of the black church, my obligation is to educate them and to bring them to a point where they see the big picture and know that it is not a black/white [issue] – it is us."[109]

Marylee Orr, Director of LEAN, said that, even though the organization has black board members, a foundation that funds environmental justice organizations has questioned the fact that LEAN is not staffed by people of color. She said that she told the foundation, "If you can find us an African American chemist who gives six figures worth of time practically for free . . . and give us a chemical engineer who gets compensated very little when he could be doing something else, I'd take them in a heartbeat. But I haven't found it." She added,

I think that you have to be careful not to be divided by race and you have to be careful not to apologize. You should not have to apologize because you are white. If I were black, I shouldn't have to apologize because I'm black. There's some level of respect that we need to reach as a society that's not there at many levels. So, I've dealt with it [racial tension] so much in a very volatile way that I've gotten pretty definite feelings about the race issue. The premise of LEAN is that we are a family and what makes us unified or so strong is our diversity. If we begin to apologize or to always notice the other's color, then, there is no purpose in our diversity.[110]

Several activists, both black and white, have said that, although there is significant racial tension within the state and, at times, within the movement, the movement ultimately has the potential to bring the races together. Albertha Hasten, a very vocal, dedicated, black environmental justice advocate and LEAN board member proclaimed,

You don't have time when you're really committed and dedicated – you don't have time to have racial tension. The air does not have no color in it – it's killing everybody slowly. This water we drink don't have no color on it – its been killing everybody slowly. And the food we eat don't have no color on it. But we put the color into it. We say,"well because I'm black maybe I might last a little longer than you or because you are white, you might last a little longer than me." There's people putting the color into it. But, mother nature and industry and large corporations didn't put no color in it.[111]

Hasten viewed the main problem for the movement as the color green – not black and white. She explained,

It's an issue of saying what is fair and equal justice for all. We have never gotten to that – fair and equal justice. We have never gotten to it because we take the rich and make them richer and we take the poor and make them poorer and we take the working class people and put them in the middle. Which whether you are white or black, hate it or not, you're in a trap. And because you're white, you feel very inferior because you are now being deprived of the pie some and if you are black, you've been deprived for over 200 years and you're still seeing the pie, but you can say it's hurting you more, but really this injustice is hurting all of us. Fair and equal justice for all through all the letter E's of education, environment, economics have never empowered the people. We must stand up and quit denying to ourselves that there's no problem. There is a problem, and the problem is the green, the economics of the green, we must face that.[112]

Hasten sees the movement as multiracial. She is chairperson of Louisiana Communities United, an organization that brings together and supports community organizations and grassroots groups in their efforts to find solutions to their community's problems. She stated,

It's important to show unity, because when you're showing unity and diversity, people cannot take that. Unity is diversity – those words are very powerful. When you say Louisiana Communities United – unity with diversity – their eyes see white and black pulling together – that's nerve racking. That's power and they [the power holders] can't deal with that. They can't take that power – that's people power.

Florence Robinson agreed that a unified multiracial movement will be most successful. She argued,

I think if people are really sincere and really interested in solving the problem, it can go beyond race, and they will work beyond race. Gradually they will overcome their prejudices. You know, people aren't all of a sudden going to change their opinion about how they felt for generations – that's not going to happen. But, people can make progress and I've seen an awful lot of progress made.[113]

Orr, a white activist, echoed Robinson's prediction that the movement can work beyond racial tension. She explained,

We can't limit ourselves if we really want to win. You've got to examine yourselves, too. If you really want to win for people's health and safety, then you got to lay aside a lot of crap – your egos and different kinds of things. We've kind of demanded that with people and I've been pretty harsh with other leaders and I think that's made me not popular to a degree – because I don't want to see us divided in that way.[114]

Harold Green of the Southern Christian Leadership Conference (Martin Luther King, Jr.'s group) proposed that the movement is currently in a transitional phase. He places great faith in the potential of the next generation of black youth. Green worked with the Deep South Center for Environmental Justice to develop a curriculum on environmental justice for children in grades K–12. He believes that the future of the movement depends on the young blacks who are growing up learning about environmental injustices. Darryl Malek-Wiley, a white environmental justice activist, agreed that African-American youth are the key to the success of the movement. He stated, "I think the sleeping strengths [for the movement] are the African-American colleges."

Even though many environmental justice activists whom we interviewed disliked the occurrence of racial tension within the movement, they did acknowledge that the racial tension in the larger society causes environmental injustice and that sense of injustice drives the environmental justice movement. Our point is that activists should not be surprised at the difficulty of reaching across a divide created by centuries of mistreatment and miscommunication. Although the cases in this book took place in the last decade of the twentieth century, they have been heavily influenced by the way Africans were brought here and treated for 300 years and more recently by the struggles that occurred, the organizations that were created, and the coalitions that formed since that birth of the toxics and environmental justice movements. The cases that follow have pushed the movement forward and have shaped the issue of environmental justice in Louisiana and the nation. We are left with an open question: *Does this movement have the ability to rise above or alter the social toxins of the racist environment in which they exist?*

3

The Nation's First Major Environmental Justice Judgment

THE LES URANIUM ENRICHMENT FACILITY

Top: Dorothy Hamilton (left) and her four-year-old granddaughter, Toriuanna Hamilton, at the Shreveport hearing on July 20, 1994. [Billy Upshaw, photographer, courtesy *Shreveport Times*]

Bottom: Map from Sierra Club Legal Defense Fund letter to the Louisiana Department of Environmental Quality of August 12, 1994, showing the location of homes nearest the proposed LES uranium plant site. [Original map by Norton Tompkins]

INTRODUCTION

Lumber trucks speeding by the window shake our car as the four-lane narrows to two-lanes and we twist through the piney woods of north Louisiana past huge paper mills, lonely, old small towns and the K-mart strip malls that have sapped their energy. Reaching the northernmost point in the state, Claiborne Parish, we called ahead to our contact, who said he'd meet us at a place called the Linder Motor Lodge. "I'll be driving a gray towncar." The unassuming one-story brick motel sat alone at the crossroads of two rural highways at a place appropriately called Deer Crossing. There the gray car was running, parked well away from the front windows of the motel office and from what appeared to be a popular coffee shop for truckers. He stepped out of his car, said hello, and we suggested we talk in the coffee shop.

"No, check into your room, we'll talk there." He said with a serious smile. "That place has ears – this is a small town; you never know who's listening around here."

Back outside with the key, we circled our cars around to the back to the end of the parking lot and the last room. In the low-ceilinged, wood-paneled, mildew-smelling room, to the steady rumble of the air conditioner, our informant plunged into a story that began more than a decade earlier. It was a story of a bizarre and shadowy project, one that had all the features of an episode of the *X-Files*, a spy novel, or a major motion picture . . .

* * *

On the sunny hot day of June 9, 1989, flyers appeared around the Claiborne Parish courthouse and the surrounding shops on the picturesque but spare town square of Homer, Louisiana. The word spread quickly that a big barbecue was going to happen that evening at 5:30

in honor of U.S. Senator J. Bennett Johnston's birthday, at which he would make a major announcement to the community.

As the crowd gathered around the hastily constructed wooden stage, the lanky senator took off his jacket and climbed on stage with his red suspenders. After welcoming the guests and acknowledging his friends and the local dignitaries, Johnston announced that the parish would be the site of a $750 million "uranium enrichment facility," which would be entirely safe and would bring 400 jobs and millions in tax revenues. The construction jobs would be plentiful, and the tax revenues enormous for the depressed rural community. The cheerfully named Claiborne Enrichment Facility would be run by a group of investors called LES, for Louisiana Energy Services. LES was a German-led consortium that included British and Dutch interests, as well as utilities from North Carolina, Minnesota, and Louisiana.

Yelling up from the crowd, local second-grade-teacher Barbara Monsly asked what the plant would do for the local schools.

"This will be worth eleven times the tax base of Claiborne Parish," Johnston confidently shot back.[1] Johnston told the townspeople that among the benefits of the project would be $5 million in tax revenues to their beleaguered schools. The plant might even bring more industrial development with it, which would employ residents and create a new economic boom for the north of the state, with their town in the middle of it all.

Senator Johnston chose to spend his birthday in tiny Homer, Louisiana, because the success of this project was important to him, for three reasons. First, though he was known in Washington for his huge successes in bringing billions of dollars in "pork" federal development projects back to his home state, he had been repeatedly and increasingly criticized in north Louisiana for only bringing development to the distant corridor between Baton Rouge and New Orleans.[2] LES was to be his beacon for North Louisiana.

Second, as a conservative and as chairman of the Energy Subcommittee, Johnston sought to bring change to two bastions of federal bureaucracy: the Energy Department and the Nuclear Regulatory Commission. Those agencies held a complete monopoly on the production of nuclear power plant fuels since the beginning, and there was a strong push during the Reagan-Bush years to privatize their supply.

Finally, Johnston owed some of his political fortune to these energy companies who would benefit from privatizing enriched uranium to supply to nuclear power plants in the United States. *The Washington Post* reported that in a fifteen-month period in 1989–90, "Johnston collected $236,500 from oil, gas, utility and other energy industry PACs . . . more than any other senator received from any interest group."[3] Walker F. Nolan, executive Vice President for Edison Electric Institute, a trade association, organized a fund-raiser for the Senator that year. "If you're going to do fund-raisers, you're doing it for people who have jurisdiction over your issues," he admitted candidly. "He's chairman of the Energy Committee."[4]

The crowd in Homer excitedly cheered Johnston and ate barbecue as the evening air cooled. Many in attendance were not surprised by the announcement: they had been told that a large facility was coming, but they had been told until then only that it was a "chemical plant."[5] A series of informal gatherings had already taken place with wealthy residents and owners of local businesses. The town council, industrial development group, the police jury (roughly like county commissioners), the state representative and state senator for the district, the congressman, and senator were all on board for this project. Many were already planning how they would spend the $5 million boost to the school budget and imagining the benefits of four hundred new jobs.

The town leaders knew and trusted the senator. The sheriff in Homer was the father of Johnston's top aide, Executive Administrator Jim Oaks. Fortunately for LES, those who made decisions in the town were a small handful of business and political leaders. The town's Industrial Development Board, which like a chamber of commerce represented the town's "growth machine," was a group of businessmen who sought to build the local economy and eagerly recruited the consortium.

As the senator later told us, "There was competition between several places, so I knew the 'community fathers' supported it . . . this was very much desired." When we asked him if what he meant by the community fathers was the Industrial Development Board, he nodded and said, "Yes."

Johnston, the political establishment, and the developers failed to even consider those who lived closest to the proposed site. Five miles outside of Homer are Forest Grove and Center Springs, two small, hundred-year-old, rural African-American communities that are connected by a narrow road upon which the enormous factory was designed to sit. Those residents were neither at the announcement nor invited to the gatherings in the weeks beforehand in Homer, the parish seat.

"All the plans had been made, no one never told us nothing" a retired schoolteacher and granddaughter of Georgian slaves whose farm overlooked the plant site, told us from her porch rocker.[6] Essie Youngblood put it this way to a *London Sunday Times* reporter, "They wanted to put it there because they thought we wouldn't be able to afford a lawyer to fight them. They thought nobody here had an education, and that we wouldn't know what to do."[7] Most of the Forest Grove and Center Springs residents first heard about the plant from the local newspaper, or third-hand from their alarmed neighbors. Juanita Hamilton, another schoolteacher and Center Springs resident told us, "I just heard about it on the ten o'clock news. What pissed me off was they talked to people in Homer, but didn't even talk with us about it."[8]

The fascinating and twisting tale of LES shows how NIMBY (not-in-my-backyard) and environmental justice groups can form powerful alliances forcing national agencies and corporations to address their health concerns. It shows the importance of experts, and it shows the potential of President Clinton's 1994 executive order on environmental justice. It raises all the themes posed in the introduction to this book: the politics of siting and of science, of who speaks for the community, and of how the fear of the contamination and the struggle itself influences individuals and the communities. Finally, it is a study in shifting, creative strategies used by environmental justice groups in the nebulous game Fontenot described in Chapter 1. Still undecided is whether the balance of power swung decidedly in the 1990s toward local control over threats to community health and environment, bringing lasting power to previously ignored minority communities. As Ed Davis, president of the American Nuclear Energy Council, an industry group despaired in the *Washington Post* midway through the struggle, "If we can't get a site for a facility like this, an enrichment facility, how are we ever going to get a site for another reactor."[9] Observers on both sides of the environmental justice battle want to know: what kind of precedent has the LES case set?

In the crowd at Johnston's barbecue, however, was a white real estate agent and property assessor named Toney Johnson. His family has been in Homer for one hundred years, they were in the timber business, and his great-grandfather was a state legislator and mayor of Homer. Toney came from "old money," which had not translated into new fortunes: Wal-Mart was killing his hardware store, and his real estate business was only making ends meet.[10]

Toney Johnson's experience with real estate development led him to question the claims of huge windfalls to the schools and general government budget; they simply did not add up and it "smelled fishy." He knew the school taxing districts and realized that with recent redistricting the plant would be outside the town's lines. Unlike most of the crowd, Toney also knew that in Louisiana new factories are granted ten years of operation without having to pay any property taxes at all, and that school taxes were included in the exemption. In fact, new plants were taxed only on materials, not on the labor to build the plant. As he investigated further, Johnson learned that the labor and engineering could come up to $650 million of the entire $750 million construction bill. So, instead of the $5 or $15 million in direct taxes many expected from the plant each year, Toney believed his community would only see $1 million.

Johnson began poking around looking into the details of the plant and writing letters to the editor of the local newspaper. Meanwhile, Essie Youngblood and the residents of Forest Grove and Center Springs were getting organized, meeting alternately in their two small churches, which shared a minister. They invited Toney Johnson to a meeting where they formed an opposition group named Citizens Against Nuclear Trash (CANT). A white exmanager and chemical engineer at an aluminum plant in Jamaica named Norton Tompkins also joined the group, providing technical help and assistance with the media. Tompkins was worried about radioactive materials leaking out of the plant and into a nearby creek that flowed into Lake Claiborne, where he built a retirement house on the water he shared with two thousand other middle-class white retirees. Very few of them, however, publicly expressed concern about the plant.

So the core of CANT was in place. This tiny group CANT – "as in you CANT build it here"[11] – eventually secured the legal support of Nathalie Walker of the Sierra Club Legal Defense Fund (now called Earthjustice), Greenpeace, the Nuclear Information Service (an old antinuke group), and several other local, national, and international groups. Their coalition crossed race and class lines and survived nearly a decade of battle before the matter was finally settled. Willie Fontenot, the special assistant to the state Attorney General, told Tompkins that "all you need is three or four dedicated individuals" to fight and win this battle.

Walker summarized the anti-LES case this way: "The feed material, the uranium, is coming from Oklahoma and Illinois and the destination for the enriched uranium is Connecticut, the state of Washington, North and South Carolina. But where do they put a facility that will have radioactive [wastes] for years and years? A poor African-American community in Louisiana."[12]

A SENATOR'S WORK, A GADFLY'S BUZZ

Since the dawn of the nuclear era in World War II, the mining, refining, and distribution of uranium had been tightly controlled by the U.S. government. The greatest fear, of course, was of "proliferation," the spread of the technology and materials to "rogue nations" or terrorist groups, which would make nuclear bombs capable of killing millions of people. Decades after 1945, when the United States proved the devastating potential of the bomb in Hiroshima and Nagasaki, the number of nations with the technology and the uranium to do so still numbered around a dozen.

But conservative winds of change were blowing across America in the Reagan decade, and the Department of Energy's (DOE) monopoly on nuclear fuel production was being increasingly criticized. The DOE was criticized for being too expensive and too difficult to work with. The European consortium Urenco had a newer, much more efficient technology to enrich uranium and wanted to expand into the huge U.S. market.[13]

Urenco president Peter Jelinek, a tall blond Austrian, contacted the North Carolina utility company Duke Power and set up a plan with other investors designed for their mutual benefit. The idea involved using Urenco's "ultra-centrifuges" to concentrate uranium at a much lower price than the DOE's other "gas-process" plants such as the one in Paducah, Kentucky. Duke Power was contracted to do the licensing, and Louisiana Power and Light (LP&L) was set to sell the huge amounts of electricity the plant would require. Chemical plant construction giant Fluor-Daniels invested in the project and would gain a huge contract for the building of the plant. The three utilities – Duke Power, Northern States Power (out of Minnesota), and LP&L – together operate eleven nuclear reactors.[14] LP&L is part of Entergy Systems consortium, which has three more reactors. Together these fourteen nuclear reactors could consume nearly 80 percent of the uranium produced at the plant. Urenco would also gain entry into the massive U.S. market for nuclear fuels (its core goal), selling fuel from its European plants at its normal rate of profit.

Urenco and its consortium partners knew from the start that getting a private plant approved and sited would require significant help from Congress, and especially from the Senate Energy Committee. As Chairman of the committee, Louisiana Senator J. Bennett Johnston learned of Urenco's idea early. The German firm's proposition seemed an opportunity to bring home economic benefits to his district, and Johnston saw no problems with the risks:

I found out, I was aware that the Urenco crowd was looking for a place to site the uranium enrichment plant in the U.S. and so I became interested in trying to locate that in Louisiana. I was trying to bring industrial development to Louisiana. . . . So I went to look at the Urenco process. I looked at their plants . . . they're very bucolic things, cows all around, no smokestacks. . . . There's no impact. You've got this very nice plant, it looks nice, there's no negative impact of this. I talked to their people, told them we'd like to have them in Louisiana and so I got a commitment that they'd like to come, then we set about with a process to find the place.[15]

Back in North Louisiana, many locals believed strongly that Johnston's influence, both direct and indirect, was behind all the decisions from that point forward. He is spoken of in the north of the state like the Wizard of Oz: his power is assumed to be omnipotent. For example, opponents of the plant quickly discovered that the site where the team proposed to put the enormous factory was owned by Joe LaSage, the son of one of Johnston's staffers. They did not believe it was a coincidence that the father of one of Johnston's aides was sheriff of Claiborne parish and owned one of the land tracts considered. Joe LeSage had been a classmate of Senator Johnston's back in his days as a law student at Louisiana State University. Their suspicions of corruption were piqued when they found out that LES had bought the 442-acre LeSage tract in 1990 for $536,462, over twice the going rate for cutover timber lands.[16] And they let Joe LeSage cut the timber on the land after the sale, which LeSage sold for another $369,000 to a local paper mill.[17] By the critics' reckoning, that brought the price of the land to four or five times the going rate. It appeared to critics that local businesspeople used their political connections to make a hefty profit, directing the plant toward the lands they owned at the expense of the two black communities.[18]

How was the LaSage tract selected? This question turned out to be the crux of the environmental justice battle that was brewing. A massive report prepared by LES describes a scientific process of narrowing down the sites based on such criteria as the size of the tract, access to highways, and seismic stability, since the slightest earthquake jiggle could damage the centrifuges. The description presents a siting driven by technical criteria in a political and social vacuum, when in fact Johnston and others admitted that the list of sites was immediately limited to North Louisiana for political reasons.

In fact, Homer resident and LES spokesman Blake Hemphill described how he and the Industrial Development Board developed a list of several possible sites around Claiborne Parish to present to LES.[19] The final list consisted of just three sites. One was near the prison, one near Lake Claiborne and its thousands of retirees, and finally there was the LaSage tract. A Fluor Daniels employee, Larry Engwall, drove around the sites and gave them numerical scores based on "eyeballing" property values and estimating the numbers of people who would be affected. The other sites were rated higher: the ramshackle houses of the Center Springs roads nearest the plant site did not seem as valuable as did the retirees' middle-class homes. He gave the poor rural black homes a 9 and the middle-class white vacation and retirement homes along Lake Claiborne a 7. He later described that "We just felt, opinion-wise, people probably would not want this plant to be close to their pride and joy of their lake where they go fishing."[20] This ranking process turned out to be pivotal in claims of environmental racism raised by local residents.

The other reason the Claiborne Parish site was chosen was the welcoming nature of local politicians and business interests. Nuclear plants around the country had faced paralyzing protests since the 1970s, and many could never open. Antinuclear groups had, for example, managed to drive the Seabrook reactor in New Hampshire to shut down and delayed its reopening for years. After several of these battles, and after the terrifying near leak at Three Mile Island in 1979, the Nuclear Regulatory Commission cracked down more tightly on plants' safety measures. As a result, the economics of nuclear power shifted.[21] With the increased safety requirements, it was immeasurably more expensive to open and operate nuclear plants, and no new plants had been built in the United States in nearly two decades. There were, however, more than 120 plants still operating, and fuel costs were high because of the government monopoly.

Throughout the country, intense local opposition sprang up nearly everywhere that was even rumored to be a potential site for the dumping of nuclear waste. Spent fuel rods were kept in tanks of water at plants around the country with nowhere to go since even remote locations like Yucca Mountain in Nevada saw extended protests. Even low-level waste, like that produced in hospitals and research universities, was piling up with nowhere to be sent. To shift the problem down, the federal government divided the nation into multistate "compacts," leaving it up to them to decide where to dump the low-level waste. Louisiana joined a compact with Nebraska, Kansas, Arkansas, and Oklahoma and sought a site to dump the low-level waste.[22] One site considered in 1987 was in Claiborne Parish south of Homer. Since there were few potential jobs and little revenue for the locality, opposition arose quickly in Homer and was communicated to Johnston. Johnston wrote a letter to the local newspaper saying that if the local people did not want it, he would take Claiborne Parish off the list for the five-parish compact low-level dump. He wrote to the local paper: "I am extremely concerned that the health and welfare of the citizens of Claiborne Parish be the utmost priority in this process."[23] Now fifteen years later, the dump still has not been sited since all 150 locations rejected it. Anything with the word "nuclear" attached had become virtually un-citeable.

In December 1989, as LES bought the LeSage land, they initially saw no opposition. But a Duke Power engineer told local LES representative Blake Hemphill, "'they'll come out of the woodwork.' And they did."[24]

So, aware of the experiences around the country, LES sought a "streamlined" process to get its government permits to build and operate the plant in Claiborne Parish. Federal regulations required "two-step" permitting for any nuclear facilities, which many industry observers believed accounted for the protesters' success in blocking any atomic plants. Each of the two steps required public input, and a complicated and expensive Environmental Impact Assessment was mandatory. The LES group sought instead to permit its uranium enrichment plant according to the "one-step" process used in siting chemical plants. One of the crucial differences between the two permitting processes was the amount of time citizens were provided to make public comments and how those comments were treated.

LES went to Johnston and asked to have the law changed to allow them the one-step permitting. On December 11, 1987, Johnston replied on Senate letterhead to Joe Bader of Urenco that he would help open the U.S. uranium market to privately owned facilities.[25] Johnston set out to change the law quietly to make it more difficult for protesters to block the plant. He slipped an exception for the LES plant in the Minnesota Lands Act, an obscure piece of legislation giving an island in Lake Superior back to the state of Minnesota. Johnston's amendment also would have allowed the LES plant to be built without even the preparation of an Environmental Impact Statement.[26] Based on his substantial power as chair of the Energy Subcommittee, Johnston's amendment sailed through the Senate without opposition, on his word that it was noncontroversial and completely safe.

Staffers for California Representative George Miller, who had just taken over control of the House Interior Subcommittee, noticed the completely unrelated section in the bill and began to raise questions. Representative John Dingell, of the Energy and Commerce Committee, wanted to slap Johnston's wrist for attempting to slip the bill through and asked him to come testify in the House on its behalf. Senators are almost never asked to testify in the House; it is considered an insult to have to do so. The antinuclear group Nuclear Information and Resource Service (NIRS) requested to have a member of CANT testify at the hearing along with representatives of LES, government agencies, and Senator Johnston, "not knowing if CANT could even afford to send someone to the hearing."[27] Arizona Democrat Morris Udall's office, still nominally in charge of the committee, refused. NIRS threatened "to bring up a busload of African-Americans from the area and hold a press conference outside the hearing room so they can explain why they're not being allowed to testify."[28] A week before the hearing, the committee backed down and allowed CANT to send a representative. They chose Toney Johnson.

The *Washington Post* carried a long article about LES on the day of the hearing. Representative Miller sat as temporary chair for the dramatic meeting of the House Interior Subcommittee on Energy and the Environment when J. Bennett Johnston was called to testify. Johnston's goal was to show people that radioactivity was all around us, not explosive, and nothing to be hysterical about.[29] Johnston turned on a Geiger counter he had brought into the hearing room. It buzzed, which Johnston said was due to radioactivity in the granite walls of the Capitol.[30] He then turned to the president of LES, who handed him what Johnston said was the fuel product of the uranium enrichment plant: uranium hexafloride. The Geiger counter popped slightly louder. He then held up an 18-inch-long armor-piercing bullet, made with depleted uranium – a by-product of uranium enrichment. The Geiger counter popped slightly more. Then he held up a plate about which he said "you can buy in any supermarket." The Geiger counter buzzed louder and faster. So the factory's materials appeared less radioactive than everyday items like a dinner plate.

Johnston said that unlike the DOE's uranium enrichment plants, the LES facility would be contamination- and pollution-free, and so an Environmental Impact Statement was unnecessary. He commented that Louisiana needed the jobs, and that any local opposition would be better off without the long hearings of two-step permitting since then they would be saved the expense of hiring a lawyer.[31]

Critics of the nuclear industry, however, had two surprise responses for Johnston. Toney Johnson's sister lived in Washington, and she had called and talked to Michael Marriotte of the NIRS there. "I realized we had to win this outside Homer, Louisiana." Marriotte got Toney on the agenda for the committee meeting the next day. He flew half the night, and worked all the next day with Marriotte to prepare the testimony. Putting on his best "aw shucks" country boy affect, Toney Johnson sat at the other end of the hearing room table from Senator Johnston and refuted his claims about the safety of the plant, the destiny of its waste products, and the lack of local opposition.

The other unpleasant surprise for Johnston was that, with the help of the Washington-based antinuke group NIRS, the plate was revealed to be uranium oxide-coated Fiestaware, which had not been manufactured since the 1940s. In fact, it had been banned in the 1960s. It was also revealed that if Johnston had brought real uranium hexafloride into the Capitol Hill hearing room, it would have eaten through his hand and might have killed everyone in the room.[32]

When the press got the word on the error, Johnston's plate testimony was called the "Gaff of the Day" on a Washinton TV station. When he returned to North Louisiana, a local KTBS-TV reporter asked Johnston at the Shreveport airport why he said that the plate could be bought in any store. "I didn't say that." On the evening news, the station ran Johnston's denial and then immediately ran the clip of his words in the congressional hearing. The Shreveport reporter was fired within a month. But a national CBS news piece "Eye on America" on the LES project used the airport denial and congressional testimony in the same way: to cast doubt on Johnston's testimony. Though his point had been to express his comfort with radioactivity and his confidence in the safety of the LES project, Johnston had been caught by the TV cameras giving misleading testimony he had been handed by the nuclear industry. He justified the need to quiet irrational fears of radioactivity because he saw the plant as safe: "I stake my political life on it, my integrity . . . this is not a subject on which reasonable minds can disagree."[33]

Johnston was a popular target among consumer groups in Washington, such as the National Taxpayers Union and Ralph Nader's group Public Citizen. Both had criticized legislation he sponsored allowing the nuclear industry to write off most of a $9 billion debt to the federal government who provided them with enrichment services.[34] The consumer groups believed that the LES project was little more than a "consumer scam," and that LES had no intention of selling enriched uranium on the open market. Rather, they believed that the companies would merely raise their utility rates to charge the consumers for the investments in LES. They believed, therefore, that the customers were helping the German firm Urenco sell its products in the United States.[35] From their perspective the evidence began to accumulate that this was true: Northern States Power asked the Minnesota commission for $200,000 in a rate increase for its initial investment in the LES project.[36] Duke Power asked North Carolina Utilities Commission for $9.2 million in rate increases to its customers to cover the risky investment.[37]

Angered at Johnston's attempt to deceive his committee, Representative Miller held up Johnston's amendment and stripped it from the Minnesota Lands Act.[38] Miller gave him a tough compromise: Johnston would get one-step permitting, which was being phased in for nuclear plants in two years anyway, but the plant would have to go through public hearings and prepare a full Environmental Impact Statement. On the last day of the congressional session in 1990, Johnston got the one-step permitting amendment passed as an add-on to a bill, ironically the Bill to Encourage Wind and Geothermal Power.[39]

Exhausted after nights of travel and preparing his testimony, Toney Johnson flew back to North Louisiana with a message: "They're going back to Washington and laughing at us. They're looking for a parish where the politicians will take a plant that's so dangerous that if it blows up the whole parish will be contaminated, not for ten years, but for a million years."[40] Back home, a friend told him, "It's gonna hurt your business." Toney immediately felt the chill for his treason. "They

cut me off from appraisal work. All of a sudden, I'm having trouble getting loans approved."[41] The battle was just beginning to get ugly.

A NEW ACTOR IN AN UNLIKELY PLACE:
CITIZENS AGAINST NUCLEAR TRASH

Back in Homer, a movement was growing among those no one both-
ered to ask about the plant: the poorest of the poor black folks living
in trailers and ramshackle shacks along the back roads of Forest Grove
and Center Springs. Their towns, though ignored by the white establishment, had been around over one hundred years. The land and
communities means something more to more "rooted" Amerians than
it does for the more transient of us. Some of the support for the protest
against LES came from family members who had been forced to migrate far from home in search of work, but who still dreamt of returning to their beloved rural lives later, maybe only upon retirement.

The retired schoolteacher Essie Youngblood told her family's history
this way. "My mother and daddy farmed and raised cotton for four
cents per pound trying to make payments on this land. My brother in
Detroit would finish out the payment. Their advice to us was to keep
this land. If the water table and everything is ruined I don't feel like
we could."[42]

Calvin D. Applewhite, a U.S. Marine stationed 2,000 miles from
Homer, said, "We want to come back and build our homes here and
raise our families here, but with the plant here we don't want to come
back."[43]

The courage of the black communities must be appreciated, since
many were intimidated; they were afraid of repercussions, of the Ku
Klux Klan, or of less organized racism. During the battle over LES,
there were two Klan rallies in the parish. The men were especially cau-
tious, a legacy of the bad old days when black men were lynched for
troublemaking.[44] More recent than lynchings, job blackmail was still
common in this town where work was extremely scarce and precious.
"All the government workers are under the politicians, and peoples'
families were afraid they'd lose their jobs," said Essie Youngblood.[45]
Norton Tompkins called it like he saw it to a Shreveport newspaper reporter: "At least 20 percent employed in Homer are on a government
payroll. Everyone is kin to, works for, or sleeps with people in power."

Intimidation came other ways, anonymous phone calls with racial epithets, threats to whites, blacks, elderly women, and to people's businesses.[46] The CANT members feared their churches would fall victim to arson, of which there was a long history (and a current wave) in the South. Still, Essie Youngblood would get on her phone and could get dozens of people out in a matter of hours for a weeknight meeting. She explained, "The younger people were too busy raising families. But they'd show up for meetings and protests."[47]

Some of the job fears proved well justified. Elmira Wafir, a social security official with the state government, was active in the opposition group. She reported that the local sheriff called the state health department to try to get her fired. She was passed over for promotion. She filed a formal complaint; her boss got upset at the sheriff and vowed to support her. He helped get her a good job in Shreveport, 45 miles away.[48]

A pivotal moment was at one of the first meetings of the group Citizens Against Nuclear Trash. After seeing Toney Johnson's letter to the editor in the newspaper warning of the plant's dangers, Elmira Wafir asked him to come to the meeting in the humble frame Center Springs church. Mary Boyd, public relations officer of the LES consortium, walked in and swiftly took over the meeting. CANT members had already called the TV cameras. Boyd claimed that there would be no environmental nor health effects. Toney stood up and said she was lying about the lack of negative health effects. An older black man stood up at the back of the church. He was enraged: "You've been doing this for one hundred years. You white people are taking this land. This land is all we've got." Mary Boyd was offended by the charges of racism and left the meeting angry.[49]

The black churches played a pivotal and sometimes contradictory role in the LES struggle. The Center Springs and Forest Grove Christian Methodist Episcopal Churches shared one minister, the Reverend E. D. McWoodson of nearby Minden, who would alternate preaching at each sanctuary. First, LES promised recreation equipment for the churches, and the minister said he was for the plant. Then LES sent a check for $500 to each church in early 1991, a not inconsequential contribution for these congregations. However, CANT members ran the books of the churches, and before the minister could cash the checks, they called for a vote on whether to accept the donations. The 147 members rejected it.[50] Reverend McWoodson told a local newspaper reporter that he "would have kept the money if it had been his decision to make." He continued, "They do what they want . . . I have never in my whole life turned down a contribution to the church."

When the same reporter asked LES spokeswoman Mary Boyd why the consortium had made the offer, she said the company made the offer "in the spirit of wanting to be good citizens in the parish." She went on to describe $8,000 in donations to twenty-two community service agencies in the parish to that point. These included supporting a group of school students to go to Alabama for camp at the NASA Space Center, important help for the Claiborne Parish Fair, support efforts for Desert Storm and Shield troops fighting in Kuwait, and ads in the local school newsletters and yearbooks. Later, a full-page ad in the local newspaper detailed $70,000 in donations to local groups, such as the Girl Scouts and lighting for the courthouse.[51]

The congregations of the black churches went around their minister and used the churches as powerful moral pulpits and networking tools. Virtually every meeting of CANT was held in one of the black churches. The women of the congregations would make box lunches and raise money selling them through the churches. They reached out to the Episcopal Bishop Gillmore in Shreveport, who donated $1,000 and worked to help CANT.[52] They used the budget of the Forest Grove Church to help pay for a school bus to bring children to a critical hearing in the courthouse in Shreveport. Several retired women in CANT would go to the library in Homer and read and copy the letters from public record from the Nuclear Regulatory Commission. They would bring them to the meetings, to hear what their neighbors were saying about them, and to strategize their next steps.

With the skills they learned running the churches' finances, the Forest Grove and Center Spring women ran CANT as a tight ship. The black community raised money, built around a core of twelve families who had each pledged $100 per month, for two years, to keep the group alive. The box lunches raised $1,700. Toney Johnson's office was the communications center; he provided his copier, fax, and phone. Norton Tompkins wrote some grants to national antinuclear foundations, some of which were funded. He later remarked, "We're the only group ever to pay all our bills."

But the religious affiliation of the group provided them something perhaps even more crucial: a common language and faith that helped them reach across race, income, and political boundaries. "I'm saying this in all sincerity: God led us. We had divine guidance. We tell that to everyone who interviews us, but it never ends up in print."[53] Religion brought them together and guided them.

Finally, the group cultivated contacts with national and international groups. They begged Nathalie Walker of the Sierra Club Legal Defense Fund's recently opened New Orleans office to come up and visit. When she did, she could not resist taking up the case. It would drain her organization's budget and staff time for years, bringing legal claims to the NRC, the state environmental agency DEQ, and to EPA.[54]

TESTIMONY AND BACKLASH: SIMMERING TENSIONS
BECOME OPEN HOSTILITY

In the heat of the summer of 1991, The Nuclear Regulatory Commission announced that it would hold a "scoping meeting" in Homer, at the unairconditioned Homer High School cafeteria. CANT took out an ad in the local newspaper, the *Homer Guardian-Journal*. While blasting the plant's potential effects on their health, the advertisement admonished readers that "CANT encourages everyone to be POLITE and COURTEOUS at the NRC meeting."[55] An hour before the hearing, CANT members planned a "Citizens Rally" at the Homer High School football stadium, across the street.

The school cafeteria was so hot that a retired man collapsed in the back and was carried off. Essie Youngblood, the small, soft-spoken but tough farm woman, stood at the microphone to make her testimony:

My name is Essie Youngblood. I live within two miles of the proposed plant site. I am a full grown senior citizen, a retired schoolteacher. The purpose of this meeting is to express local environmental concerns. I consider black human beings as much a part of the environment as land, air, and water. The uranium enrichment plant will be located in the dead center of a rural black community consisting of over 150 families. I have read the Environmental Report included in the 15-volume NRC License Application and not one word is written about the fact that the plant will threaten and disrupt a rural black community that has been in existence over 100 years. To the contrary, the report goes to great length to emphasize how sparsely the area is populated. . . . The residents of our community have never been consulted as to whether or not we wanted the plant in our midst . . . and when we attended the police jury [parish council] meeting to voice our concern, we were assured that the vast majority of the people wanted the plant, thusly revealing the fact that our community is expendable, because the establishment favors the plant. If there is one ounce of human decency in the NRC or the DEQ, the LES uranium enrichment plant will not be licensed to be built in the heart of our black, minority neighborhood that is adamantly opposed to it.

Alean Jones, secretary of the Forest Grove Christian Methodist Episcopal Church, stood up with a copy of a January 25, 1991, "Policy Issue [Information] Bulletin" from the NRC in her hand. The memo, written by James M. Taylor of the NRC, said that there was a great surplus of the uranium waste tailings, which the LES consortium said they would sell to make bomb casings. Refuting Senator J. Bennett Johnston's testimony in the House, she read that "It should be noted that HF [hydrogen floride] is a very reactive and corrosive chemical that may cause unusually severe burns." Finally, she also read from that memo that this depleted uranium [DUF6] was likely to soon be treated as a waste, since there was such a surplus of depleted uranium available, and that "it is also likely that the enrichment plant would agree to keep these tails . . . final disposition of the tails may be cumbersome." Then she went on to speak for herself:

My name is Mrs. Alean Jones. My husband and I, with our two children, live in the Forest Grove Community less than one mile from the proposed plantsite. . . . I can foresee a possibility that is frightening. If the five-state compact should refuse waste from this plant, then the State of Louisiana could declare this plantsite a low-level waste disposal site and the [depleted uranium hexafloride] tails could remain in Forest Grove forever. Before NRC issues a license, we beg you to do whatever is necessary to prevent our community being turned into a radioactive waste dump.

The backlash was immediate and pervasive. The Claiborne Parish Industrial Development Foundation (CPIDF) took out a full-page ad in the *Homer Guardian-Journal* billed as an "Open Letter to the Citizens of Claiborne Parish." It read: "A small handful of people is attempting to take the future of Claiborne Parish hostage to their own hidden agenda of fears and political preferences . . . [using] innuendoes, half truths, facts taken out of context, and misrepresentations."[56] During the run-up to the NRC scoping meeting in Homer, Louisiana, July 30, 1991, a barrage of letters to the editor and to the NRC flew around the town and around the country. Plant proponent Charles M. Kendrick sent a letter July 16, 1991, to the NRC which read:

I wanted to appear before the meeting and state that I own my home, two rent houses, and four commercial office buildings and that I am a supporter of the proposed plant. . . . The ringleaders of the opposition to the plant went into the area near the selected site, occupied mostly by families of African origin. They were told that the site selected has been purposely chosen because it was in an area populated by "black people" and it would not have been put where most of the neighbors were "white". My point is that "fear" has been generated, and largely through unfair examples.

Just after the hearing, the letters multiplied. After the NRC hearing, pro-LES residents sent a stream of letters directly to the NRC. Homer resident Lawson Guice was moved by the hearing to write directly to the NRC. His letter said:

I attended the "scoping meeting" held in Homer on July 30th. Due to conditions under which this hearing was held, I feel a true opinion of the residents of Claiborne Parish was not evident due to the fact that many supportive citizens did not attend. They were aware of the manner in which those opposed to LES had monopolized the speaking time and would not allow proper response at prior information meetings, so they did not wish to witness another such spectacle.

The frustration could be heard in many other residents seeing their hoped-for future economic growth being undermined. Homer resident Jean Blockwelder wrote an August 22, 1991, letter to Charles Haughney of the NRC, which said:

I along with my whole family and lots of friends want this plant. The only people opposed to the plant are uneducated and do not want to be educated to this process. I love these people but they do not know what this will mean to the state. Please help to bring this plant to the state. I will get a list of people for this plant if I have to. I want the world to know this is a safe plant.

In a passionate August 10, 1991, letter to Haughney, Judy and Jerry Whitton, owners and operators of the Linder Motor Lodge, summarized quite a lot of the feeling among business owners in Homer.

As business owners we have and will benefit from the growth that this plant will bring to our area, but even if we did not have a business, we would still support this plant due to all the good things that it will eventually do or cause to happen in the parish. . . . Over five years ago when we bought this business I began serving on the Board of the Chamber of Commerce. Through those years I worked on finding ways to encourage growth in the community, but controlled growth. I still want this type of growth and from all indications we could achieve this with this plant. Many of those who are against its location here do not want change of any kind – but we know that changes will take place – the town will die or it will progress – either direction is a change. My husband and I are guilty as many others are of letting the dissenters be more vocal than the supporters, but we want to point out that there are many more people who want this plant than those who don't – they just are not speaking up.

Meanwhile, the CANT members were reading and copying these letters at the public library, and reading them at their meetings. Another read:

The Euranem [sic] plant was welcomed by the vast majority of Claiborne Pariah [sic]. A small group of less than fifty oppose it. There are about five leaders in Homer (men who have never been too successful and glory in publicity) who are very vocal. The majority of this are the people who live around the land of the proposed plant. They have been brain washed to believe it is there because they are black and it will ruin their land or kill them. LES has done everything to prove plant is safe, but leaders keep them hysterical. We WANT the plant, please. They gathered some money and have put horrible looking ads in papers. Sincerely, Dorothy Thomas. August 21, 1991.

Neither side had any idea that the battle, which was polarizing their community, had only just begun.

A LONG WAR, A WAR OF ATTRITION

Already in the spring of 1991, LES had been hit by a March 21 Nuclear Regulatory Commission memo saying that their license application "appears to contain incomplete or inadequate information." That summer, the antinuke group NIRS wrote that:

The LES project is already on shaky economic ground, and it is unclear whether it could survive a lengthy delay in the licensing process. Two of the five consortium members – Duke Power and Northern States Power – are already making plans to drop out of the project if and when a construction permit is granted . . . the LES project would probably become the nation's single largest commercial generator of radioactive waste.[57]

Among the items slowing down the construction of the LES plant was the lack of the permits needed from the State of Louisiana and the NRC. The Louisiana Department of Environmental Quality was the key agency from which they needed to get air and water pollution permits. The agency, normally extremely proindustry, was in turmoil because, for the first time, a reform-minded governor, Buddy Roemer, had appointed Paul Templet, the strongly proenvironment professor from Lousiana State University, as its secretary. Templet had quickly drawn the ire of the oil and chemical industries in the state by cracking down on polluters and linking their tax breaks to environmental performance.

One effect of the July scoping meeting at Homer High School was that Templet's agency, the LDEQ, was moved to request more information from the NRC. At Templet's direction, assistant secretary Vicki Arroyo wrote to Peter Loyson of the NRC just two weeks after the scoping meeting. "While these meetings have been quite informative, they have brought to light several issues which LDEQ feels should be part of the NRC scoping process . . . many of these issues will have to be confronted before future operational permits from the LDEQ may be granted."[58] Further, the DEQ used the pivotal "IT decision" discussed in Chapter 2, which mandates that the DEQ consider the potential adverse effects, cost-benefit analysis of environmental costs against social and economic benefits, whether any alternatives technologies or sites are available, or whether greater protections could be added.[59] This may be one of the few times that the SOS/IT ruling was fully utilized in the state's history.

Among the thirty-four detailed questions raised by DEQ in its attached memo[60] was a series of questions on how the site was selected, including details on all the sites which were considered and the environmental impacts of several sorts for each. The questions implied clearly that politics and racism may have influenced the decision to choose the LaSage tract. And DEQ requested that the NRC respond to fears about possible evacuation routes and health impacts on locals.

The memo asked for a true analysis of the net economic effect on the state, given the substantial tax breaks the plant would receive and comparing them to the reported economic advantages. It also requested the number of permanent jobs that would be created and whether they would be likely to be filled by locals or outsiders. The DEQ memo wanted to know who would pay the cleanup costs of the plant "if the project failed at any time, or the LES partnership encountered financial difficulties." The DEQ was also concerned about the nature of the "limited partnership and the legal liability of the partners." The *Nuclear Monitor* accurately said that the DEQ memo contained "the veiled threat that the proposed plant may not meet Louisiana criteria."[61] These are some of the toughest questions ever asked of any development project in Louisiana history. Even though several CANT members expressed that the DEQ never did anything for them, it is clear that they were fortunate that their struggle originated during a sympathetic administration. The state environmental agency will play a quite different role in the cases described in the other chapters, which unfolded under less environmentally friendly governors.

CANT and its allies in Washington were not standing still waiting for the DEQ, however. In mid-1992, they sent letters to many lenders on Wall Street to warn them of the project's shaky financial foundations.[62] On July 9, 1992, they sent a letter to more than 450 energy industry financial analysts, saying:

From River Bend to Grand Gulf to Seabrook to Shoreham, the nuclear power industry has proven itself to be an economic albatross on our nation's utilities. Now, a new nuclear company, Louisiana Energy Services, has appeared, promising that its "new" technology will usher in a new era of nuclear profits. Don't bet your money on it . . .[63]

Opponents continued taking the battle to new ground. In mid-1993, there was a minor earthquake nearby, and evidence was unearthed about how the region was, in fact, not entirely free from seismic risk in that it lies near the New Madrid fault line.[64] They also developed the environmental racism case. CANT brought in speakers from the NAACP national office and the Sierra Club Legal Defense Fund to discuss patterns of environmental racism in the siting of dangerous factories.[65] They featured Lance Hughes from Native Americans for a Clean Environment, who talked about accidents at a uranium processing plant in Oklahoma. He said, "Our experience with Sequoyah Fuels is a warning to this community in Homer: nuclear factories are dangerous, and the federal government doesn't have the ability or the will to ensure that you will be protected when an accident happens."

LES shot back with a letter to hundreds of residents of Claiborne Parish saying that the chemical means of processing the uranium at the Oklahoma plant was entirely different than LES's new ultra-centrifuges. The most severe injury in these types of plants over thirty years in Europe "has been a broken ankle from a fall from a ladder," the letter read.[66] Responding to racism charges in locating the plant, LES called the statements "untrue and repugnant . . . close to being defamatory." They continued:

For technical reasons, the CEC [Claiborne Enrichment Center] will be in Northern Louisiana, an area of relative seismic stability . . . then with the help of the Louisiana Department of Economic Development, several communities were identified as receptive to new industry. The areas around these communities were rated for soil stability, access and proximity to Interstate 20, and having a large enough population to provide future employees . . . [for the] 400 jobs during construction . . . and 180 permanent positions.

Critics rebutted that the firm would not commit to any firm numbers of jobs that would come from Claiborne Parish, saying only that employees would be carefully selected from Claiborne and the surrounding twenty-three parishes and counties in adjoining states.

The letter ended emphatically and appealed to the citizens' pride of self and community. "LES selected Claiborne Parish out of confidence that its residents and many nearby are fully capable of filling a number of positions at the CEC; how ironic that members of the CANT group, claiming to represent you, are confident that you are not capable!" The five-page letter was signed by LES's vice president for community relations Mary Boyd. "The irony continues when you consider that LES is being branded racist for providing the education and opportunities that will empower local residents to fight racism and poverty. To us it appears that those who are accusing LES of racism are doing the most to perpetuate conditions that would support racism." This point reflects the deep disagreement on what needs to be done about the problems of racism in the community.

Also in 1993, the local representative of the Industrial Development Foundation who recruited the landowners to sell their land to LES – in essence the man who was behind much of the site selection process – sent a bitter letter to Roy Mardis of CANT defending his intentions. "Anyone who says the site for Claiborne Enrichment Center was picked with disregard for the interests and welfare of its neighbors will, to my certain personal knowledge, be stating a falsehood that causes a direct personal reflection on my motives, character and actions." He ended with a single ominous sentence, which CANT members read as intimidation: "In such a case I will obtain and follow the advice of competent counsel regarding legal remedy for slander and/or libel. Very truly yours, Travis M. Tinsley."[67]

As will be seen in the Shintech case described in Chapter 4, the National Association for the Advancement of Colored People was the battleground for much conflict over this environmental justice claim. The local NAACP president, Anthony Hollis, was taken to Europe by LES in mid-April 1994 and upon his return made a public statement in favor of the plant. "It appears that no stone was left unturned in terms of trying to provide the safest plant." Later his own chapter in Shreveport's executive committee went public with the opposite conclusion, calling his position "his own personal opinion."[68] Finally, in 1993, the NAACP supported CANT. In trying to convince the NAACP to take a stand, environmental justice activist Robert Bullard proclaimed, "This is a perfect example where NAACP can draw a line in the dirt to stop environmental racism. If this were such a great opportunity, believe me, white people would have it. It's all smoke and mirrors."[69]

Gaining the official support of the national NAACP and its executive director Benjamin Chavis was a crucial boost to CANT and its supporters in 1993. "There could be health effects, and on children yet unborn. We are unalterably opposed to the project," said NAACP's Rupert Richardson.[70] The Sierra Club Legal Defense Fund made much of the announcement: "We know that the Clinton Administration is taking a serious look at environmental justice. Now that one of the most recognized leaders [Chavis] has gone on record with his organization opposing this facility, I don't think there can be any question that this proposed uranium plant will get closer scrutiny." The conviction of those charging environmental racism was strengthened when the fifteen-volume Draft Environmental Impact Statement (DEIS) for the LES plant did not even mention or show Center Springs or Forest Grove on its thirty-nine maps. "The DEIS is a sham; incredibly, it doesn't even mention impacts on the communities of Forest Grove and Center Springs."[71]

Many observers note that protest movements are successful only when there is a split within the powerful, and in the LES case, the federal government was showing signs of division over the issues the plant was raising. EPA's regional administrator Jane Saginaw castigated the NRC's impact statement for not considering environmental justice.[72] Among dozens of specific requests for more information, the EPA administrator required more evaluation of the two other sites besides the LeSage tract.[73] Saginaw's letter to the NRC reveals how the EPA was concerned about negative press coverage and fearful of the damaging lawsuits:

As you know, the issue has been raised in the media. . . . EPA is closely scrutinizing our own actions with regard to this issue. We believe it is prudent for other agencies to do so as well. A conscientious effort to deal with this issue in regard to community or site selection could possibly avoid potential reactions to this or any project, such as expense, in money and time, and law suits.

LES was also busy, of course, doing its own public relations work. The firm sent its public relations team to meet with the Homer Lions and Rotary Clubs,[74] and also reached out to the children of the community. One piece in the local *Homer Guardian-Journal* revealed attempts of LES to incorporate the environmental images of their opponents. "Animals, birds and wildflowers found at the site of the Claiborne Enrichment Center near Homer, the site of a proposed uranium enrichment plant, now have starring roles in coloring books available for young visitors at the LES information office. . . . Henry, the great blue heron, leads a tour of the site."[75]

The distance between the perspectives of the two sides could be seen in another hearing with LES officials and the NRC, this one in the mid-June heat of 1994. The chiefs of the NRC's enrichment branch, John Hickey and Yawar Faraz, tromped through the woods of the site, trailed by LES representatives and a CBS news team following up on their earlier "Eye on America" story.[76] That night, they met at the low-brick Forest Grove Christian Methodist Episcopal Church near the site to hear from CANT and the black communities. "The NRC has recognized that [environmental racism] is a valid concern" said Hickey after hearing dozens of impassioned arguments about safety, jobs, fishing, well water, and the plant's lack of an evacuation plan.[77] In response to a complaint that LES had never released the details of a survey on parishwide opinion about the plant, Faraz said, "We're here to see if the Forest Grove and Center Springs communities want this plant. It doesn't really matter if everyone else in the parish wants it. We don't make our decisions on opinion polls." Providing such assurances of community input in siting decision making suggested that inside the NRC positions were shifting dramatically.

At another hearing at Homer High School, 12-year-old Forest Grove resident Kimmerly Walker said, "180 jobs at the cost of two communities is genocide."[78]

"I would not mind at all if that facility was next to my house in Shreveport," said Jim Purgerson of the Chamber of Commerce–Shreveport.

"Take it!" shouted some members of the audience.

Many people involved say the pivotal moment in the struggle was the next month, five years after it had begun: a full hearing in Shreveport's courthouse with the NRCs judges.[79] For several years, LES had been paying for community members to go to Europe to see the other Urenco plants. Most were impressed, but most were favorably inclined toward the plant to begin with. However, those supporters of LES did not show up in Shreveport. CANT understood the importance of the hearing, and the need for an all-out show of passionate but thoughtful opposition to the plant. They had some luck in that the hearings fell during spring break, so the churches were able to send two busloads of schoolchildren, who were brought into the courtroom ten at a time. CANT had over seventy-five people there each day. Damu Smith of Greenpeace helped organize the protest, bringing toxic waste removal suits with gas masks and some protest signs and banners. Connie Tucker of the civil rights group Southern Organizing Committee also helped get people out for the protests on the courthouse steps.[80] Catholic nun Sister Margaret, called "Shreveport's Mother Theresa" by many, came every day to support the group. The NAACP brought people, Global Response brought some, and every newspaper and TV station was there with cameras. An LES lawyer lamented to one CANT member: "You've got what I don't have: loyalty."

Upon arriving at the courthouse square in downtown Shreveport, Toney Johnson was concerned. The sheriff in Homer was a marshall in Shreveport, and he had called for the riot police to be there to control the courthouse square. Johnson described walking up to "a 300 pound cop in riot gear" and saying, "There ain't gonna be no trouble today, Snap's [the sheriff] just stirring things up here." The cop told his men to "clear out."

Inside, the hearings were passionate and long. LES made their case for the need for the plant in the United States, the safety of its construction and operation, the fairness of its siting, and the role it would play in the development of the region. Sierra Club Legal Defense Fund's Nathalie Walker and Diane Curran refuted it, focusing on the costs of the plant, the uncertain future of the massive piles of radioactive wastes, legal issues on how the siting decision was made, and the intentional and unintentional racism it indicated.

A key moment in the hearings came with the testimony of sociologist Robert Bullard of Clark Atlanta University. Bullard reported the results of an investigation into the narrowing of the list of sites for the plant from seventy-eight sites to the final one – the LeSage tract. At each stage of the narrowing process, the percentage of black neighbors rose, until the one site between the two towns was left, which was 97 percent black.[81] Bullard went on to testify that the construction firm Fluor Daniel's employee Larry Engwall's means of rating sites in 1989 discriminated against black residents. He cited Engwall's sworn testimony described earlier in which he said that he did an "eyeball assessment," driving through two sites and doing visual scoring

National groups also got in the act of putting pressure on the NRC judges. Working Assets Long Distance did a "call in" directly to the judges' chambers, swamping them with over 8,000 calls.[82] The San Francisco group Global Response and the Southern Organization Committee pushed a letter writing campaign to NRC, which received over 500 letters. A group of sympathetic senators wrote to the NRC on environmental justice.[83] After hearings in July 1994 and March 1995, CANT had made its point directly to the NRC, and its substantial armada of supporting groups was growing with the wave of the environmental justice movement. The timing with President Clinton's 1994 executive order on environmental justice would be critical.

A PRECEDENT-SETTING RULING? PARTIAL DECISION, BACKLASH, OUTCOME

The battle over LES swung back and forth in the following years. LES faced several setbacks in the next two years, but they persisted and won some important battles to move their permits along. In 1995, the Louisiana Department of Environmental Quality expressed concern that it might end up with the uranium hexafloride tailings to clean up by itself if the LES group chose to leave the state, or if it collapsed financially. Estimates of the cost of cleanup were skyrocketing, from $40 million estimated in 1990, to over $400 million in 1995 and after. Some predictions ran as high as $1 billion to clean up the site after just a 30-year productive life for the plant. Decommissioning, the careful dismantling and decontamination of nuclear facilities, would take years. Some state officials feared the worst, but later in the year the state accepted LES's word that they would have insurance and a fund for cleanup. DEQ issued the pollution permits late in 1995. CANT and the Sierra Club Legal Defense Fund appealed the permits and won their reversal in 1996 when the First Circuit Court of Appeals revoked them. Also in 1996 the NRC ruled that LES was financially unstable.

Finally on May 2, 1997, the NRC released a "partial" ruling on the plants which was "widely viewed as a national precedent in the area of environmental justice."[84] In it, the NRC cited evidence that "racial considerations had played a part in the site selection process." The NRC board cited LES official Engwall's testimony that he had used the "eyeball" method to count population at two possible sites, saying it "raises a strong inference that race and economic status played a role in the scoring of the two sites." NRC judges expressed that they had wanted to address the spirit of Clinton's executive order on environmental justice[85] and admitted that they were on totally new ground.

Declaring a partial victory, CANT members celebrated the ruling. Toney Johnson said,

You can never beat the NRC on technical issues. We broke the rules. We beat them on environmental racism. We never dreamed they'd agree with us. . . . We won this on environmental justice. The NRC judges saw the passion of the black people. And we argued a good case. Plus the NRC and the Energy Department didn't want this plant.

Understanding well the fragility of the "partial decision" (other elements were still to be decided), which they knew would come under intense attack from business interests, anti-LES coalition organizers did not sit back and let NRC lightly change its mind. NIRS sent out an e-mail plea around the world, and 180 organizations from thirty-four states and twenty countries signed a letter to the NRC dated July 1, 1997. The letter urged the commissioners to uphold the May 2 decision denying the permit on environmental justice grounds. Another July 29, 1997, letter to the NRC had nationally acclaimed civil and human rights advocates, members of Congress, and mayors from New Orleans and Minneapolis urging the NRC to uphold the decision.[86]

Plant supporters mounted their own campaigns to reverse the partial ruling. LES President Jensen said that the partners in the project were "outraged by the accusations of racism. . . . Racism was not an issue in this whole thing."[87] Homer's economic development panel leader J. T. Taylor said of environmental justice: "That was the furthest from the truth that was possible. The opponents were either ignorant or just against J. Bennett Johnston."[88] Taylor blasted the decision in a letter to NRC chairwoman Shirley Jackson, the only black woman to ever head the federal agency, soon after the decision. Taylor's opinion reflects much of the opinion of the business community about environmental justice issues, citing a different kind of injustice – to the firms and their workers:

Racial matters played no part whatsoever in selection of the plant site – the intervenor have presented no proof of this because there is none. As a matter of fact, it would be difficult to find any suitable rural tract in this part of the country that did not have homes of black citizens in the surrounding area . . . [the site] was selected because of its size, its terrain and the area's seismic stability, NOT because of racial makeup of any nearby small communities. If licensing for CEC is rejected, great injustice will be done to the LES consortium which has spent more than $30 million and more than seven years on the project; to the 400 persons who would not find work helping build it; to the 180 persons who would not find the permanent good jobs to be offered to black and white alike; to American industry which would not find an improved source of nuclear fuel.[89]

A month later, another letter from Taylor to Jackson took on a more desperate sound and spoke more to what he perceived might be her own perspective on whose justice was important in the LES case:

If denial of licensing for Claiborne Enrichment Center because of the unsupported claim of environmental racism is allowed to stand, incalculable harm will be done to future efforts toward economic development in our parish, throughout Louisiana, and possibly anywhere there is an appreciable number of African-American citizens. We plead for real justice through approval of Louisiana Energy Services' appeal.[90]

Taylor made the point that environmental justice rulings can hurt the communities they seek to protect by undermining job creation efforts. This paradox will arise in case after case, and its solution has never been simple.

Local residents Barry and Susan Roberts assembled signatures and sent a petition to Shirley Jackson in August. Their petition reflects the views of much of the white community in Homer and was signed by a new group designed to counter the publicity afforded CANT. They named their group Citizens in Favor of Economic Development (CFED):

It seems that the ones publicly voicing their opinion are the opponents of the Claiborne Enrichment Center and the LES. Myself and those undersigned believe that the construction and operation of the plant will be far more beneficial than detrimental to the community. Please overturn the ASLB [Atomic Safety and Licensing Board] May 1 decision regarding LES and environmental justice.

The Roberts's signature drive netted 300 signatures on the petition, and the plea was expedited to the NRC by J. T. Taylor through Louisiana's other senator John Breaux's office.[91] In a pointed cover letter, Senator Breaux asked the NRC to "Please investigate the included information sent to me [by J. T. Taylor] and let me know of the commission's response to Mr. Taylor. Please give the views and concerns of my constituent every appropriate consideration within the commission's guidelines."

After the appeals and the continuing battle over the partial ruling, in early April 1998, the NRC ordered LES to examine effects of rerouting the road, but stopped short of forcing it to study whether the siting was discriminatory. Some argued that it was still a precedent-setting ruling, but LES was quick to put out a press release on April 9, 1998, to make the media and the public aware that the NRC had ruled that "no racial bias occurred in the siting process."[92]

So in 1997 LES was ruled by the NRC to have used racial bias in their plant siting, but the decision was partially reversed in early 1998. To many people's surprise, LES finally put out a terse but angry press release on April 22, 1998 (plant opponents immediately noted the appropriateness of its being Earth Day). It read: "LES officials today ended their seven-year quest for a license from the U.S. NRC to build and operate what would have been the nation's first privately owned centrifuge enrichment plant." They attached a letter to the three commissioners of the NRC, a chronology of the licensing quest, and the April 9, 1998, press release regarding NRC's reversal on environmental justice from just two weeks before. Echoing the words of Formosa Plastics about the EPA, LES blasted the NRC for what were

incredible delays . . . the inability of the licensing process to operate in a predictable, efficient and timely manner . . . even a facility as safe and as attractive as the CEC can be delayed indefinitely, beyond the patience of the most committed and able private partners and investors . . . judging from the LES experience, nuclear projects are presently at an extreme disadvantage and could be lost in this run-away nuclear licensing process. Unless serious reforms are undertaken . . . there may be little interest in the private business community for future nuclear facility investments in the United States.[93]

Finally, they stated their opinion of the ruling on the charge of environmental racism:

[We] have been outraged by the accusations of racism in site selection and the licensing board's unfounded ruling on this issue. The partners took quite seriously the need to expose the shoddy foundation for this charge. The commission has corrected this erroneous and unsupportable finding . . . unfortunately . . . we conclude that continuing . . . has become futile at this late date.

Upon giving up their siting in Claiborne Parish, LES officials called for a drastic reform of the licensing process. "Our attorneys advised us that they don't see this licensing process coming to an end for a minimum of two to three more years. Our partners felt they could no longer fund this with no end in sight." They had expended a decade, $34 million dollars, and an impressive amount of political muscle to try to get the application approved, without success.[94]

The opposition had spent a decade, about 1/150th of what LES did (around $200,000), and flexed a surprising new type of political muscle by combining national civil rights leaders, environmentalists, environmental lawyers, and persistent grassroots organizing, which kept the struggle alive. Sierra Club Legal Defense Fund had spent just over $100,000 on the case; CANT estimated that they had raised and spent about another $75,000.[95] Of course, the other national groups had expended several thousand dollars, but the total was a tiny fraction of that spent by LES.

The opponents of the plant rejoiced because the official announcement gave them the chance to celebrate and mark the end of the seemingly endless, exhausting struggle. CANT members held a mock jazz funeral for LES on May 2, 1998. Toney Johnson built a mock casket painted with LES's name; they played Al Hirt music on a boom box and carried the pall to the burying ground.[96] The bishop from Shreveport led the procession. But they were also aware that they didn't want to anger further their neighbors who had supported the project, so they avoided thumbing their noses.[97]

LEGACIES OF THE STRUGGLE

The implications of the outcome, and all the reasons for LES's decision are still open for interpretation. After the Earth Day LES press release, both sides rushed in to release statements. "It is the first time a federal agency ruled that when you are looking at the disenfranchised poor, you have to give particular and close scrutiny to those communities," said Nathalie Walker, the lead counsel of the Sierra Club Legal Defense Fund.[98] In fact, SCLDF had recently been renamed Earthjustice Legal Defense Fund in part to reach beyond the lily-white profile many associated with the Sierra Club. The NRC judges' referring to Bullard's testimony in the 1997 partial ruling had shown the importance of demographic analysis in plant-siting decisions. Speaking to both sides, Walker said, "We hope that hazardous industrial companies and regulatory agencies pay close attention to this case. The license withdrawal sends a positive message to other communities of color that they too can win environmental justice victories."[99]

"Federal agencies can no longer idly sit by as communities of color and poor communities are targeted by hazardous industrial companies. If the NRC can make the right decision, then other agencies can also do the right thing," said Robert Bullard.[100] NAACP lawyer Kary Moss, talking about a Michigan power plant case, said the ruling is "definitely a precedent." For her, the ruling supported the contention that all federal agencies must uphold Clinton's 1994 order, to "remove that bias."[101]

In an impassioned e-mail Michael Marriott of NIRS expressed his belief that the case meant profound changes in how our system works:

Those of you who know me know I have spent much of my last 8 years on this effort. We started with a small multi-racial group eight years ago, whose aim was to learn more about LES and its plans. It evolved into a small multi-racial group . . . which has turned the world's nuclear industry on its head. . . . No longer will multi-national corporations be able to simply build whatever they want wherever they want: from now on, local communities will have a say too.[102]

Senator J. Bennett Johnston, at the end of the process, criticized the NRC's licensing process as a "regulatory morass."[103] He told us that "This is a great example of a regulatory process which just was irresponsible, uncontrolled, they just went on and on – seven years. Everybody knew that there was no real danger from this . . ."[104]

The newspaper staff in the nearby town of Minden harshly attacked the ruling and the plant's opposition in a letter to the *Homer Guardian-Journal*. "North Louisiana has blown it big time with LES decision. . . . LES announced today that it's giving up a seven year battle against over-regulators and radical environmental activists."[105] They showed that locals would not soon forget the blow from the NRC to their plans for local development. "We call on our congressional delegation to vote against all future funding for the U.S. Nuclear Regulatory Commission and demand that the agency be shut down. . . . Just because the feds and the environazi movement beat LES doesn't mean they can hold North Louisiana back forever."

The environmental justice coalition had been successful, it seemed, partly by utilizing what was evolving into a strategic *delay tactic*, which made the project economically unfeasible by tying up its permits in the courts. LES's president Roland Jensen admitted the success of the delay tactic. "They certainly did drag it out. . . . Delaying a project like this is tantamount to killing it." Again echoing the Formosa Plastics case, Nathalie Walker argued that the delays were LES's own fault, by their only providing partial information when requests were filed. LES President Roland Jensen shot back, "that's a bald-faced lie."[106]

How important was the environmental justice argument in stopping LES? Its true importance is uncertain because a series of other factors made the project potentially unviable for investors. The plant was probably no longer needed in a world market for uranium that was glutted by dismantled Soviet warheads. Interviews on both sides suggested that this was the case from about 1991 onward when the world price for uranium plummeted. Senator Johnston told us:

I think they would have persisted if the economics of uranium enrichment would have been better. I think the environmental justice part of it would have been reversed by the NRC. This was just a recommendation of the hearing judges. . . . This plant was not beaten by the opponents. It was not turned down by the NRC. . . . It was always a question of economics. . . . There was just a flood of [enriched uranium from the ex-USSR] and I think, chances are it would not have been built, even if, if you went back six or seven years ago, if it had been licensed then, maybe they would have gone ahead on it.

So, the question of environmental justice's role in its cancellation remains open for Johnston, but it is clear that environmental justice was an effective part of the delay tactic, which worked to change the economic context of the project. Still, it was not clear whether the environmental justice charges would stick if LES had persisted in the permitting effort.

But the question then remains of why LES continued the fight on an uneconomical project. By doing so and clearing themselves of the racism charge just two weeks before canceling the project, Urenco succeeded in opening up the U.S. uranium market, for decades closed except to the government monopoly. Johnston's bills had managed to give a quarter of the uranium sales in the United States to Urenco, which has begun selling the nuclear fuel from its European supplies.[107] Other observers believe that the NRC was against Johnston and the project the whole way through, and that the agency used citizen participation and environmental justice as a way to allow the agency to hold on to most of its monopoly. LES may have been driven to clear itself on environmental justice charges and was waiting to see if the market conditions for uranium improved as the years went by.

So in the end, the LES case was the first and so far the only one in which a federal agency denied permits for a major project on the grounds of environmental justice. However, because of the partial reversal by the NRC, the extent to which it sets a legal precedent, despite the efforts of environmental justice activists, is uncertain. In fact, the landmark case remains largely ignored in the literature on environmental justice, despite the enormity of the victory.[108] Of course, for CANT and those against the building of another nuclear fuel plant, the case was an unmistakable victory.

The decade-long battle over the plant left its clearest mark in the social fabric of the small town of Homer, Louisiana, and its rural surrounds. Interviews with locals suggest the depth of the feelings from the LES struggle. Some expressed how old social networks had been broken: "We had all been friends . . . it'll never be the same." Another said, "LES took nine years of my life." And another said, "I will never forgive LES for what they've done to our community. I don't know if we'll ever get over this."[109]

Toney Johnson described a personal change that came with fighting LES in CANT.

I got a lot more liberal. I'm from the Old South, and being a businessman, I didn't believe what liberals were saying. I've come to fear big companies. Big companies are taking over the world. When you have stockholders, all the decisions are based on cold economics. That's no way to run a world. . . . You've got to have a little anger. These are gross injustices against humanity, and someone's got to fight them.

Johnson also believes that race relations are beginning to change. "For years in Homer, it was the blacks against the whites. We didn't trust each other in CANT. Every time, someone made a stupid remark that would insult the other side . . . but we worked it out. Now . . . they're my friends for life. That was not the case before this."

Essie Youngblood, leaning back on her white porch overlooking her family's fields in Forest Grove and the site where LES would have been built over on the next hill, talked of the change in the community. "Ever since we had this fight, things are not just thrown on people. As far as CANT is concerned, we will always have that special feeling. We have made some genuine friends and I feel proud of it. I feel our relationships have spilled over into the community here. Racial harmony has improved." She continued, "We get lonesome sometimes. I miss the contact."

Juanita Hamilton, from the other side of the plant site in Center Springs, hugged Norton Tompkins and pointed to the site. She said, "We have been brought together in love. And we have fought this for nine years and still have that binding love – and hope to keep it."[110]

The public involvement of some people previously considered unempowered is an important legacy. Roy Mardis, a Center Springs resident had moved back from Pasadena, California, in 1987 to be back in his country home before the LES sitting attempt. After the community's representative on the local police jury (city council) voted to move the road connecting Forest Grove and Center Springs, Mardis decided to run for the seat. He won. And Juanita Hamilton was elected to the local school board.

Mardis talked of the effectiveness of the coalition approach and the empowerment the community felt.

Our coalition of CANT community leaders, lawyers, experts, and friends worked together for more than eight years to prevent LES from turning our homes into a radioactive nightmare and toxic waste dump. We proved to the world that working together, grassroots groups can win; even when the odds are stacked against them. Environmental racism had rendered our communities invisible. The grassroots struggle for environmental justice proved that not only do Forest Grove and Center Springs exist, but they along with their neighbors made their presence and voices heard when it counts.[111]

Because some similar points arise in the other cases, we will discuss these kinds of impacts from the struggles on communities further in Chapter 7.

There are, of course, other points to consider in the legacy of the epic LES struggle, among them the fate of the land, the campaign money, and the future of the nuclear industry, an inevitable generator of uranium waste.

The land was finally sold in 1999 to Woodard Walker, a Seattle-based timber company that intends to keep the land in wood production indefinitely. J. Bennett Johnston decided not to run again for senator so that he could focus on lobbying work, establishing a high-profile office just a half a block from the White House. His clients include huge energy and mining firms. By not running for reelection, he was able to keep $2.5 million in campaign donations.

Does protecting one's backyard mean another community will have to be exposed to an undesired polluter? At the time of the Earth Day announcement in 1998, LES president Roland Jensen said that for now, the partners had no plans for another site. "I don't know what we're going to do now."[112] The nuclear industry continues to attempt to revive their industry but has failed nearly everywhere. In fact, in Urenco's home in Germany, where the Green Party has taken a pivotal role in the Bundestag [parliament], the nation recently announced that it will phase out all its nuclear reactors. Back in the United States, there is still no five-state compact for where to site the low-level nuclear waste, and the high-level nuclear fuel continues to pile up at reactors around the nation.[113] As Toney Johnson delightedly put it, "Nuclear energy is gonna die, but it's just gonna die without polluting one more place."

4

EPA's Environmental Justice Test Case

THE SHINTECH PVC PLANT

Top: Emelda West speaks at the protest at the Governor's Mansion on June 20, 1998. [Photo by Tim Mueller, used with permission of the *Baton Rouge Advocate*]

Bottom: Protest against Shintech's proposed siting in Plaquemine. [Photo by Jeffrey M. Weiss]

Coming from a long line of sugar farmers, Dale Hymel is the President of the Council for St. James Parish, lying roughly halfway between New Orleans and Baton Rouge. In spite of his tie to farming, Hymel recognizes that "the majority of people realize that industry in this area is the driving force in the parish. Without industry we would have to go back to where we were before in the thirties and forties with just agriculture and trapping and logging. That doesn't pay a whole lot of money in wages."[1] The industry Hymel refers to is eighteen chemical plants and manufacturers of all sizes, which employ approximately 1,800 people and contribute significantly to the local tax base.[2]

To keep the parish economy growing, Hymel believes that the parish government should assist all business and industry in developing in any way it can. He said that the government will provide companies with access to office space, phone, and copy machines while they are getting set up in the parish. He also believes that local government representatives should "walk" companies through the permitting process, making them aware of parish ordinances and regulations, and generally make the businesses feel welcome.[3]

Hymel believes that community residents have a minimal role in decision making concerning which industries should be welcomed into the parish. He views the community's role as electing leaders, such as himself, who will, in turn, make the development decisions for the parish.

We are elected as officials to represent them [residents]. They trusted us to make the right decision. Now every four years, if we don't make the right decision, then they will get us out and put somebody [in] who they think will. I think that is their voice in government of who they elect as leaders to make the right decision.[4]

Emelda West, a feisty and fiercely religious 74-year-old African-American mother of seven, has a very different view of development and the role of communities in her parish. "There is industry here from all over. They have their industry here because they can't have them in their countries or hometowns so they just want to come here. Why? Cheap land, cheap labor. That's what it's all about. Why do we have to be the cesspool?"[5] She has seen very few of the people she knows getting jobs at the plant, and those who do work at the plants come from far away, taking their money with them. "I got five sons and why is it they can't make a decent living?"[6] She described how her son who has a Master's degree in Public Administration, could not get a job locally. "I am a taxpayer, a property owner, and I vote. And not one of my sons can get a job here. If a Caucasian boy can come out of high school and get a job in a plant, don't tell me my child is overly qualified. You understand me – yes, its racism."[7]

Carol Gaudin, the vice president of a group favoring the siting of the Shintech Chemical plant, had a different view. She agreed with West that, historically, African Americans have not received employment in the local plants, but she believed that it was time to change that. She saw the siting of a new plant as an opportunity to make industry more accountable to the black communities that are their neighbors. She didn't agree with the environmentalists, whom she saw as outsiders, that the plants would poison them. She stated,

We've lived with [industrial] plants. We're there and we know and we see, we feel like we can decide. We don't need environmentalists to tell us how harmful it all is. I don't care what anybody says, I don't care what level of formal education there is or is not, people usually know what they need and what they want for themselves.[8]

This is a story about a small parish on the banks of the Mississippi River where residents were clamoring for a say in what kinds of plants are allowed to come in. Governmental leaders and residents in the parish were of two opinions. The parish officials, many business owners, and a group of residents were satisfied with the quality of their air and water, and they wanted to pursue economic development aggressively. They were eager to reap the benefits of the proposed $700 million Shintech chemical plant, which they anticipated would provide jobs for their families, tax dollars for their schools, and a chance for area businesses to grow.

The other group, made up mostly of very determined mothers and grandmothers, argued that their neighborhoods were already being poisoned by the chemical and petroleum plants stationed nearby. The proposed plant, they exclaimed, would simply add to the already contaminated surroundings that daily threatened the health of their families and children while providing few jobs for their breadwinners.

During the struggle, each group aligned itself with powerful outside allies who provided them with important political connections, money, and training on how to pursue their fight. The pro-Shintech coalition had strong friends in high places. Louisiana Governor Mike Foster personally took on their fight and used state agencies and his bully pulpit to try to discredit plant opponents and pave the way for the plant's construction. Plant protesters enmeshed themselves in a strong and determined network of state environmental groups who had experience fighting similar battles and were willing to share resources, knowledge, and staff to support this fledgling group. National environmental and social justice groups gave support to the protesting group in the form of much needed political and financial resources.

In a struggle as charged as this, it is virtually impossible to discern the "absolute truth" regarding the events that occurred. Each side in the struggle has its own account of the events that took place and its own opinions regarding the motives of the other side. In the rest of the chapter, we will examine the events as they unfolded in this struggle and explore the attitudes and perceptions of people on both sides.

RACE AND THE UNFOLDING OF ECONOMIC DEVELOPMENT
IN ST. JAMES PARISH

St. James Parish is located halfway between Baton Rouge and New Orleans on the banks of the Mississippi River and occupies approximately 246 square miles. The community, which tries to balance the often conflicting demands of agriculture and industry, is home to approximately 6,934 households.[9] During the 1960s and 1970s, when other areas of the country were losing manufacturing plants, St. James Parish was experiencing an industrial sector boom.[10] During these years, St. James was among the top ten parishes with the most industrial growth in the state.[11] Companies continued to locate to the parish in the early 1980s, and, besides new plants, existing industry is constantly expanding their production by adding huge units. Then, during the first half of the nineties, the arrival of new industrial facilities slowed. Shintech would have been the first large chemical plant to locate to the area in the past seventeen years.[12]

In St. James Parish, there is no governmental zoning ordinances or official development plans. Therefore, the economic development officer is charged with directing economic development along with the planning commission, and the parish council. Although industries have to get air, water, and hazardous waste permits for their operations from the Louisiana Department of Environmental Quality, they must also obtain a Coastal Zone Permit if the facility is to be built in a designated coastal zone area. The local Coastal Zone Permit Committee makes a recommendation to the parish president regarding the issuance of a permit and then the parish president either approves or denies the permit.

Race has colored development in St. James Parish. As in many other plantation communities, poor black communities sprang up surrounding the sugar cane plantations. Initially these communities allowed black workers to be close to their work sites; however, as the plantations were converted to industrial sites, these communities remained, even though few blacks worked at the plants, excluded by lack of skills and some racist hiring practices.

Two explanations exist for the lack of hiring. Carol Gaudin, a black, middle-aged member of the pro-Shintech group alluded to this lack of attention on the part of industry and parish government when she stated,

Because historically coming from the whole plantation system, black people, in my opinion, were not to be looked out for. It never occurred to anybody else that these plants were locating right here, right next to black people and these people were not benefitting at all. It never occurred to the government to see that we need to hire around the plant.[13]

Oliver Cooper, a black councilperson, implied that the sugar cane growers discouraged the industrial plants from hiring their workers. He stated,

In the past, our people who filled out an application were either overqualified or underqualified. I think the reason for that to happen is you have a lot of sugar cane growers in the area and there is a lot of people that would want the opportunity [to work at a plant] – that is less people you would have working in the sugar cane fields.[14]

Regardless of the explanation, statistical records found in the St. James Parish Economic Development office support claims that blacks are not often hired at the plants. In August 1997, the percentage of black employees in eleven St. James Parish manufacturing plants ranged from 4.2 percent to 19.4 percent. This is quite low considering that blacks make up approximately 50 percent of the population in the parish. Whether the plantations are used as sugar cane fields or manufacturing sites for chemicals, blacks clearly still remain on the losing end of economic development: they get low wages in the fields and few opportunities to work within the plants. In addition, they must live in close proximity to the dirt, noise, and pollution from these plants.

Many locals argue that race is used to maintain power concentrated in a few sets of hands. A white protest group member stated, "We definitely have a race problem here. Everybody creeps around it. But it is definitely here. And the problem is our politicians use race to keep us divided. I know that as a white person looking in – I can see how race is used a lot to keep the black people down."[15] Several black residents who were interviewed portrayed the relationship between blacks and local political leaders as being based on "payoffs" rather than upon true democratic representation. Emelda West declared, "The black community just falls for anything you tell them – chick feed, chump change, and money. My people – you give them jambalaya, some beer and a little chump change, enough to buy a few more bottles of beer, and they'll sell their mother down the river."[16] Carol Gaudin explained why some blacks were willing to trade their votes for money, stating, "I think it's because they believe that anybody who gets elected regardless to who it is – it really is not going to make a difference in their lives. Their lives are still going to be the same. So, I'm going to take this, uh . . . whatever, few dollars that are handed to me to drive the car, drive the voters, or whatever."[17]

The Shintech struggle marks an important step for the black community in St. James Parish. In this struggle, no matter which side one was on, the common goal was to end "business as usual" where locals were ignored by industry. The proindustry group would accept the proposed plant siting if they could share equally with the white community in terms of the economic benefits that the new prospect promised. The anti-Shintech group did not believe that the exploitative race relations inherent in economic development in the parish since its founding would change. They chose to reject the prospect of an industry that guaranteed only to bring more pollution to their community.

A COMMUNITY DIVIDED

The first stirrings of a community conflict began on the evening of July 22, 1996. Erik Poche, a St. James Parish Council member and local sugar cane farmer, learned that Shintech was planning to build on land that he leased for cane farming. Concerned that he might have a hard time finding other land to farm, he organized an informal meeting of parish residents at Hymel's Restaurant after closing time. School board members, a representative from the Tulane Environmental Law Clinic, and other local residents attended. The word had gotten out that a subsidiary of a Japanese manufacturer, Shin-Etsu Chemical Company, was proposing a $700 million chemical plant for the parish. The company, Shintech, Inc., was considering a location in the town of Convent to set up a plant that would manufacture chlorine, caustic soda, ethylene dichloride, vinyl chloride monomer, and polyvinyl chloride. This meeting brought together local residents and potential activists and produced the spark that ignited a wild fire of opposition to the siting of the plant.

Following this informal meeting, Pat Melancon, an energetic white mother of six whose husband works at a local aluminum plant, organized two public hearings to discuss the proposed plant. Parish and state officials, Shintech representatives, and community representatives all attended. The residents who were against the plant were shocked to see the early commitment that their parish officials had already made to company officials. Parish officials were standing at the doors as people were coming in and handing them little, round stickers to put on their shirts that said, "St. James Parish Supports Industry."

Melancon became the first president of the protest group they formed called St. James Citizens for Jobs and the Environment (SJCJE). She reflected on the actions of the parish government when she declared, "I mean, it's a very intimate relationship between industry and the parish governing officials. They [the officials] are supposed to be the first line of protection and defense that people have – is the parish government. That is nothing, as far as we're concerned. Because they are definitely in bed with industry."[18]

Thus, very early in the conflict, the first major tension developed between the protest group and the parish government – the fear that the government was not adequately protecting the environment and public health of the people of St. James Parish.

The anti-Shintech coalition was particularly concerned with the nature of the chemicals that the plant would produce. In the production of polyvinyl chloride, chlorine and other organochlorides are produced and these yield dioxins. One of SJCJE allies, the Louisiana Environmental Action Network, released a flyer entitled, "PVC: Poison in Disguise." The flyer stated that dioxin acts as a powerful environmental hormone, which can have strong effects on the endocrine system, causing fertility problems, developmental abnormalities, immune system suppression, and cancer. They reported that two of the nearby PVC plants had had a total of fifty-eight toxic releases and spills between the years of 1987 and 1996. Dow, a PVC plant in the nearby town of Plaquemine, had been fined several times by the DEQ and EPA for noncompliance with regulations and for violating clean air regulations.

As the struggle unfolded, the protest group discovered that the preponderance of industrial plants in their parish were located in close proximity to poor, black communities. It was this awareness that provided the grounds for their claims of environmental injustice and the filing of a Title VI civil rights complaint with the EPA. Gloria Roberts, an SJCJE member, described how they came to that conclusion. She reported,

We went on each street from the Romeville part. . . . I counted how many blacks and how many whites. [We covered] both sides of the river within that 2 mile radius. Because this is what we are talking about, this is where you are going to impact . . . well that was the beginning of talking about Title VI.[19]

It is important to note, however, that the group was not just interested in environmental justice for minorities. Even though they felt that poor and African-American communities were being dumped on by industry, they also felt that no one, regardless of their race or income level, should be dumped on.[20]

According to the members of SJCJE, the relationship between community residents and industrial plants had been strained for quite some time. The president of the group stated,

We haven't had any real good association, especially with people who live in the shadows of the industries. The people who live in the shadows of the industries suffer from the [chemical] releases that go on constantly. The nighttime releases, the weekend releases and they [the companies] refuse to work with us when we try to find out what it is they are releasing. You know they just deny everything. The parish officials do not help us at all.[21]

The anti-Shintech group was unusual because it was composed of both whites and blacks: in St. James parish it is rare for people of both races to come together to form a group of any kind. The president, Pat Melancon, was white, but the group claimed to have a majority of African-American members.

Early on in the struggle, the St. James Parish protest group realized that they would need legal assistance in their fight against Shintech. They approached the Tulane Environmental Law Clinic (TELC) to ask for free legal assistance because the group couldn't afford a lawyer. Brenda Huguet, a group member, described how the group felt initially:

When we first started, nobody helped us. We started on our own. I can remember going to bed at night and we needed legal representation and we didn't know where to go. I kept saying, "we can't keep this up, we don't have a lawyer. We need a lawyer to be helping us." I just couldn't get over this – what are we going to do? Every night I prayed. . . . It took so long for Tulane to say – "yes."[22]

Tulane finally did say "yes" in November 1996. In addition to the clinic, a large coalition of environmental and social justice groups assisted SJCJE. Greenpeace was one of their most visible and controversial allies. Initially, the protest group members were less than impressed with the international environmental organization. Gloria Roberts, one of the leaders stated,

The first time Greenpeace sent someone here she made a mess and we called them back and said, "No, we don't want Greenpeace." Well, I remember once we refused and then he [Damu Smith, National Associate Director] came back and wrote a letter and said, "I will not do anything you don't want me to do." He has kept his promise. We have had no marches, we have had no laying wn anywhere, any of that kind of stuff, because we told him that we weren't ng to do that.[23]

onique Harden, a former Greenpeace environmental lawyer, de- ed her organization's relationship with SJCJE as one of support. id that "the coalition was supporting the community – they [the nity members] were very strong, feisty, smart, spiritual com- leaders. They made our job very easy."[24]
ruggle fit perfectly into Greenpeace's broader environmental f eliminating dioxin-producing material. The national organ-

ization created and maintained advantageous political connections for the St. James group by coordinating weekly conference calls among coalition members and arranging meetings for SJCJE members with members of congress, national and international rights groups, and the media. Greenpeace got word of the struggle out to celebrities who helped to publicize the case. Bonnie Raitt, Michelle Shocked, The Dave Matthews Band, and Winton and Brandon Marsalis all donated money and publicity to the cause. The artists distributed postcards at their concerts for people to sign and mail to the EPA voicing their opposition to Shintech. This produced a groundswell of national support for the protest group. People from as far away as Vermont, California, and Indiana voiced their concerns to the EPA on this environmental justice case.

At least twenty-three local, state, and national groups supported SJCJE. SJCJE member Gloria Roberts recalled the coalition's assistance:

Greenpeace supplied us with all of the information we needed to know. Dan Nicolai [Labor Neighbor/OCAW] was our fiscal agent. When any grants were gotten, he kept the money and he printed notices of meetings for us. . . . Mary Lee [Louisiana Environmental Action Network], well, what can I say, she furnished money, she was there every time we needed her. There are people in her office like Dr. Gary Miller who would look things up for us.

Monique Harden described the participation of outside groups when stating, "Every group had to be accepted and invited by the leadership of that community group. By leadership, I am not talking about one person – I am talking about active people. It does take a coalition that is very respectful and very resourceful."

The Deep South Center for Environmental Justice at Xavier University in New Orleans also conducted valuable research on the case. The center's director, Dr. Beverly Wright, who has done research on the racially disparate impact of industrial facilities in the river parishes for a number of years, led a field investigation armed with a video recorder and camera. Because she believed that census data does not always tell the whole story, she compared her findings with 1990 census data, which described the demographics of the communities. She provided the protest group and their lawyers with her results.[25]

The protest group was very religious, determined, and tenacious. Lisa Lavie, the supervising attorney at the Tulane Environmental Law Clinic described these characteristics of the group. She recalled,

I would go to these meetings with the clients and I got very close to them. That was my life. We would always start a meeting with a prayer and Miss West – she usually led the prayer. She would always end the prayer with "I take authority over Shintech in Jesus' name. Shintech will not locate here!" She said it with such conviction after about twenty times being in on this prayer and just kind of seeing the way they just never would consider [that Shintech would be able to locate in the parish] and they always talked about the Lord. I'm not a religious person, but I started to believe that. You know I really did. Part of me started to believe – I just couldn't envision them [Shintech] coming. It just didn't match with the whole attitude of the group.[26]

On the other side, the plant proponents did not view the coalition of outside groups as merely supporters of the SJCJE group. Rather, they felt invaded by outside groups who were coming in with their own agendas and using the community's struggle for their own benefit. During the struggle, Governor Foster waged a relentless attack on the Tulane Environmental Law Clinic. In a radio interview, he responded to a statement in which the reporter stated that the St. James parish group sought out the help of the clinic. Foster stated,

May I simply tell you, "baloney" – if you do a good investigative report, you'll find they [the law clinic] solicit clients. This is their whole purpose in life. They love to go around, pick things, make a judgment, decide whether it's something they want personally and make a big scene over it and make it difficult for us to attract jobs to the state. I disagree with that, I don't mind them doing it on their own, I just don't want to see a major university, with a major tax break, people that sort of become a law within themselves – and that's my problem with this.[27]

In the same interview he called the law students and professors "modern day vigilantes."[28]

Governor Foster revealed his dedication to the siting of this plant early on when the law clinic received an inquiry from his special counsel and deputy chief of staff as to whether the clinic would accept the case. When the law clinic proceeded to work on the case, Foster called the president of Tulane University to inquire if he knew what the law clinic was doing. The president, Eamon Kelly, assured the governor that he was aware of the situation and said that he could do little to stop the clinic's actions. As the struggle unfolded, Foster actually discouraged alumni and local business owners at a New Orleans Business Council meeting from supporting the school.[29] He was joined by Dan Borne, the president of the Louisiana Chemical Association, who said that he often tells members to "consider long and hard before you feed the mouth of the entity that's going to be consistently trying to shut you down."[30]

The secretary of the LDED also tried to persuade the President of Tulane to request that the Louisiana Supreme Court review the activities of TELC. He accused the clinic of "conducting legalistic guerrilla attacks against environmentally-responsible industry and the DEQ" and "damaging the prospects of the citizens of Louisiana – who don't have the security of tenured jobs – for obtaining well-paying employment." He suggested that "Tulane request the Louisiana Supreme Court review the activities of the Environmental Law Clinic to determine if the clinic has overstepped the charter the court originally gave it."[31]

Locally, the parish economic development officer thought that outside groups were simply trying to pursue their own agendas in their small parish. She stated,

I think that St. James Citizen for Jobs and the Environment are mainly driven by Greenpeace whose mission is to stop chlorine production worldwide. Shintech will manufacture chlorine, that is why they are being targeted. This is not just a local environmental group – power is coming from Tulane Environmental Law Clinic, Greenpeace, and Sierra Club. The special interest groups have their own agenda. SJCJE is very small, people don't realize that the same thirty to forty people are at the meetings. Personally, I believe that they represent only forty people.[32]

The pro-Shintech coalition also accused the SJCJE members of not really being part of the community that was closest to the proposed site. Pat Melancon, Emelda West, and Brenda Huguet, three of the group's leaders, all lived in Convent; however, they did not live in the Freetown area, which is closest to the Shintech site. They cited this fact, along with the participation of the outside groups, as a reason that SJCJE should not be considered to speak for the community most likely to be affected by the plant.

Three local groups strongly supported Shintech. The St. James Citizen Coalition had approximately twenty members, all African Americans, with about five or six core people. Carol Gaudin, the vice president and spokesperson for the group, stated that she got involved when she first heard that Shintech was locating in the community. She said that she thought, "Wait a minute! Let's see what's going on here. Let's get in on the ground floor." She tried to persuade the councilperson from that district that they had to get in touch with the company and let them know that the company had to have a positive impact on the community – that they needed to contribute something. She stated, "We don't need another plant in our back yards if they don't help us to do and be what we want to be."[33]

The councilperson was unresponsive. However, Gaudin did find someone who was thinking like her – Gladys Maddie. She ran into Miss Maddie in the grocery store, and they started talking. Maddie, an African-American grandmother, who lives within a mile of the proposed plant site, had already written a letter to Shintech. Miss Maddie, angered because she saw environmentalists who were saying that they didn't want the plant in the community, told Carol that nobody had asked her if she wanted the plant. After receiving her letter, the plant manager, David Wise, gave a presentation at her house describing the plant and answering questions about the possible hazards. Several residents who attended that night formed a group called St. James Citizen Coalition. Members of the group later traveled to Freeport, Texas, to visit a PVC plant owned by Shintech. They said that on the trip they saw a standard of living that they would want for their community.[34] Wise and Maddie became fast friends. He attributes eighteen of the twenty-four pounds he gained during the two-and-one-half-year conflict to her tasty home cooking and hospitality.[35]

Ernest Johnson, the president of the state chapter of the National Association for the Advancement of Colored People knocked on doors with Govenor Foster and asked residents what they thought of the proposed plant. In June 1997, the state NAACP chapter appeared to support the anti-Shintech group when they invited them to present their case at an "Environmental Justice Summit" at Southern University in Baton Rouge.[36] A mere three months later, the state chapter announced that they would remain neutral on the issue. Additionally, Johnson came out with some scathing statements condemning the environmental racism claims of plant opponents.

The announcement of the state NAACP neutrality coincided with the award of a $2.5 million state-funded loan to an organization with which Johnson is affiliated.[37] Governor Foster and Johnson adamantly denied any connection between the state chapter's position on Shintech and the loan, which they say was in the works for some time before the NAACP's position on Shintech was made public.[38] However, the plant opponents had doubts and suspicions about the coincidence of timing of the award and Johnson's statements. Additionally, the local chapter president, Grayling R. Brown, endorsed the project on September 8, 1997. The local chapter based its decision on an economic development program proposed by Shintech to provide jobs, job training, and other economic benefits to African Americans in the parish.[39]

Similar to the accusations of Shintech supporters that outsiders were butting into a local conflict, the anti-Shintech group charged that outsiders were actually stirring up local support for the siting proposal. The anti-Shintech coalition believed that the Louisiana Department of Environmental Quality's Office of Community/Industry Relations was intricately involved in organizing the proindustry community group. The anti-Shintech coalition accused the CIR office of being biased towards the pro-Shintech community group. They cited numerous comments made by the environmental justice coordinator and ombudsman that indicated that the CIR office was squarely in favor of having Shintech in the community. For example, the CIR's Janice Dickerson referred to members of the anti-Shintech coalition as "little Hitlers" and "little dictators" during a speech at Southern University. Additionally, the law clinic arduously tracked the phone records, time sheets, and correspondence of staff in the CIR office during the struggle and documented a pattern of correspondence of office staff with the pro-Shintech group, Shintech officials, Shintech's public relations firms, and DEQ and EPA officials.[40]

The clinic accused Dickerson of ghost writing a highly critical editorial for the proindustry group's president, Gladys Maddie. The clinic lawyers showed that Dickerson had been in Maddie's neighborhood on numerous occasions, including meetings as late as 2:00 A.M. just prior to mailing the letter. They also documented that Dickerson told Shintech representatives that the CIR office was available to assist the company in dealing with environmental justice issues.[41]

The CIR office representatives adamantly denied that Dickerson wrote the letter. In a memo from Dickerson to Herman Robinson, EPA assistant secretary of legal affairs and enforcement, she challenged the integrity of the Tulane Environmental Law Clinic:

Based upon my years of prior experience as an environmental activist, I am not surprised by Kuehn's [the clinic's director] groundless accusations. Through my eyes, the Tulane Environmental Law Clinic's history is one drenched in racism and exclusion of African Americans. . . . Tulane's action in the Shintech matter is tantamount to an environmental racist act because it decided to represent a white middle class woman and her "group" at the expense of shunning an entire black community – the community most impacted![42]

Throughout the struggle, both the pro and anti groups fired off press releases and letters to the editor stating that they spoke for the community closest to the proposed site. Each group accused the other of being led by outside forces and not truly speaking for the community. The pro-Shintech community group said that they lived closer to the plant than members of the other group. The anti-Shintech group refuted the claims of the pro-group's leader that she was the matriarch of the community. An SJCJE member stated, "She [Maddie] wants to say she is the matriarch and she only been there for twenty some years. I was here thirty years!"[43]

This points to one of the most difficult issues in this type of struggle – which community is most affected and does it have a single voice? Both groups had petitions signed by "community members" that represented their side's points of view. The pro group's petition declared, "I am interested in Employment and Business Opportunities Shintech has to offer," whereas the protest group's petition read, "As a resident of St. James Parish, I believe the proposed Shintech PVC Facility is not in the best interest of our parish; therefore, I join with other St. James Citizens to oppose Shintech and to ask Shintech not to locate in St. James."

Various people and organizations polled the community. The NAACP and the governor walked door to door in the Freetown area and claimed they found overwhelming support for Shintech in their informal polls; however, they failed to provide information on their method of sampling respondents or the margin of error involved in their findings. Two polls commissioned by Shintech and conducted by Southern Media & Opinion Research, Inc., showed that at the beginning of the struggle in September 1996, 49 percent of registered voters in St. James Parish who had heard of the Shintech siting proposal were in favor of the plant, 32 percent opposed it, and 20 percent were unsure. In January 1997, the approval rating for Shintech increased to 60 percent of those who had knowledge of the plant, 24 percent opposed it, and 15 percent didn't know.[44] However, a *New Orleans Times-Picayune* poll conducted in January 1998 showed a different picture of opinion regarding the plant. Although they found that 53 percent of the parish residents supported the plant, when they looked specifically at the district of the proposed site, they found that a majority of residents were against the plant. In this district, 52 percent of the residents opposed the plant, 38 percent favored it, and 10 percent didn't have an opinion.[45]

It is important to note the limitations of these survey results. The informal surveys are wide open to bias due to a lack of uniformity in selecting which houses to visit. Several SJCJE members who live on the street that the governor visited reported that he did not knock on their doors. The telephone surveys are also open to bias because they survey only registered voters and individuals with phones. In St. James parish, approximately 10 percent of the residents do not have phones. Therefore, the opinions of the poorest residents were probably not surveyed.

CONTESTED RISKS AND BENEFITS

The state and local officials argued that the benefits of industry greatly outweighed the costs. And besides, the costs of having industry were constantly being decreased due to the advent of new technologies and stricter regulations. Both the parish president and Gus Von Bodungen, assistant secretary, DEQ, said that pollution was decreasing in the area. Dale Hymel described pollution in the parish, saying, "Certainly the parish is much cleaner now than 25 years ago. Industry has been spending a lot of money to upgrade pollution controls, equipment monitors, and scrubbers to keep some emissions out."[46] Von Bodungen agreed with Hymel's comments. He stated, "The emissions are down to a fraction of what they were."[47] In a report he submitted to the EPA, he elaborated further in describing the trends in emissions for the parish. He demonstrated in that report that there was a 74 percent reduction in volatile organic compounds emitted in the parish from 1972 through 1998.[48]

State and local officials also had very different views concerning the health effects of pollution in St. James Parish. The parish president blamed the health problems that the protest group members complained of on lifestyle issues, such as drinking alcohol, eating high-fat food, and not having proper medical care. He stated, "So industry gets blamed for a lot of health problems when some people are not taking care of their bodies, themselves."[49] Von Bodungen echoed Hymel's opinion. He stated, "See, they claim all kinds of health threats, and the plant is not even built . . . it's always lifestyle – excess smoking, excess drinking, whatever, you know, drugs, and anybody that does a study and leaves drugs out is really leaving out a major part of lifestyle."[50]

The parish government officials excitedly looked forward to the tax revenues that the proposed plant would bring to the parish coffers.

Shintech's public relations firm, Harris, Deville and Associates, Inc., predicted that the effects of the new plant on the local economy would amount to $3.8 million in local tax revenue, $7,600,000 in sales tax revenue for the area schools, 2,000 construction jobs, and $506 million of indirect or secondary spending during the construction phase. During the operating phase, the parish would see $292 million in direct spending, 165 permanent jobs, 90 contract jobs, and $2.6 million annually in local (sales) tax revenue.[51]

Shintech needed a Coastal Zone Permit issued by the parish government. The protest group feared that the parish officials' excitement over the project would prevent them from being objective when reviewing the company's permit application. On November 13, 1996, parish officials held a public hearing for the Coastal Zone Permit. The minutes from the meeting reveal that the majority of the individuals who spoke were against the facility. The reasons for their opposition were echoed in hearings, meetings, and lawsuits throughout the two-year battle. Residents feared spills or major catastrophes as a result of plant operations, one woman from Convent asked, "Where in the name of providence are our evacuation sites if we would have a major catastrophe here?"[52]

Concerned that there was already too much pollution in the parish, one member of SJCJE stated, "If we get rid of all the other plants, good, bring Shintech in. But we got all these other plants lined up in a row within a six-mile area. How many plants we got all jammed up together and Shintech wants to be in-between all of them?" Residents were concerned about the effects of the pollution on their family's health. A woman from Convent stated,

The question I have to ask is one: We go to bed sometimes feeling fine and the next morning we are waking up with headaches and nausea and don't know where the problem is coming from. . . In the last two years, how many people have died of lung cancer, not only lung cancer but cancer, in general? How much more pollution does the citizens in St. James Parish have to eat and drink?[53]

Plant opponents doubted that DEQ would do an adequate job of regulating the plant. One man, who worked with the Union/Convent Volunteer Fire and Rescue Unit, complained,

Now, as far as the people doing their surveys – tell them to come and follow me on the levee. I will show them every plant that is throwing trash in this river. DEQ gets called. All these other people get called. They take an hour or two coming out of Baton Rouge. They [the companies] shut these things down before they get here.

An SJCJE member stated, "But in regards to DEQ, they do not protect us. They allow the plants to hire their own people to monitor emissions, and if they want to keep their jobs, they have to say what the company wants them to say."[54]

Two individuals who spoke in favor of the plant worked at C-K Associates, an engineering consulting firm hired by Shintech to assist in the writing of the applications for environmental permits. They stated views that were echoed by company officials, state and local government, and the pro-Shintech residents' group during the two-year struggle:

Every day all of us citizens have to rely on the government to fulfill their responsibilities. Their responsibilities are mandated by the US Congress by the constitution. The responsibilities that we ask our government to fulfill include building roads, and maintaining the national defense, and controlling crime, and also protecting the environment. The US government created the Environmental Protection Agency [EPA] and charged them specifically with protecting the environment. The EPA has turned over the air and water programs for the state of Louisiana to the Department of Environmental Quality [DEQ]. EPA continues to provide a lot of oversight to insure that those responsibilities are fulfilled.[55]

They expressed total confidence that the LDEQ and EPA more than adequately protect the environment by enforcing existing regulations, which are very stringent.

In spite of the overwhelmingly negative feedback from the public at the Coastal Zone Permit hearing, the very same month the Parish Coastal Zone Advisory Committee recommended approval of the permit. In December, the parish president approved the permit. Immediately, SJCJE filed a request for an appeal of the decision to grant the permit. They based their request for appeal on the following objections. First, they argued that public and/or private statements and actions by parish officials showed their overwhelming support for Shintech and made it impossible for citizens to receive due process, including fair and impartial hearings and decisions. Second, they alleged that the parish government had not followed correct procedures in considering the Shintech permit. Lastly, they cited legal and technical problems and/or deficiencies with the Shintech permit that prohibited it from protecting the coastal zone.

The parish council held an appeal hearing in which they considered the protestor's claims; however, they voted to reject the citizens' appeal and upheld the permit. The protest group, along with the statewide Louisiana Environmental Action Network, filed a petition for Judicial Review and Injunctive Relief of the Coastal Use Permit. In the lawsuit, the protestors claimed that parish officials were biased and did not adequately analyze the impact of the plant on the local area. The plaintiffs asked for revocation of the Coastal Zone Permit issued by the parish government.[56]

To support the claims of bias on the part of local officials, the protestors cited several incidents, including a letter written early on by parish president Dale Hymel on April 9, 1996, to Shintech pledging his support for the proposed siting. Additionally, group members found a fax sent on May 3, 1996, from the parish director of operations to Shintech's legal representative that contained dossiers on public officials on the St. James Parish Coastal Zone Management Advisory Committee and Planning Committee and other parish officials. The fax outlined the race, occupation, and temperament of the officials. For example, one entry read, "Roland Malancon – represents District 6, black/male. Employed with Shell Pipeline Co. Primary Concern: hiring local individuals."[57] The plant opponents charged that conveying this information to the company represented a "secret permitting and lobbying process not open to the concerned public." Additionally, they cited instances when parish councilpersons had made public statements in favor of Shintech and against plant protestors.[58]

There was also evidence that the parish president received continuous communications from Shintech's public relations firm, Harris, Deville, and Associates, Inc. The firm kept the president abreast of the activities of Shintech's opponents. For example, they sent a copy of meeting minutes from an August 1996 public information meeting held by SJCJE.[59] Other correspondence from the public relations firm included information that the president had requested, such as "key information from the Economic Impact Study on the proposed Shintech plant," articles from newspapers and magazines on the battle, and a summary of a public opinion survey commissioned by Shintech.[60]

The tone of the correspondence was always friendly and suggested that the parish government was part of the "Shintech team." For example, in a memo to the parish president and economic development officer, Brad Lambert of the public relations firm discussed the participation of Greenpeace in opposing Shintech. He stated,

Greenpeace could be considered among the most radical environmental groups. They tend to utilize publicity stunts and confrontation. Whether they have any other plans for St. James Parish, we'll just have to wait and see. But just in case, Harris, Deville, and Associates is beginning to put together a Greenpeace strategy for Shintech and we would, of course, be happy to share my information with you. I will continue to visit Greenpeace's Internet Site, and I will forward any other pertinent information I find.[61]

David Wise, the Shintech plant manager, said that he needed the assistance of the public relations firm because he was in Louisiana by himself and had no support services. The firm kept him up to date by sending him news clippings, facilitating meetings, supplying logistical support, and, generally, keeping people informed.[62] These efforts helped to keep the many members of the pro-Shintech coalition, including the local government, informed. They were acting as a coordinated "growth machine" as described by Logan and Molotch (see Chapter 1). In essence, anti Shintech community residents were accusing the local government of working too hard on their duties to support economic development in the parish at the expense of carrying out their responsibility to protect the health and welfare of the parish residents.

It was quite clear that the parish government was not representing the views of plant opponents. In fact, they appeared to be going out of their way at times to create roadblocks to their activities. The parish charged community residents seventy-five cents per page for copies of the public record. This proved to be prohibitively expensive for the protest group. Additionally, the group had a difficult time getting the complete public record from the parish, and there was an instance when a parish employee admitted to destroying a document. The group won a lawsuit against the parish, which decreased the cost of copies to five cents a page. A lawsuit against the parish for destroying a public document is still pending.[63]

Evidence uncovered by the Tulane Environmental Law Clinic revealed that, during the conflict, state agencies such as DED and DEQ met with business groups and Shintech to try to push the siting forward. The director of international investment at DED wrote a fax to a lobbyist that described an upcoming strategy meeting between coalition members. He stated, "Today at 2:00 P.M. there will be a meeting to discuss a strategy to move forward the permit approval process. It will include representatives of DEQ, DED, consultants to Shintech, the Louisiana Chemical Association, and Louisiana Association of Business and Industry." The fax also indicated that the DED was working at a national political level to promote the Shintech siting. The DED official wrote, "In preparing for this meeting, I spoke with Shintech's government relations consultant, Mr. Tom Spradley, and he expressed interest in talking with you about a strategy to deal with these issues in Washington, D.C. I briefly described your involvement in lobbying at the federal level and suggested that you might be an excellent resource."[64]

State agencies and the governor also tried to hinder the Tulane Environmental Law Clinic and other supportive nonprofit organizations. Louisiana secretary of economic development, Kevin Reilly, initiated targeted investigations into the legal filings of TELC and the Louisiana Coalition of Tax Justice, both opponents of the plant. Reilly acknowledged his actions when he stated to a reporter, "You're darned right I looked up their records. . . . I'm going to use every legitimate method at my command to defeat them."[65]

In the midst of the permitting process, the governor assured Shintech of the "cooperation" of the Department of Environmental Quality. In a letter to Shintech president Kanagawa, Governor Foster stated,

From the state of Louisiana's perspective, environmental permitting continues to proceed smoothly. I can assure you, and I believe Mr. Mason [Shintech Controller] has confirmed, that the Louisiana Department of Environmental Quality has been cooperative during this process. . . . I am proud of the degree of cooperation that Shintech has reported receiving from Louisiana agencies.[66]

The DEQ sponsored a public hearing regarding the Shintech air permit on December, 9, 1996. At this highly charged meeting, the opponents and proponents of the plant came head to head for approximately seven hours – from 6 P.M. to after 1 A.M. Depending on who you ask, there were forty-two or forty-four speakers in support of Shintech and thirty-four or thirty-five speakers against the plant. At least fifteen of the individuals who spoke in favor of Shintech were paid employees, many of whom were flown in from the Freeport, Texas, plant.[67] The plant opponents included eleven members of SJCJE, nine other concerned citizens, eight persons affiliated with environmental activities in other areas of the state, two representatives of the Tulane Environmental Law Clinic, and four individuals affiliated with national environmental groups.[68]

The major dispute at the meeting, other than the siting of the plant, was the manner in which DEQ conducted the meeting. Pro-Shintech voices monopolized the first one hour and ten minutes of the meeting. The DEQ representative allowed individuals to speak in the order that they had signed in at the meeting. The DEQ hearing officer said that Shintech inquired several weeks before the meeting as to the manner in which the order of speakers would be determined. Then, the night of the meeting, many pro-Shintech supporters showed up early at the hall and signed in. As the meeting wore on, the anti-Shintech contingent began to complain that they were not being allowed to speak. Many were mothers who had to get home to feed and put the children to bed. At about 7:10 P.M., the DEQ officer agreed to alternate speakers in terms of their support or opposition of the plant. Plant opponents also complained that the hearing officer unfairly imposed a five-minute time limit on them but not on the plant proponents.

Both Greenpeace and Mary Lee Orr of LEAN voiced complaints with the EPA's Office of Environmental Justice regarding the meeting. A summary of the meeting prepared by another anti-Shintech organization, Labor Neighbor, stated that:

as a result of DEQ's actions favoring speakers paid by industry, at least 16 concerned citizens who signed up to speak were excluded from the hearing. These people's names were called after 11:15 and [they] had already left the hearing because of jobs, family obligations, to eat, etc. Note that by 11:40 P.M. all paid industry consultants, Shintech employees, etc., who signed up had already been allowed to speak by DEQ.[69]

The DEQ officer adamantly denied that plant opponents were treated differently.[70] As a result of the meeting, Janice Dickerson from the DEQ Community/Industry Relations office urged the agency to develop a uniform procedure for speakers at public meetings. She stated in a written critique of the meeting, "If an effort is not made to develop a uniform procedure for speakers at public meetings, we will continue to see the frustration, disorganization, confusion and public distrust of the agency that we witnessed at the public hearing held Monday, Dec. 9, 1996 in Romeville."[71]

This meeting exemplifies on a small scale the main dispute between Shintech supporters and Shintech opponents. The opponents didn't trust the state DEQ and didn't believe that it would protect their health, safety, and interests. The supporters, however, believed that the environmental regulations and procedures conducted by the DEQ were sufficient to protect the community.

In May 1997, DEQ issued the following air quality permits for the Shintech facility: a chlor-alkali permit, a polyvinyl chloride permit, and a vinyl chloride monomer permit. Gustave Von Bodungen, the assistant secretary of DEQ's Office of Air Quality and Radiation Protection, stated, "That issue [environmental justice] is another issue, not a permitting issue. We think everything is straightforward. The facility is modern and emissions minimal. We think the benefits outweigh the minuses."[72]

THE EPA, ENVIRONMENTAL JUSTICE, AND INDECISION

In May of 1997, the plant opponents, assisted by the Tulane Environmental Law Clinic, filed a petition with the EPA seeking to veto the issuance of the Title V operating permits on environmental justice and air pollution regulatory grounds. In the same month, they also filed a Title VI of the 1964 Civil Rights Act complaint with the EPA Office of Civil Rights in Washington, D.C.

Even though the state has permission to operate a Title V air permitting program, the EPA is authorized to review the state operating permits that are issued. It is highly unusual for the EPA to overturn a permitting decision made by the state agency. In fact, they had never rejected a Louisiana environmental permit.[73] Surprisingly, in September 1997, the EPA responded to the opponents' demands by agreeing with one of the technical objections that they raised and requiring a reopening of the Shintech air-permitting process.[74] The opponents claimed a vinyl-chloride monomer cracking furnace was not classified correctly and, thus, did not meet the emission requirements for such furnaces. In the course of their review, the EPA agreed with this complaint and also found forty-nine other technical deficiencies in the permit.[75] The EPA, however, denied the request by plant opponents that the permit be rejected on the basis of environmental justice claims. They stated that "While there may be authority under the Clean Air Act to consider environmental justice issues in some circumstances, Petitioners have not shown how their particular environmental justice concerns demonstrate that the Shintech permits do not comply with applicable requirements of the Act."[76]

The plant opponents were elated with the EPA's decision to reject the permits. Mary Lee Orr, from LEAN stated, "We were wondering if EPA had any teeth, and they do. I thought, what a powerful message

EPA sent out to the community."[77] Conversely, Shintech representatives were left wondering how to interpret the ruling. In trying to anticipate the delay that the ruling presented, Shintech comptroller Richard Mason stated, "I suspect three or four months (wouldn't have) a significant impact on the decision-making. If it takes 18 months, a year – that may be a different story."[78]

Although the EPA rejected the claims of environmental injustice in the air permits, they asked that Louisiana environmental officials attempt to address the concerns raised by plant opponents. Additionally, they acknowledged that they were taking seriously the Title VI environmental justice complaint that plant opponents had filed and the EPA Office of Civil Rights was investigating. The Title VI complaint proposes that the EPA suspend federal funding for the LDEQ due to their granting of the Shintech air and water permits because of the following two grievances: (1) the public comment and hearing process of LDEQ discriminated against minorities and was biased toward Shintech; (2) the permit issued by LDEQ violated the federal Clean Air Act by ignoring the plant's impact on a minority community that is already overburdened with pollution.[79]

Monique Harden, a lawyer who worked for Greenpeace at that time, described the manner in which the coalition approached the DEQ and the EPA. She said,

It took a lot of strategy in looking at how DEQ handles permits, in relation to [how] EPA Region 6 handles permitting and enforcement issues and in connection with how headquarters [the Washington office] wants all that to be done. . . . We had to say "Gee, Region 6 – look what DEQ is doing and look at this horrendous record" and giving them evidence that they already had, but making it front and center. Then going to headquarters, "Look what Region 6 is doing – this is your enforcement team – look what they are doing." So that each level had to be accountable for the other.[80]

Lisa Lavie from the Tulane Environmental Law Clinic further described the protest groups' legal strategy. She stated, "We thought we had strong claims on everything, but knowing how some judges are, especially on technical issues, the only thing I would say we really felt like we had a good chance of succeeding on, ultimately, was the Title VI complaint."

One of the most unique aspects of the case was the attempt by the protest groups' lawyers to tie environmental justice concerns with the technical aspects of the air permit. Monique Harden said that they wanted to phrase their complaints so that the EPA couldn't separate the environmental justice complaint from technical aspects of the plant. She stated,

What we would be saying – given the full background of the environmental justice issues, the health issues, the health consequences, and the hazardous impact of the chemicals that Shintech would process on the community that was ill equipped, very vulnerable, and very sick . . . that should be an important priority for EPA in reducing and preventing more pollution being heaped on them. It was very important that those technical issues be argued in a way that they say that each area of noncompliance means more hazards and more pollution on a community that should be relieved from this.[81]

In a speech to the Congressional Black Caucus Environmental Justice Forum in Washington, D.C., EPA administrator Carol Browner emphasized EPA's willingness to pursue the Shintech case. She stated, "If the concerns of the local residents are not fully addressed [in the new permitting process], EPA will expedite its review of the [civil rights] complaint."[82]

The EPA had selected Shintech as its national test case for environmental justice. Industry, state environmental regulators, and environmental justice advocates anticipated that a ruling in this case would set a precedent for the dozens of other pending Title VI cases, as well as future development in general. Bettsie Baker-Miller, a representative of the Louisiana Chemical Association stated, "Whatever happens in this case will have an extreme impact on the permitting of facilities in the U.S., whether it's existing facilities seeking permit renewals or new facilities looking for their initial permits."[83] An anonymous administrator at the EPA told a reporter, "All I can say is that it is the highest-priority investigation because it is likely to be the first decision on the merits and will be a major milestone in the development of the environmental justice program."[84]

The EPA had not developed or implemented regulations dealing with this issue previously. Similarly, the state environmental officials had never dealt with these issues and there was no case law or established federal rules to guide them. One DEQ Air Quality Division employee described the lack of guidance that the agency received from the EPA when the federal officials visited the agency for a meeting. He stated, "One time they came down to tell us how to look at environmental justice issues. The meeting started at 9:00 A.M. and lasted until 12:00. At 12:20 the meeting ended and there were questions until

3:00. I [still] hadn't heard one word on how to deal with environmental justice."[85]

Gus Von Bodungen, the assistant secretary of DEQ, felt that the IT questions that are required for permitting by Louisiana regulations actually cover environmental justice issues (see Chapter 2). He stated, "They [EPA] sent us no guidance whatsoever. We have what we call the IT decision. . . we think that's strong enough to answer all those situations where you're bringing in a new company."[86]

In January 1998, the EPA released a preliminary analysis of the emissions burden in the area surrounding the Shintech plant. Individuals on both sides of the struggle criticized the methodology employed in the analysis. The report compared the percentage of African Americans to non–African Americans within a one-mile, two-mile, and four-mile radius of toxic release inventory and toxic emissions data inventory sites in St. James Parish, the industrial corridor, and the state.[87] The report contained a multitude of tables and graphs; however, the findings presented in these figures were not summarized in an easily understandable manner. One would need statistics training to even attempt to understand the analysis. Environmental justice advocates objected to the analytical procedures that the EPA used to determine disparate impact, the multitude of different analyses that they conducted, the way they presented the data, and their emissions estimates for the proposed Shintech plant.[88] Still, one of the tables in the report revealed that African Americans in Louisiana were 50 percent more likely to reside within one mile of a Toxic Release Inventory site than whites, 41 percent more likely to live within two miles, and 20 percent more likely to live within four miles of a site.[89]

A month later in February 1998, the EPA issued draft guidelines for investigating Title VI Administrative Complaints Challenging Permits. State and local governments and the business community nationwide charged that the guidelines were vague and overly restrictive, while environmental justice advocates complained that they were not restrictive enough.[90] In these guidelines, which are reviewed in more detail in Chapter 7, the EPA stated that they would conduct a disparate impact analysis to test the validity of each environmental justice complaint. They would identify an affected population, determine the demographics of the population, and identify the universe of facilities that affect the population. Then, the agency would compare the impact of pollution on this group as compared to a nonaffected population. This procedure would allow them to consider the impact of multiple facilities. Many environmental justice advocates argue that current permitting procedures do not take into consideration the synergistic effects of a community's exposure to emissions from multiple facilities.

Due to substantial criticism that the agency received, the EPA decided to rewrite the rules and have the Federal Science Advisory Board committee study the methodology used in the analysis. This "peer review" process delayed the announcement of a decision even longer.[91] In August 1998, the deputy director of the EPA's Office on Environmental Justice anticipated that a decision would be delayed until the next spring.[92]

Monique Harden was not surprised by the delays. She stated, "No one was surprised by that [the delays] or, at least, I hope they weren't. This was certainly a decision that they didn't want to make."[93]

They really wanted to be status quo by the books and not responsive to the real consequences of having this pollution on communities where homes have been turned into mini medical clinics with respiratory devices, prescription medicine, people with very itchy eyes, troubled breathing, cancers, tumors. They didn't want to look at the flesh and blood consequences. And we [plant opponents] were there doing the streets, in congress, in the petitions, in the legal strategy that make them have to be responsible and have to face to prioritize those kinds of consequences.[94]

Federal environmental representatives at several levels (for example, White House, regional EPA office, EPA civil rights specialist, EPA administrator) floated a possible solution: emission-reduction tradeoffs. This would require existing plants in the Convent area to reduce their emissions to make the emissions impact from the Shintech plant less intense. EPA's director for civil rights stated, "It appears to EPA that impacts associated with hazardous air emissions could be substantially ameliorated if, for example, offsetting emission risk reductions were secured at other facilitates . . . in the immediate vicinity of the proposed Shintech plant."[95]

Neither side in the dispute received this idea warmly. DEQ officials didn't want to be forced to use emission-reduction tradeoffs in an area that had no extraordinary compliance requirements from the Clean Air Act. A DEQ representative stated, "That makes a mockery of all the regulations that Congress and the states have put in place as to the Clean Air Act. It presents a real problems for regulators."[96] Environmental justice advocates adamantly opposed the suggestion that a

PVC plant be allowed to pollute their community, even if other plants reduced their emissions. St. Charles Parish environmentalist Adam Chandler likened the suggestion for emission-reduction tradeoffs to saying "it will be legal for more drunk drivers to drive through low-income, African-American communities as long as they obey the speed limit."[97]

IS THERE A MIDDLE GROUND?

In an attempt to reach a resolution in the struggle that was growing more contentious by the day, the EPA hired a public conflict resolution organization out of Atlanta to mediate between the two sides. Gregory Bourne and David Anderson Hooker from the Southeast Negotiation Network (SNN) conducted a series of meetings with the stakeholders. After a series of interviews with TELC lawyers, DEQ representatives, parish officials, Shintech representatives, and representatives from the two community groups and state environmental network, the mediators proposed a schedule of formal meetings that would eventually bring all the stakeholders together.[98]

The mediators explained the motivation behind the conflict resolution process in their Draft Convening Assessment Report. They wrote,

At this time, it appears some parties prefer legal remedies to stop the facility from being sited given concerns about potential risks to the environment and human health that outweigh any potential economic benefits. If this remains unchanged, the issue of whether or not to site the Shintech facility will be resolved outside the process. On the other hand, value might be attributed to participating in a process that provides everyone with a better understanding of the issues and options, and that lays the foundation for more normalized relationships and communications among all parties.[99]

SJCJE members were not in any mood to compromise with Shintech. Brenda Huguet stated, "They wanted us to compromise. But there was nothing we could talk about – how could we compromise on health? Now, the main thing is they don't talk about health issues. They just talk about the dollar sign and nothing that has ever been addressed to us about health."[100]

It is not hard to understand why the mediation efforts were not successful. Shintech opponents refused to sit down to a table with state officials whom they believed they could not trust and a company that they didn't want anywhere near them. The opponents backed up these views by filing a legal motion in early 1998, asking the state's top three environmental officials to recuse themselves from further Shintech Air Permit proceedings due to their bias toward Shintech. When DEQ officials refused to step down, the Tulane Environmental Law Clinic filed a lawsuit in the Nineteenth Judicial District Court of the State of Louisiana. In June 1998, State District Court judge Kay Bates ordered a hearing be held on the bias complaint. This ruling effectively put a halt to DEQ's processing of the permit while the legal case was being resolved. Then in September, the same judge refused to consider a motion filed by DEQ to stay her ruling. The judge stated that she couldn't understand why DEQ was so opposed to the hearing. A DEQ representative argued that a premature hearing would disrupt the permitting process, and that the opponents were welcome to raise their complaints in an appeal once the permit was issued.[101]

Meanwhile, as the struggle over permits and the mediation efforts was unfolding, Shintech signed an agreement with the St. James chapter of the NAACP and the pro-Shintech citizens' group, the company pledged $500,000 to fund a nonprofit corporation called the St. James Environmental Economic Development Program, Inc. that would be devoted to job training and small business creation. They said that the board of directors for the organization would have representatives from the NAACP, Shintech, the Citizen Coalition, St. James Business Coalition, and the St. James Parish president's office. The NAACP made the announcement of the agreement in a "friend of the court brief" on the appeal of the DEQ water permit brought by plant opponents. In the brief, the NAACP and Citizen Coalition defended their stance by stating, "Unlike other groups organized to fight any attempt by Shintech to construct in St. James, thereby eliminating the potential for economic benefits by African Americans and other minority citizens, [we] have applied logic and reasoning in reaching the decision to support [the project]."[102]

THE UNEXPECTED RESOLUTION AND SHINTECH'S LEGACY

The Shintech struggle that raged for two years with the fury of a wildfire ended abruptly and unexpectedly. There was no compromise among industry, the state, and protest activists. There was no landmark precedent-setting decision from the EPA. The environmental justice advocates were not plowed over in the name of development. Rather, quietly and calmly, Shintech officials announced their plans to abandon the site in Convent and to locate a smaller plant near Dow Chemical Company in the town of Plaquemine, approximately twenty-five miles up the river. They said that the proposed $250 million plant would employ fifty workers and twenty-five contract workers and would rely on the Dow Chemical Company to make the raw materials for the finished plastic that the plant would produce. Previously, Shintech had planned to manufacture both the raw materials and the plastic. The proposed annual production of polyvinyl chloride remained unchanged at about 1.3 billion pounds. However, Dow officials agreed to reduce their existing emissions so that the proposed Shintech plant would put out no new emissions in the area.

The new Shintech siting was conducted very differently from the attempt in St. James. Before they even applied for permits, the company hired a private firm to conduct six meetings in which members of the community could hear about the siting proposal and ask a Shintech representative questions. They used a National Environmental Justice Advisory Committee booklet on public participation to design the public meetings. Following the meetings, Shintech released two response documents that addressed the over one thousand questions that they had received.[103] The new siting also differed from the old siting because the land for the plant was purchased from Dow Chemical Company. Dow representatives, who enjoy a long-standing reputation as supporting the local community, also helped Shintech present the siting and address questions in these community meetings.

As this book goes to press, the new Shintech plant has received the necessary air and water permits, and the company has begun construction in the new location. A small but staunch group of protestors have filed a lawsuit against the DEQ air permit issued for the new plant. Protest group members, Liz Avants, Les Ann Kirkland, and Albertha Hasten are long-time environmental activists who attended many of the protest meetings in nearby St. James Parish during the first siting struggle. Although they were denied legal assistance by the Tulane Environmental Law Clinic due to the Rule XX changes instigated by the state's business leaders (see Chapter 7), the group has managed to obtain legal assistance from trial lawyer, Jerry McKernan.[104]

There are many different opinions on the lasting legacy of the Shintech struggle. The struggle lasted over two years and created tremendous division between groups in the parish, state, and nation. Much was at stake – millions of dollars in taxes for the parish and state governments, millions of dollars in profits for local and statewide businesses, the image of Louisiana as a business friendly state, the health and safety of the residents of St. James Parish, and the future of all environmental justice and Title VI complaints brought by other community groups from around the country.

Wise said that the struggle greatly changed him and Shintech as a company. He stated, "Because of what we went through, we are different people. We understand more how people feel – I'm a better person because of it." He said that when the company first came, they naively thought that everyone in Louisiana would love them like they did in his hometown of Freeport, Texas. He said that he learned that he had to listen to the community. He also said that the failed siting in St. James was not a victory for environmental justice advocates. He explained that the real environmental injustice lay in the community that would now be deprived of jobs that could help raise residents out of a quagmire of poverty and unemployment.[105]

The pro-Shintech citizen's group agreed that the struggle had changed the company. Carol Gaudin thought that Shintech came in as one company and left as a different one. She stated,

There was an opportunity for them to understand more about this human environment that they were going to locate into. They had just heard about it . . . and barely thought about it. The only thing they thought about was their bottom line, not that they were going to locate next to real human beings with thoughts, feelings, wants, needs, desires – you know – hopes and aspirations of their own. The company is thinking of their bottom line. But, there are some other things that they understand [now], I think.[106]

Shintech proponents were disappointed with the company's decision to locate elsewhere.

A DEQ representative felt that the decision would have a negative impact on economic development in the parish. He stated, "They succeeded in keeping the plant out. That plant probably would have helped the poor in the community. . . . you can't build an industry without economic benefit, even if it creates only five jobs."[107] Another representative from the DEQ CIR office said that the activists had killed the goose that laid the golden eggs.[108]

Parish president Dale Hymel lamented, "I don't see it as a major [environmental justice] victory at all; the EPA dropped the ball. I still stand behind industrial growth along the river. Just because Shintech is gone, that doesn't mean we're going to stop looking." He also expressed confusion over the meaning of the permitting of Shintech in its new location. He stated,

Shintech has moved to Iberville and got their permit. So why? It don't make too much sense to me to be giving a permit to operate in Iberville parish – if it is safe to operate in Iberville, why is it not safe in St. James. . . so if you not going to let them build next to a black community because you gonna kill them, but you gonna let them build next to a white community [in Plaquemine] – that's what people can't understand.[109]

A spokesperson for Governor Foster said that the decision was "a disappointment to the governor . . . it would have had significant economic development. It's a loss for that area, a loss for Louisiana." He added that the decision may have a negative impact on other industrial expansions throughout the United States.[110]

When Shintech pulled out of St. James, protest activists claimed "a major victory for environmental justice, the people of Convent, and St. James Parish, and a blow against the PVC industry."[111] EPA administrator Carol Browner was also pleased. She stated, "I want to commend Shintech Inc. for their efforts in finding a community-based, constructive approach for ensuring industrial growth while protecting the rights of communities."[112] EPA general counsel, Gary Guzy explained, "We are quite proud of the approach that is taking root there, and would encourage companies thinking about this – who want to be environmental leaders, to be engaged, to be good neighbors – to look at Shintech as a lesson in how to approach these issues."[113]

Environmental justice activists felt that the tremendous visibility of the case brought this issue to the forefront and onto the national political agenda. However, they were less than satisfied with the behavior of Shintech representatives. They felt that instead of learning how to truly work with the community, Shintech learned what they needed to do to co-opt and persuade the community. This was apparent to them when they saw how Shintech attempted to locate their new plant in Plaquemine. Activists argued that the community meetings that Shintech conducted served only to co-opt the residents due to the unequal balance in technical knowledge between the company and community residents. They accused the company of presenting a rosy picture of their experience with PVC production and failing to admit that there could ever be any difficulties or harmful effects from the production process.

Monique Harden, former Greenpeace lawyer, stated,

> The lesson that Shintech has learned is one that many other industries have learned – they have to present a very strong, very positive public relations campaign and they have to go in [to the community] in small doses. That's what Shintech learned. Is that a lesson of environmental justice? No, but that is certainly the response of industrial groups and associations that are trying to get around it, just as they would any other environmental law or regulation.[114]

Another lasting legacy that the Shintech struggle left in Louisiana was the change to Rule XX, the Louisiana Supreme Court regulation that governs the activities of student lawyers. This rule change is explained extensively in Chapter 7. In brief, the change made the financial eligibility criteria for potential clients more stringent, ultimately limiting the range of individuals/groups that can receive free legal services from law students. Lisa Lavie from TELC stated, "Unfortunately, that has been the biggest lasting legacy in some senses of this case. We are boot strapped."[115]

The Shintech struggle also left legacies on an individual level. The struggle had changed the lives of the members of SJCJE. For the last two years they had battled a corporate giant and the state of Louisiana. In an interview with several SJCJE group members, we asked them what they learned from their experience. Here are some of their responses:

"God was with us."

"I found out that I cannot trust the people that govern St. James Parish or the state."

"People of different races can work together – that we are all people no matter what color we are."

"I was tougher than I thought I was. After seeing all of this, it toughened me up a lot . . . and I would like to add – where there is unity, there is strength."

"I would like to say that I found out why I was here. Because God gives everybody a gift and sometimes we don't know what that gift is but I am so glad that I had become spiritual and now I see that as long as we put God in the lead and let him lead us, we can't fail, we can't fail. That is why we will not fail. I try to instill that everywhere I go because man is stumbling – he can't do everything."[116]

This is a very complicated case that has far-reaching implications for future environmental justice conflicts. It is hard to say who the winners in this struggle are. We will return to this question as we describe and weigh the backlash to Shintech in Chapter 7. A simplified interpretation may be that environmental justice advocates won the battle but lost the war. They won the battle because they prevented the facility from being sited in their neighborhood. However, they lost the war because another Louisiana community will be exposed to the plant's pollution. A fiery backlash has reached from Washington, D.C., to all fifty state capitals. The EPA never issued a landmark environmental justice ruling, and development forces were able to change the rules of the game to limit access to legal resources for future protest groups. However, this analysis is too simple.

The Shintech struggle has had broad, nonquantifiable implications. The fight changed the awareness of all sides in the development game. First, both environmental justice and industry advocates learned information that will help them strategize for future fights. Second, it is almost certain that this highly publicized victory will encourage other community groups to wage war against developers of unwanted land-uses. Finally, as a result of the struggle, both EPA and state DEQ representatives have realized that environmental justice is an issue that will not go away any time soon, and they must now figure out how to deal with it.

5

Media Savvy Cajuns and Houma Indians

FIGHTING AN OILFIELD WASTE DUMP IN GRAND BOIS

Top: Tanker truck dumping in waste pit at U.S. Liquids at Grand Bois. [Photo by Thom Scott, used with permission of the *New Orleans Times-Picayune*]

Bottom: Clarice Friloux and family with protest sign. [Photo by Timmons Roberts]

"TOXIC IN ALABAMA, NONTOXIC IN LOUISIANA"

Over a period of a week and a half, eighty-one sleek white tanker trucks, with red diamond-shaped warning placards, rolled down the highway from an Exxon oil-drilling site at Big Escambia Creek in Alabama. Crossing the Louisiana line on Interstate 10, their cargo was magically transformed from "hazardous" to "nonhazardous" by the different definitions found in the laws of the two different states. By crossing state lines, the price of disposing of the contents also magically plunged, from $85 a barrel to just $6.50.[1]

This alchemy was possible due to an enormous loophole negotiated by oil companies after frantic days of political maneuvering in Congress leading up to the votes on the 1980 amendments to the Resource Conservation and Recovery Act (RCRA). In the loophole, with the obscure name Rule 29-B under Section 3001(b)(2)(A) of RCRA, the regulation of "oilfield waste" is left to the individual states. Alabama had defined the by-product of oil drilling as hazardous material, whereas Louisiana, the site of decades of oil exploration, elected to label oilfield waste as nonhazardous.[2] EPA secretary Carol Browner put it simply: "Big Oil got a sweetheart deal."[3]

The trucks, with no markings indicating that they carried Exxon's waste,[4] and no placards on the outside detailing what was in them,[5] turned off Interstate 10 to cross the Mississippi River onto Highway 90, and then turned left onto the tiny Louisiana Highway 24 surrounded by marshy willows, from Houma to the tiny bayou fishing town of LaRose. The road passes directly through the middle of a minuscule town called Grand Bois, the home for generations of families with roots in the intermarriage of the Houma Indian tribe and Cajun French settlers. Just a chain-link fence separates the homes of Grand Bois and the massive waste dump pits of a company called Campbell

Wells, where millions of barrels of waste had been dumped over a span of the nearly two decades.

The trucks with the Exxon waste pulled up to the Campbell Wells office in mid-March 1994, where the drivers, wearing white protective jump suits, got instructions on where to dump their loads. The drivers backed the trucks up to the designated pit, and then got out to open the dumping hatch at the back of the truck. When they opened the hatch, several were struck by the stench and were forced to run to the front of the truck, according to a state environmental official who was at the site taking air samples.[6]

Fifty-six hundred barrels of Exxon's waste were dumped at Campbell Wells that week, saving Exxon something over a half million dollars compared to what it would have cost to dump the waste in one of Alabama's more tightly regulated facilities. Alabama's Oil and Gas Board had been pushing Exxon to clean up its temporary pits at Big Escambia Creek since 1993, and now the job was done.[7]

The smell from Exxon's waste being dumped wafted across Louisiana Highway 24, where a woman trucker passing by was sickened by the smell. Virgie Fulmer, then fifty-five years old, was driving her truck from Amelia to Fourchon. Approaching the facility at about forty miles per hour, Fulmer said she was startled by the strong odor. "I was burning all over, inside and out. It was like the air was pulled out of my body . . . I asked the Lord to save me."[8] Fulmer felt pains in her chest and noticed that she got dizzy. But she opened the window of her truck and kept going on to Fourchon. Returning to Morgan City, she went to the hospital. Doctors there told her that hers was only an allergic reaction. They gave her a shot and some pills.[9]

The fumes then drifted through the tiny town of Grand Bois, home to 300 residents. Children coming home from school dashed from their school bus to their homes, covering their faces with their shirts or a handkerchief. Coming home from work on March 19, Anna Matherne said the smell from the pits "burned your nose. You would breathe and it was like there was nothing in the air."[10] She says that "chemical" and "rotten-egg" odors destroyed her sense of smell, and that she was left with headaches and problems with her sinuses, chest, lungs, stomach, and joints. She later told a jury that she had suffered uncontrolled diarrhea since that March 1994 period. "I keep an extra set of clothes in the car."

All these symptoms are typical of acute exposure to hydrogen sulfide (H_2S). Hydrogen sulfide is a common by-product of drilling for oil, treating animal and human waste, and making paper.[11] It accounts for the common "rotten egg" smell at many industrial, sewage, and drilling sites.[12] Known for centuries as "swamp gas, stink damp, rotten-egg gas and hydrosulfuric acid, the compound has left a long and well-marked trail of anguish."[13] It is listed as a dangerous substance under Occupational Safety and Health Administration (OSHA), Superfund, RCRA, Department of Transportation (DOT), and the Clean Air Act and called "one of the most toxic of the gases" since 1924.[14] A 1977 government warning said it was "a leading cause of sudden death in the workplace."

The human nose can detect hydrogen sulfide at only three to four parts per million parts of air.[15] At these levels it can be a "potent eye and mucous membrane irritant." State regulations say the level should be less than one tenth of that. The oil industry fiercely resisted attempts to get hydrogen sulfide regulated at the federal level, pressuring Congress to strip it out of the 1990 Clean Air Act. "It was a political deal,"[16] in spite of the fact that, at higher levels (around 100 ppm), the nose is no longer able to sense H_2S, and so it no longer serves to warn the victim. Researchers report that only one or two breaths of massive exposures can kill a person.

What happened at Grand Bois was not in that league. But at lower levels, hydrogen sulfide can cause "sudden fatigue, headache, dizziness, intense anxiety, loss of olfactory function, nausea, abrupt loss of consciousness, disturbances of the optic nerves, hypertension, insomnia, mental disturbances, pulmonary edema, coma, convulsions, and respiratory arrest, followed by cardiac failure and often death."[17]

There are some mixed findings on what happens after a lower-level exposure to hydrogen sulfide. EPA's technical report says that "If exposure is terminated promptly, recovery occurs quickly."[18] However, neurological effects (brain damage) have been reported to persist. Dr. Bob Borda, a neuropsychologist in Stafford, Texas, did psychological and aptitude testing of victims of hydrogen sulfide poisoning. He found that an H_2S-poisoned brain was like an "outdated computer program: It runs, but it is maddeningly slow and inefficient."[19] The townspeople of Grand Bois also believed they were exposed to benzene, lead and arsenic, and the latter two have been associated with subtle forms, of nervous system damage.[20] Benzene is on a short list of chemicals well known to cause cancer.

Back in Grand Bois, Anna Matherne didn't know how to cope with the acrid smell coming into her non-air-conditioned home, so she hung up sheets of fabric softener from her clothes dryer in her windows.[21]

Startled, other residents of Grand Bois repeatedly called the state's Department of Environmental Quality. Paul Muhler, staffing the department's emergency hotline, was sent down from the DEQ to Grand Bois. He reported in his notes that the DEQ did four one-minute air samples at the time of the dumping.[22] Inspectors did not look for hydrogen sulfide because DEQ inspectors had been specifically instructed not to test for H_2S.[23] No one discovered the source of the note on the form that field inspectors were given, directly instructing them not to test for hydrogen sulfide.

Finding no help from the state environmental agency, the outraged residents turned to a doctor from the region who had recently been elected to the state senate. Tall and thin with a full head of graying hair over his deeply lined face, Dr. Michael Robichaux had a thriving local medical practice just up the road from Grand Bois. Robichaux, a new father, is married to a woman of Houma Indian descent, who has family in Grand Bois. Grand Bois residents asked Robichaux to change the laws in the state, to close the loophole for oilfield wastes, and, more immediately, to close the pits at Campbell Wells.

The residents also sought the assistance of a young trial lawyer from New Orleans, Gladstone Jones. Jones, who had little trial experience, was the stepson of the former dean of the Tulane Law School. They told Jones that they wanted to sue to get the pits shut down. The question was whether Exxon or Campbell Wells could be responsible if it was perfectly legal to dump these "nonhazardous" oilfield wastes in Louisiana. Taking on what was to become the case of his life, and one that sapped much of the resources of his firm, Jones and all 301 residents of Grand Bois spent four years developing a case against Campbell Wells, Exxon, and several other defendants. "The list of defendants in this case reads like a Who's Who of the oil industry . . . this is a trillion dollar a year industry," said Jones.[24]

60 Minutes reporter Ed Bradley and his "CBS Investigative Reports" news team followed the story of Grand Bois for over a year, finally showing the hour-long special to a national audience just before Christmas in 1997. The piece portrayed a paradise lost: Cajun accents and fiddle music frame tranquil scenes of an idyllic family town where the people have lived close to the land since around 1900, swimming, fishing, and hunting on the bayous and tree-lined canals.

This is the story of a community that attempted to change the laws and, frustrated in that approach, waged a five-year battle of protest and lawyers against state government and the private firms they believed took away their bayou paradise. In doing so, they've taken on what is perhaps the ultimate Goliath: Exxon Corporation, one of the world's largest firms, whose assets and sales run up into the hundreds of billions of dollars. "We had to sue," said Clarice Friloux, a leader of the town's persistent movement. "Nobody would listen to us."[25]

Although their twisting story seems to have concluded with a long trial against Exxon and an out-of-court settlement with Campbell Wells in the summer of 1998, the battle continues to simmer as the people of Grand Bois have not gotten what they wanted: the closure of the site. The ripples this case has sent through state government, and on EPA's regulation of the oil industry, are substantial but uncertain. Driving the waves is the persistent frustration of the townspeople, and their attachment to the land. "We're going for closure. These 300 middle- to lower-class people are making a fuss. That surprised them," said Clarice Friloux, wiping her nose as she spoke of her family's health problems.[26] As Lyes Verdin, whose home is just 333 feet from the pit where Exxon dumped its eighty-one truckloads in 1994, put it, "They came here after us. They're doing wrong. I'm going to fight them all the way."[27]

AN IDYLL, A STENCH

Grand Bois was chosen for a settlement by a handful of families of Houma Indian descent around the turn of the century because it offered good fishing and hunting and some land to plant. One writer described the current residents of Grand Bois: "Although they speak with bayou accents, the residents have the deep-set brown eyes, sharply angular features and thick, dark hair of their forefathers." She continued, "On important occasions in the community, they often perform complex dances and drum ceremonies that have been passed down through their families for generations. There is a somber air about them that is striking."[28] The residents survived with a mix of hunting, fishing, farming, and working in the oil industry, commercial fishing, and local services in the nearby city of Houma.

Grand Bois remained relatively untouched by the modern world until 1981, when just next to the town a start-up firm, called Intracoastal Oilfield Fluids (IOF), sought a license to inject oilfield wastes into

2,000-feet-deep wells.[29] The residents didn't fear the new neighbor initially, since oil production had been going on around the area for generations, and oilfield waste was not considered to be terribly dangerous. Several Grand Bois residents were later to testify that they thought the facility only disposed of salt water from oil drilling.[30]

The firm, however, sought another permit in 1983, this time to dump the waste into open-air pits and to use bacteria to break down the oil waste by "biological remediation," a process that needs oxygen. Beginning with ten pits, each around five acres in area, the site expanded to eighteen pits in 1987. A firm called Campbell Wells bought the site in 1991 and significantly increased its use: by 1994 it was pumping 1.4 million barrels a year of waste into the Grand Bois ponds. That was 77 million gallons of oilfield waste per year.

Campbell Wells, in turn, was bought in 1994 by U.S. Liquids, which operates five other sites – four of them in Louisiana. Then came the loads of waste from Exxon.

Blake Matherne, the forty-year-old stepson of Anne Matherne, termed the odors he smelled as "an ammonia-type of smell. It was just a real, real strong smell I never smelled before."[31] He said he had a "scratchy throat" and a "cotton mouth," reporting that he never had sinus problems before March 1994, but he developed them afterward. Dale Matherne, uncle of Blake and brother-in-law to Anna, went outside to cut the grass one day that month and "started vomiting." He felt his eyes burning and smelled something "somewhat like sulfur." He said he was worried "not only for my health, but also my kids' and my grandkids'."

Reflecting the fear of exposures, which will be a persistent theme in the next chapter's case on the Agriculture Street Landfill, Roland Molinere said he would wake up in the middle of the night, and "like a guard dog [check] on my kids to make sure they were still breathing."[32] Molinere ran outside on one day they were dumping with a video camera and caught the trucks unloading the waste, footage which would later run on the CBS special. Taping the event, he said, his "eyes were on fire, my throat and my sinuses were freaking out," and he had to use his shirt to cover his mouth. "It was like when you drink Coke and it comes back through your nose."

U.S. Liquids and Exxon representatives did not appear to take the complaints of the residents seriously. Faced with the angry townspeople's demands, Jerry Brazzel, division environmental engineer at U.S. Liquids, said, "We can't even talk to those people. We've tried to talk to them."[33] Asked about what is driving their efforts in the class action lawsuit, Brazzel responded that "I guess they want some money." "It's hard to see how people are impacted adversely. They have never showed anything getting away from here [the pits] near the people." Exxon's lead attorney in the case Lou Woolf said people like Molinere are just interested in getting a lot of money. They pointed out to the jury assembled later that eight of the eleven in the first set of defendants didn't even go to a doctor. Molinere said he wanted to go to the emergency room but didn't "because I didn't want to look stupid."

DR. MIKE GOES TO BATON ROUGE:
THE HARD LEGISLATIVE ROAD

How did the oil industry get such a broad loophole for allowing oilfield wastes to avoid being regulated as a hazardous material by the federal government? In the debate running up to the original creation of Superfund rules for handling hazardous wastes in 1976, environmentalists argued that oilfield wastes needed to be treated as hazardous. However, with the nation still reeling from the 1973 energy crisis, the EPA was under intense pressure from the oil industry to give the exemption. The EPA reasoned that it was a question of the lesser of two evils. Declaring the waste hazardous would increase costs for the industry and drive more firms overseas and worsen the U.S. dependence on foreign oil, and deepen the country's trade deficit.[34] EPA calculated it might cost oil companies $12 billion dollars a year if 70 percent of the waste was considered hazardous. EPA researchers went on to project that this could reduce U.S. oil production by "as much as 18 percent by the year 2000. Because of attendant world price increases, this would result in an annual direct cost passed on to consumers of over $6 billion per year." The trade balance was expected to worsen by $18 billion a year.

Because oil taxes are set up to tax drilling in American territory, federal and state government tax revenues would also drop, especially in places like Louisiana. Lobbying by the oil and gas industry got exemptions built into the 1980 amendments on the Superfund laws. So in 1988 EPA made a "regulatory determination" that oilfield waste was exempt and left the regulation to the states.[35] This effectively pushed the battle over how the oilfield wastes would be regulated down to the states.

In Louisiana, the definition of nonhazardous oilfield waste is "oil- or water-based drilling mud and cuttings; salt water; drilling, workover and compression fluids; produced oily sands and solids; pit sludges; natural gas plant processing waste and various types of water from oil fields, among other things. No matter what toxic chemicals these waste products contain, they have been considered non-hazardous since 1980."[36]

Industry officials argue that the oil firms rely on the cheap disposal of the wastes they encounter in exploring for crude. Even though there are twenty-two permitted commercial oilfield waste disposal sites in Louisiana, only four are for "land treatment" in open pits like at Grand Bois.[37] Many others are run by the exploration firms themselves, many are underground injection wells, and there was one major incinerator (GTX/Marine Shale), which was the source of tremendous conflict and was eventually shut down due to pressure by environmentalists.[38]

Opinions on the adequacy of how Louisiana handles the problem of drilling sludge are all over the map. "Louisiana has very good, if not the best, set of oilfield regulations in the country," said the assistant commissioner of the state Department of Natural Resources in late 1997. "We feel they are adequate to protect public health and the environment."[39] Meanwhile Louisiana State University economics professor and former DEQ secretary Paul Templet argued that DNR has a conflict of interest because it promotes and regulates exploration for oil in the state.

Due to the Grand Bois situation, one lone legislator set out to change the whole system. "Dr. Mike," as Robichaux is fondly called by Grand Bois residents, was used to taking risky stands and being isolated for doing so: he got his political start founding a surprisingly effective anticorruption group in LaFourche Parish. As a result, he began to lose patients and was followed, threatened, and harassed.[40] Robichaux went into the 1997 legislative session with the intention of closing the loophole, at least for his constituents in Grand Bois. He introduced a bill in the state Senate to have the U.S. Liquids site in Grand Bois closed. A bus full of residents from Grand Bois packed the usually deserted Senate Environment Committee hearing room. They brought a CBS camera crew with them.

The industry argued that Robichaux's bill would shut down the oil drilling in the state by crippling its ability to access disposal sites around the state. Robichaux argued that his bill was "local" because he had limited it to municipalities within a tiny population band that included Grand Bois. In effect, he was only dealing with the local problem – he knew that to attempt more would be political suicide.

Although the committee was faced with the testimony of residents and supporters and an expert's list of the ailments from the 1994 Exxon dumping, they proceeded to vote down Robichaux's bill overwhelmingly. Robichaux and environmentalists pointed out the ties of committee members to the oil industry. "I really don't think that any of our legislative delegation short of William Jefferson has the guts to get into a fight with the oil and gas industry," said Robichaux. "We should have the Exxon tiger posted over the Capitol."[41]

Not giving up, Robichaux continued to fight the war by attempting to get the Grand Bois closure amended to other legislators' bills. However all those were defeated, and attempts in the next legislative session met the same fate: they never made it out of committee to a vote of the full Senate or House.

By putting all his effort into the oilfield waste issue and alienating much of the Senate, Robichaux was left isolated and ineffective on this and other issues in the legislature. Trying to protect this community by changing state laws was indeed turning out to be political suicide. In the next election, he was singled out by the governor of the state for a "jihad" (a holy war, this was Governor Foster's word for it). Working hard on a grassroots campaign, however, Robichaux managed to hold on to his seat.

What does this case tell us about the possibility for communities to reform legislation that is responsible for their exposure to hazards? Robichaux himself put it bluntly and perhaps fatalistically in a letter to the editor of the *New Orleans Times-Picayune*. "Legislative remedies to correct this problem were unsuccessful when the oil and gas industry, along with their political apologists and several state agencies, managed to convince legislators that it is acceptable to poison poor children who live in rural areas."[42] He shrugged off the potential for the legislative road to reform: "I am sure that the industry and its political puppets are lining up intellectual prostitutes and timid bureaucrats who will give them the answers they seek."

TESTING THE WATERS, TESTING THE BODIES: MEDIA PRESSURES AND AGENCY RESPONSES

Even though the legislative approach failed, the people of Grand Bois and their supporters continued to pressure the state agencies charged with regulating the oil industry.[43] The case provides a test of the extent to which attention from major network media can move an extremely antiregulatory governor. Governor Foster's ability to resist removing the exemption for oilfield waste was bolstered by his high favorability ratings, and the state's frequent scandals, which seldom lead to reform. Still, one observer commented that "the waste site has become a public relations nightmare for the governor and others charged with enforcing the state's environmental laws."[44] So after Robichaux's efforts failed, the pressure shifted from instituting new laws to better enforcement of existing ones.

Seeking to head off criticism, Governor Foster predicted before the CBS showed aired that "It is going to be an emotionally done story to try to make Louisiana look bad. We're used to that. We've just got to do the right thing and prove that we have done the right thing."[45] Preparing for the backlash, Foster looked for a fall guy, and promptly fired the director of the office that oversaw oilfield waste disposal, George Carmouche. Just months before, Carmouche and DNR director Jack Caldwell had testified in the statehouse for the adequacy of existing oilfield waste treatment, to head off Robichaux's bills.[46] Foster said he had replaced Carmouche with someone more willing to institute changes in how oilfield wastes were handled.

On the advice of advisors from the oil industry, Foster also sought to head off deeper reforms by instituting testing of the oilfield waste to see if the stuff really was a problem. Newspapers reported that the looming CBS documentary "prompted Gov. Foster to announce that oil companies would be required to test waste for certain toxic chemicals." Foster commented that "The networks would like to see the oil companies lose their exemptions, which would be very, very bad and environmentally upside down. Oilfield waste, in almost every instance, is not hazardous."

Starting at the beginning of May, the commissioner of conservation at DNR issued a series of emergency rules, because of "public concern." They all called for testing of wastes at the site of production. They were all geared toward narrowing the list of *types* of waste that must be tested. They cut back from wider tests to simpler tests, which one critic called "very fudgeable."[47]

At a public hearing with the Senate Environment Committee, the new testing regulations were opposed by several members, both with links to the oil industry. Republican Lynn Dean – the legislator given the worst voting record in the 1997 session by local environmentalists –

was led to ask "What right does the government have to do this, to impose these expenses?"[48] Department of Natural Resources secretary Jack Caldwell told him that current law allowed the state to require the testing.

On the other side, Gladstone Jones complained that the testing plan was totally backward, not testing at the site of drilling but at the site of disposal. The sludge "will be put in the pits and then it will be determined if they are hazardous or not."[49] If it's found to be dangerous, it would have to be removed from the pits and treated at a special facility.

Addressing a meeting of oil and gas operators in April 1998, DNR secretary Jack Caldwell said, "If you feel you are ever in a position where you have to shut a well because of the way you read the rules, give us a call. We will work something out."[50] These comments were reported in the April 1998 edition of the industry newsletter *Oil and Gas Reporter*. Caldwell said also that the new rules in the state would keep the EPA from closing the oilfield waste loophole. "I think it will greatly lessen the chances of the EPA's drive to revoke the exploration and production waste exemption from hazardous waste regulation."[51]

For Grand Bois residents, these words raised the question of whether there is any meaningful difference between the regulator and the regulated. Clarice Friloux, leader of the Grand Bois struggle, said regulators and oil industry/waste operators "stick together. They sit together and talk together. It's like they [state officials] are working for Campbell Wells."[52]

The Department of Environmental Quality, however, was being pressured to do more. DEQ sent air quality monitoring machines hooked to computers, which are put in an air-conditioned shed between the site and the town. An alarm is triggered if health standards levels are exceeded.[53]

Meanwhile, data from thousands of samples of oilfield waste testing were rolling in. Again, scientists were divided on what they meant: researchers ended up on both sides of the mandated testing. Louisiana State University civil engineering professor John Pardue received a federal Department of Energy grant worth $250,000 to study oilfield waste disposal, charged with creating "cost-effective, risk-based regulatory decisions."[54] James Wharton, former LSU chancellor, and Dan Reible, director of LSU Hazardous Substance Research Center, also worked with Pardue on the analysis of the data being collected at the pits. Their first finding was that of the 1,800 samples taken, many were not "validated" in terms of how they were taken or handled. Hundreds were dropped from the study.

On heavy metals, they found that 99.3 percent of the tests did not exceed the "toxicity characteristic leaching procedure (TCLP) levels" suggested by EPA.[55] However, for the known cancer-causing agent benzene, Reible and a coauthor found that there were nine types of oilfield wastes that had benzene concentrations over the EPA threshold levels of 0.5 milligrams per liter. Much of these were "produced salt water" and other production sludge and water, which are currently injected back into deep wells in the state, and so "therefore do not pose a surface exposure risk."[56] They often claimed that *mixing* wastes would lead to safe levels of benzene. Critics believe that this idea is archaic, along the lines of the old "dilution is the solution to pollution" mentality of the 1950s and 1960s.

The LSU researchers acknowledged, however, that the most common dangerous oilfield wastes were production tank sludge, gas plant processing waste, and three others types. These five types of waste together only made up 3.8 percent of all oilfield wastes treated in commercial facilities in 1998.[57] So an affordable solution seemed possible to satisfy both sides: for these small number of loads of special kinds of waste, "special handling or treatment may be necessary . . . vary[ing] from tracking the wastes to insure they are not concentrated in a single cell or land treatment facility to specific treatment of the waste."[58]

Independent toxicologist Wilma Subra, who often consulted for community and environmental groups, critiqued several aspects of the study. The raw data on which their analysis was based, she argued, showed samples with benzene levels as high as 15,000 milligrams per liter, and dozens above 50 milligrams per liter, which is 100 times higher than the EPA standard.[59] The way Subra read the results after a month of the testing was that only the RCRA loophole allowed these wastes to avoid the expensive treatment mandated in Alabama and other states.

Oil industry official Richard Metcalf said, "there are a lot of exempt wastes that fail one or more of the EPA characteristics, not just our industry. . . We are willing to relook at some of the rules" to help managers "isolate some of these waste streams from the public."[60] With the national attention shifting away from the case at least temporarily, however, DNR stopped testing just five months after it started, on October 1, 1998. They had done 1800 samples in the five months from May to October. An agency spokesperson explained that "We want to come up with results [a new program for testing and treating oilfield wastes] that will stand up to national scrutiny."[61] Since then the testing remains on hold and the emergency rules mentioned earlier have been indefinitely extended. That is, nothing has been done to change the way the oilfield wastes are handled.

* * *

Besides testing the waste, Governor Foster also sought more human *health* testing to confirm his suspicions that nothing was wrong in Grand Bois, to document a problem before tightening existing regulations. "I'm really confident that right now in Grand Bois we can make a very good case that what's happening there now is not dangerous to anyone in the community."[62] He promised to shut the dump down if there was evidence that U.S. Liquids was causing health problems. "That is a lot of attention focused in that one area," said Foster's press secretary, Marsanne Golsby. "The governor is ordering this attention because he deeply cares."[63]

Foster saw himself as a man of quick results. "We want a crash program in that community to see if there is any indication that anybody has been hurt in the past. . . . It's the kind of thing that I am not comfortable piddling around for the next year."[64] Foster and Billy Tauzin, U.S. congressman from the district, asked the U.S. Centers for Disease Control and Prevention (CDC) to provide immediate assistance to the state agencies conducting the health assessment.[65] Grand Bois residents, however, decided that they would be tested only by the scientists and agencies they trusted, and that specifically excluded the state Office of Public Health. Speaking for the residents, Robichaux said "We're not going to cooperate. We will work with the feds. We believe the state should take a subservient role."[66] Robichaux collaborated with two other doctors to do their own health study. Seeking to reassure the distrustful residents, Robichaux told them to not worry, "we are your friends and advocates."[67]

The researcher that Grand Bois residents trusted most was a woman named Patricia Williams, director of LSU Medical School's Occupational Toxicology Outreach Program. Williams had represented a series of communities facing toxic threats, including residents at the Thompson-Hayward Chemical Company in New Orleans mentioned in Chapter 1. She received funding to work with Robichaux and Mt. Sinai hospital physician Phil Landrigan, a nationally known expert.

Saying that the state Office of Public Health waited too long to help the people, Williams blasted the agency for neglecting their health. Dianne Dugas, director of the state public health agency's section on environmental epidemiology, argued that other state agencies had failed to respond to complaints about exposures until too late, so residents distrusted the state government. Her office began an internal study using existing data of lead levels, which showed no elevated levels of lead.[68]

Williams had years of data from working directly with the community, exactly the access and trust the state researchers were unable to obtain. The core of the health study led by Williams was monthly testing of blood and fingernails of Grand Bois residents to test for contamination. Nearly everyone she asked participated. Williams' study found lead in the toenails and fingernails of nearly half of the residents tested. She found 73 percent of the residents tested positive for "stippled" red blood cells, a (controversial) indicator of heavy metal poisoning, but their blood lead levels were relatively low.[69]

State government officials cringed when Williams went public several times with summaries of partial data. They argued that the data collection and analysis should be completed, and the results reviewed by a scientific panel, before its release. They also asked Williams for the original data to corroborate the findings, but she turned them away. A scientist from the CDC's environmental branch ATSDR criticized William's use of fingernails to test for lead, saying that bones and teeth were the accepted ways to do it.[70]

U.S. Liquids also bristled at a scientist such as Williams taking the position of advocate for the community. Jerry L. Brazzel, division Manager of U.S. Liquids, said, "A handpicked panel of so-called experts (several of whom lack scientific objectivity) has chosen to attack us based on a study that is incomplete, unconfirmed, and has not yet been released to the public or to our company."[71] Brazzel said that the lead levels in Grand Bois were actually ten times lower than elsewhere, and testified that no toxic odors they smelled came from U.S. Liquids. Brazzel said the smell could have come from "marsh gas, an old abandoned waste pit nearby, or somewhere else."[72]

When the state health department demanded Williams' data, she refused to provide it, saying it would violate the trust of her study's participants to hand it all over to the very state agency they so reviled.[73] Williams promised that she would send the data to Department of Health and Hospitals (DHH) secretary David Hood and public health department head Dr. Jimmy Guidry only after removing confidential information/identifiers and consulting with the rest of her team. Governor Foster warned, "I'll get to the bottom of this, whether people like it or not. It is totally unacceptable for anyone who has information not to share it with us, especially if there's allegations of a public health threat."[74] The OPH office struck back in 1999 with the passage of Senate Bill 709, which made it unlawful for researchers to withhold information from public health officials. The bill, however, was amended by Dr. Pat Williams' husband Ron Landry, who happened to be a state representative in Baton Rouge. Landry's amendment forced the state agencies to get a court order to force researchers to turn over data to the state, essentially making the bill identical to existing law.[75]

Back in the Senate Environment Committee, Williams faced skeptical questions from committee members. Democrat Senator John Siracusa from the oil town of Morgan City asked if the lead poisoning Williams found in children's bodies could have come "from old batteries lying around" in people's yards.[76] Clarice Friloux responded to the press that "My community is a mile long and you've got this waste site sitting next door and he's asking about batteries. That's ridiculous."

The saga of health monitoring in Grand Bois continues. In early June 1999, several residents stopped participating in the state and federally funded health testing. ATSDR's contractor, in November and December 1998 conducted tests on residents, but the company's contract ran out in December, and, six months later, people were still waiting for the results and analysis.[77] An editorial written in a local newspaper sympathized with the residents.

That is part of the reason for the added frustration for Grand Bois residents. That means more skepticism that the state will do anything. For years, these residents have tried to get state officials to listen. . . . Conducting business in Louisiana seems to outweigh the need to protect its citizens. That's the message residents get, loud and clear. And as they await test results, it remains unchanged.[78]

LEGAL EAGLE MEETS GOLIATH EXXON

Less than a month after the fateful Exxon trucks dumped their dross at the U.S. Liquids ponds in Grand Bois, the community had filed a class-action lawsuit. This was probably not their preferred choice for a strategy, but as the legislative and regulatory approaches failed to make any change, it was increasingly the focus of their energy. With young lawyer Gladstone Jones, they filed *Clarice Friloux et al. vs. Campbell Wells et al.* Jones tag-teamed with partner Mike Fawer, who had years of courtroom experience. The massive case would take them three years and hundreds of thousands of dollars to prepare. There were seemingly endless pretrial motions and arguments about where the trial should be heard, what damages could be obtained, and what types of evidence would be allowed. U.S. Liquids' trial was moved to Baton Rouge; Campbell Wells and Exxon would fight together. The presiding 17th Judicial District Judge Bruce Simpson disallowed evidence from LSU Dr. Patricia Williams because he considered it correlational, not proving causation.[79] Simpson ruled that the case of the 301 plaintiffs – the entire town of Grand Bois – be broken down into thirty separate trials consisting of ten victims each. Just hours before the trial, Exxon got funding for lifetime "medical monitoring" removed from the damages it would have to pay for if it lost. Jones and Fawer fought to get these damages reinstated.

When the people of Grand Bois finally did get their day in court against Exxon and Campbell Wells, the trial was held in an inauspicious upstairs low-ceilinged courtroom in the LaFourche Parish Court Annex, in the steaming hot town of Thibodeaux in July of 1998. Window air-conditioning units lumbered in the background as dozens of residents of Grand Bois packed the courtroom each day. One day the air conditioner broke down, and Simpson called a recess while repairmen were called in.

For the side of Campbell Wells and Exxon, Lou Wolff and Hoard Jarvis led a team of four lawyers. Wolff's initial questions to the potential jurors were about whether other exposures could have caused the health complaints.[80] He asked jurors if they knew that arsenic was present in foods and in the air. He asked them if they used wood preservatives or whether their children played with hobby kits. For the Grand Bois plaintiffs, Fawer asked potential jurors if smokers could still sue companies who exposed them to toxic chemicals. And he asked them if they would rely on testimony from a state Department of Environmental Quality employee more than anyone else.

After three days of jury selection there were still no panelists seated. The defendants' lawyers fought to empanel a jury that was heavy on people from the more developed north of LaFourche Parish, where many residents were seen to consider people from the area around

Grand Bois as less industrious and more interested in gaining monetary awards from corporations.[81]

After establishing their lines of argument in the opening statements, Jones and Fawer called resident after resident who described what they smelled and saw, and what happened to their health after the fateful Exxon loads were brought to Grand Bois in March 1994. Because they couldn't get any residents to refute the claims of those claiming health damage, the core of the Exxon/Campbell Wells strategy was to call witnesses who worked inside the Campbell Wells/U.S. Liquids facility. The idea was that if the waste was causing no problems inside the facility, how could it be hurting people outside. Exxon's Lou Wolff asked the jury rhetorically, "Inside the facility it doesn't appear any harm is going on. How does it cause harm outside the facility but not inside the facility?"[82]

Wolff called the manager of the trucking contractor who hauled in Exxon's waste, C. M. Penn and Sons of Baton Rouge, to the stand. He testified that none of his drivers got sick, and that they didn't use respirators or any other equipment.[83] They called Troy LeBoeuf of Cut Off, Louisiana, then manager of the U.S. Liquids site in Grand Bois, who was a mechanic at the site in 1994 when the waste was dumped. LeBoeuf said he climbed down into the cell and worked three hours fixing an excavator machine while the Exxon materials were being dumped, with no problems. LeBoeuf was wearing no protective clothing nor a respirator.[84] These were difficult arguments for Jones and Fawer to refute because they had subpoenaed Exxon and Campbell Wells for any information about workers becoming sick from the waste, but the reply was that there were none.

The plaintiffs called Dr. Richard Friend, who works locally, and who said all the patients he examined from Grand Bois had the same symptoms: headaches, dizziness, nausea, respiratory problems, numbness, and two had arsenic in their urine. Expert witnesses for the townspeople found arsenic and barium in their houses, Cell 11, and three other pits. Then Exxon brought in a series of doctors, each of whom said that they had examined the patients, but said no one was seriously sick. Dr. Douglas Swift, medical director of the Tulane Centers of Occupational Health, had earlier taped a deposition with the attorneys which was read in court most of the day of August 6.[85] Swift's affidavit showed he did blood counts, tested breathing capacity, took chest x-rays, and did full physical exams of all the plaintiffs as a doctor for Exxon. For each plaintiff, Swift was asked if he found any injuries resulting from exposures to the chemicals. For each, Swift said, "No." When asked if he thought the symptoms reported by Grand Bois plaintiffs could be caused by neurotoxins, such as hydrogen sulfide and benzene, which can cause nervous system damage. Swift said, "No." Referring to the famous New Orleans bar district, he said, "Every time you walk down Bourbon Street, you see a neurotoxin at work – alcohol." When asked the root of the complaints, Swift replied, "The truckloads of stuff did not smell good and people got upset and that's why we're here."

Fawer and Jones attacked Exxon for deceiving the Louisiana Department of Natural Resources by characterizing their waste as non-hazardous. Fawer grilled Exxon's environmental regulatory compliance engineer, Doug Callon, until he admitted that the air samples taken over the top of the container truck in Alabama found five times the hazard thresholds for some chemicals and so Exxon knew they were hazardous.[86] Callon admitted that Exxon was unaware that there was a community so close to the Campbell Wells facility. When the complaints came in, he flew over Grand Bois in an airplane because Exxon was concerned about possible exposures to residents.[87]

Each time Jones or Fawer developed a line of argument, Wolff objected. Rather than accepting or denying the objection, each time Judge Simpson called both sets of lawyers to the bench for a private conference. Many lines of questioning had to be abandoned because Simpson would not allow them or because it was too difficult after the long conferences to develop them again. The heat, pressure, and frustration were building as the overtaxed air conditioners droned on.

But then the case took a twist as if out of a Sunday-night television drama. One night in the last week of the trial, Fawer and Jones received a phone call from Florida. It was from a worker named Gary Holley, who had spent three days in Alabama using a back hoe to load the waste that went to Grand Bois.[88] Holley's wife liked to read the news on the internet, and when she saw a story about Exxon waste from Alabama, she asked her husband if he wasn't seen by the doctor after loading that material in his old job. Holley was rushed by the plaintiffs to Thibodeaux to testify. Looking ill and speaking haltingly on the witness stand, Holley said he had to quit working two years later and is today diagnosed with chemical nerve damage to the brain. "The face of chemical poisoning was on that witness stand and the defendants are running scared," said Mike Fawer to the judge when Exxon attorneys asked for extra time to address the claims.[89] One doctor who examined Holley was Dr. Swift, the Tulane occupational health specialist.[90] Swift had received the results from the lab analysis of the waste in the pit, and Swift had cited the waste in writing a report. Just the day before, Swift's testimony was that he was unaware of any workers who had been made ill by the waste. Swift's report on Holley was like that on all the other plaintiffs: his systems were normal. Further, Swift wrote that his syndrome might be the result of marital problems at the time he first became ill. Jones and Fawer, for the Grand Bois plaintiffs, charged Exxon with hiding "significant" documents that Holley had brought them. "Dr. Swift's credibility has been called into account," said the judge.

Fawer and Jones' belief that Holley's testimony, which contradicted that of Swift, put Exxon and Campbell Wells "on the run" was half right. Indeed, his appearance caused U.S. Liquids and Campbell Wells to make the residents an offer quickly while court was still in session that same day. "I got a note a short while later that said, 'we will accept the settlement on the following terms.' It was all written out," said Jones.[91] During a break, he explained it to the residents and asked them to think about it. After adjournment that day, Campbell Wells, U.S. Liquids, and plaintiffs' attorneys worked through the night to reach a deal.

The settlement from Campbell Wells and U.S. Liquids, though "sealed," was reported to include damage payments of some $7 million, but this was spread over all 301 plaintiffs. Lawyers received 40 percent and expenses, a common commission for taking this kind of high-risk case. The average to the Grand Bois residents, therefore, was less than $14,000 per person. Finally, U.S. Liquids agreed to make some important changes in how the facility would be operated in the future, the most important point for some of the plaintiffs. Specifically, the company would have to close several pits nearest the houses and to build a huge "screening berm" along its property line to keep the smells and possible flooding out of their neighborhood. U.S. Liquids also agreed to create an industry/community committee to "build positive relations and open communications with the citizens of Grand Bois," said its president, Gary Orr.[92] Finally, the settlement came with a gag order, which prohibited the plaintiffs from discussing its contents, and an agreement that they would refrain from any further legal action against the companies.

The small firm flinched, opting for a settlement they could write off and stay in business. Exxon, with a net worth of some $43 billion, hung in for the verdict.

Exxon's attorney Lou Wolff fought on alone. His closing arguments admitted that there may have been some harmful chemicals in the waste, but they were in too small amounts to really hurt the people in Grand Bois.[93] Before the lawsuit was filed, he noted, "No one went to the doctor before that – except two." Of those two, one thought she was sickened by roofing material fumes, and the other went in for an existing illness. The sinus problems and anxiety cited by the plaintiffs' own experts didn't merit the expense of long-term medical monitoring, as they were requesting. He cited the words of his final witness, who had said that lifetime monitoring of Grand Bois residents' health was too costly, and totally unnecessary.[94]

Should Exxon "be punished because they complied with the law?" he asked. Rather, he argued, if plaintiffs don't like the law, they should change it.

Mike Fawer, in his closing arguments, told the jury about the ways the Exxon waste of March 1994 had changed life in the community, and about the health and psychological effects on the plaintiffs, Nora Bonin, Lyes Verdin, and Anna Matherne. "The impact on these individuals has been devastating."[95] He asked the jury to consider $150,000 for lifetime medical monitoring of each community member, $100,000 to $500,000 per year over the past four years for pain and suffering, and $80 million in punitive or exemplary damages. That shouldn't hurt Exxon too much, he argued, because it was just 1 percent of Exxon's 1997 profits. But since it was just the first ten plaintiffs of the 300 members of the class action lawsuit, it should send a message to the firm and others who would do the same. The total suggested by Jones to the jury for these ten plaintiffs was $84 million. If that pattern was repeated for the other 290 plaintiffs, the total judgement against Exxon could reach $2.5 billion. Exxon's annual profits were running about $7 billion a year in 1994.

Fawer's voice rose to the dramatic conclusion: "What you have seen in this courtroom is the unabashed – unabashed – arrogance of Exxon . . . Exxon poisoned that community. . . . Send a message to Exxon, the governor of this state, the legislators, the regulators – we will not be the dumping ground for anyone else's wastes: Do pure and simple and beautiful justice."[96]

The next day, the jury came back with a verdict. The packed courtroom fell silent as Judge Bruce Simpson asked the series of questions he'd sent the jury in to answer. His clerk read the verdicts one by one.[97]

"Was Exxon negligent in its handling and disposal of the waste from Alabama?"

"No."

"Did Exxon hurt Collette Friloux?"

"No."

"Did Exxon hurt Joyceline Dominique?"

"No."

"Did Exxon hurt Timothy Billiot?"

"No."

Tears started to well in some of the Grand Bois plaintiffs' eyes. Heads fell. Some walked out of the courtroom as the list of "No's" grew. Others just stared in shock at the jury. Finally on the last three names, there were "yes" responses.[98]

Then the clerk read the verdicts on the amounts that Exxon was responsible for in harming those three residents. For Bonin, the woman truck driver driving by, only $15,000. For the other two, only $7,500. This was virtually nothing compared to the $84 million or the $2.5 billion the lawyers had suggested they charge the oil giant.[99]

Exxon declared victory. Asked if they would appeal the tiny penalties, Exxon's attorney said no. "We feel Exxon is vindicated absolutely."[100]

Colette Friloux, a plaintiff who walked out of the courtroom before all the verdicts were read, said simply, "We're not stopping. We're not giving up. It would be like giving up our lives." Trying hard to put on a glad face after years of work, Fawer said, "We're more than satisfied" with the $7 million settlement.[101] The community wanted to try again with the next ten plaintiffs, but their lawyers hesitated. Rather, Jones fought with Simpson to reopen the trial because of the documents Exxon had kept from him.

Some Grand Bois residents felt the trial was unfair because Simpson had not allowed LSU Dr. Patricia Williams' study as evidence.[102] Others said that "this is an oil town" and that the doctors for Exxon "had amnesia." Tying these two facts together, Anna Matherne believed that the doctors in town are afraid to be critical of the industry here or they might lose their business. One bitter resident said, "It's too bad we couldn't take that waste and drop it by the jurors' houses."[103]

Only a few jurors were willing to speak to the press. One said, "We all felt something needs to be done to prevent this from happening, but to punish a company that is following the guidelines" would be a mistake. Jury foreman Terry Lendsey said "I never heard anytime where they [Exxon] were cited for breaking the law."[104] Beverlyn Eymard of Cut Off said, "The law has to be changed. People's lives are at stake."[105]

LEGACIES AND NONLEGACIES:
BETTER LAWS OR FEWER LAWSUITS?

As the uncertain dust cleared from the exhausting summer courtroom marathon, it was clear that all the efforts of the citizens of Grand Bois had gotten them only so far. What they had achieved was due to their ability to attract dedicated lawyers and state and national media attention, but they lacked the support of a national or international environmental group to sustain the pressure put on the governor from the newspapers and the Ed Bradley CBS piece. As chemist Wilma Subra put it, this was their bad luck: "no national group has adopted oilfield waste" as a long-term campaign, the way Greenpeace took on PVC production and dioxin, which meshed so well for the residents of Convent in their fight against Shintech (Chapter 4), or NIRS' dedication to the anti-LES group CANT because it fit their antinuke focus.[106] They also had not been adopted by the environmental justice movement. Grand Bois' residents had failed, therefore, by no fault of their own, to take the battle to Washington the way the anti-LES coalition had. Instead, they fought the waste pits on legal grounds and with state agencies for the better testing and enforcement of state environmental laws. One picture of Clarice Friloux in the November 25, 1997, issue of *The New Orleans Gambit Weekly* showed her standing by a huge protest sign in front of her house with the pictures of 15 children in the town.[107] It read, "President Clinton Please Help Us!! No one else seems to want to." Her quote beside it read, "We had to sue. Nobody would listen to us."

Grand Bois residents learned quickly that, even with a tireless, courageous proponent, the legislative road was completely closed due to the strength of the oil lobby. Most observers believe that Exxon was absolved in the trial because it had not broken any laws, and most agree, therefore, that new laws need to be put on the books. However, all agreed that moving such a law would be politically suicidal with the massive power of oil lobby and campaign war chests. Caldwell's comments also revealed that the state agency was working with industry to undermine efforts by the EPA to tighten regulations on the industry. Federal departments directing the nation's energy policies remain under pressure to protect oil production inside the United States because the price is going up just as the nation's dependence on foreign oil has jumped. Just eight days after the Grand Bois verdict, a Department of Energy press release said that Louisiana had about 27,000 marginal wells that might shut down if controls were tighter: "These wells are especially susceptible to even small increases in environmental compliance costs," they concluded.[108] The agreement between the federal and state governments and the oil industry was that discussed earlier: to study carefully and find out which parts of the waste flows need regulating. If only 3 percent of all wastes were causing troubles such as the Grand Bois case, then perhaps they could be treated as hazardous, without jeopardizing the viability of the whole industry. But even these reforms have stalled.

Several other issues suggest that the pressure of protest and media exerted by the Grand Bois community on the state government was not effective in the face of a conservative governor. The pressure on the state worked for a time, but as soon as press coverage started to wane, Governor Foster and his DNR and DEQ moved on to other issues. The head of the section at the state department that governs oilfield wastes was canned, but the DNR remained in an extremely pro-oil industry posture, as witnessed by Caldwell's quote above promising the regulators could "work something out" if the new rules became burdensome for oil companies.[109] In fact, in 1999, Foster and the oil industry went on the offensive against the claims of Grand Bois residents and those of any community that might make similar demands. An important backlash from the case was in the area of whether possible victims of toxic poisoning could seek "punitive" damages in lawsuits like that brought by Jones and Fawer, specifically those to pay for monitoring their health to see if they developed illnesses later in life from their exposures. Governor Foster's first legislative priority upon being elected was to enact strict limits on what kinds of penalties victims could seek in class-action lawsuits. He succeeded in passing this "Tort Reform," closing one avenue for redress in future contamination cases in Louisiana.

As mentioned earlier, just before the case went to trial, Judge Simpson said that the plaintiffs could *not* seek money to cover physical exams in the future.[110] An angered Mike Fawer said that "what you have done is taken away the most crucial element of this trial." Fawer and Jones took it to the First Circuit Court of Appeals, and won a ruling that they could seek "medical monitoring" compensation for the Grand Bois residents.[111] But Governor Foster and oil industry lobbyists proposed and passed a bill in the 1999 Louisiana legislature which effectively cut off the ability of plaintiffs in the state to sue for medical monitoring expenses, unless doctors observed symptoms immediately upon the exposure. Environmentalists in the state argued that many exposures, such as to benzene and asbestos, are famous for causing cancer only several years after exposures, with few if any immediate symptoms. This represents a step backward for citizens' rights from where they were when the Grand Bois case began. The attempt to use Senate Bill 709 from the state health department to force Dr. Williams and any others to hand over their data to them was another important effort by industry and the state to regain control.[112] In both of these cases of legislation, the governor was no longer on the defensive against the claimants from Grand Bois: he was preventing them from going further and other communities from following in their footsteps.

So it appears the Grand Bois residents pushed the state agencies as far as they could, at least under the current administration. "We've gotten no support from the state at all," said Clarice Friloux. "We feel we have the EPA on our side in some ways, but as far as the DEQ – no. The Office of Conservation – no. The Department of Health and Hospitals – no. We not only have to fight the company, we have to fight the state, too."[113] Certainly the residents have lost their faith in their state government to protect them, and their distrust of the federal government is growing with the battle over the ATSDR health study.[114] Residents believed that study was merely a ploy by the state government to override the findings of their trusted scientist.

Probably the most positive outcome of the case is the awareness that Grand Bois has raised in the state of Louisiana about the nature of oilfield waste and what it must be like to live in a contaminated community. People learned, during the Grand Bois struggle, about what a small town can do, even without the strong help of a national or international environmental group. On the downside, the townspeople's awareness has led to some lingering psychological impacts of the contamination and the struggle. Joyceline Dominique testified that the Campbell Wells waste disposal site "just about destroyed our lives. We're always sick, we've lost our home. We can't enjoy our yard. I've been diagnosed with chemical exposure."[115]

Environmental justice experts have argued that private lawsuits are almost never satisfactory, for individual residents, or for the cohesiveness of the community.[116] This issue comes up even more forcefully in Chapter 6, and we discuss it again at some length in Chapter 7. This is only speculation, but the "legal eagle" glamour of the case as covered in the Ed Bradley report and other press reports might lead more communities to attempt this approach, and more young people to enter environmental law. The prospects for many of these communities is not good: many of them will not be as effectively organized as Grand Bois, and they will rely more entirely on their lawyers to move their cases forward. And some of their lawyers will certainly not be as dedicated as were Jones and Fawer. On the other hand, most companies would have sought to settle out of court before Exxon did. The daily barrage of bad publicity for a firm once its case goes to trial serves as a strong deterrent for most firms, and they opt to settle quietly and keep their cases out of court. That Exxon, Campbell Wells, and U.S. Liquids were willing to try this case may have been related to the size of the penalty ($2.5 billion) that Fawer and Jones were suggesting the jury levy the firm. Interestingly, neither side suggested moving into binding arbitration, an increasingly common process where a hired judge hears both sides and assigns a settlement.

Communities taking the class-action lawsuit approach often are frustrated in the end by out-of-court settlements because they sometimes create jealousy, and, when they are "sealed," they block further organizing. Having not secured a public interest law firm or clinic (as in the case of LES and Shintech), the community also had not been able to make a strong environmental justice case by filing a Title VI complaint against Campbell Wells, Exxon, or the state DEQ. This has also kept the firm's battle essentially local.

There is a final twist in the story of the settlement between Grand Bois residents and U.S. Liquids: the firm promised to build a huge "screening berm" along the fenceline, to keep odors and possible flooding out of the town. Its plans have been filed, and they include using waste from the pits to construct the huge mound. The residents are livid at the prospect of stirring up tons of contaminated sediments to build a wall that might drain into their yards.

6

Stress and the Politics of Living On a Superfund Site

THE AGRICULTURE STREET MUNICIPAL LANDFILL

✳   *with Amanda Leiker*   ✳

Top: Peggy GrandPre, center, talks to neighbors during a community meeting at the Agriculture Street Landfill site in New Orleans. [Photo by Thom Scott, used with permission of the *New Orleans Times-Picayune*]

Bottom: Residents of the Agriculture Street Landfill neighborhood take their protest to the White House with the help of Greenpeace. [Photo by Thom Scott, used with permission of the *New Oreans Times-Picayune*]

TWO MOTHERS ON A LANDFILL

Elodia Blanco was born in New Orleans to a Creole Catholic nurse and her husband, a Guatemalan seaman.[1] The family lived two blocks from the Lafitte public housing project until her parents divorced when she was at an early age. The kids would alternate summers, spending one with her father in San Francisco and the next in Guatemala or traveling with him as he worked as a chef on the ships. By age sixteen, Elodia was married, and two years later she had two baby boys. After a disagreement with her husband, she took her boys to California to live with her father and her "Nanny," his wife. "I knew I had to get out of New Orleans." They were the only African-Americans in that part of Marin County, where she lived for a decade. After earning her high school equivalence and studying for several years of college around the Bay Area, Elodia remarried her trucker ex husband and they had a daughter. She moved the family back to New Orleans when her mother took ill. Upon her return, Elodia landed a good job in Mayor Dutch Morial's office as a program manager.

There, she learned about a new federally supported housing development called Gordon Plaza, which sounded perfect for their family's needs and fit within their means. They looked at the blueprints, drove out and looked at the staked-out lots, and picked out a nice big corner one. Building began in 1980, and she "came by every week to watch the progress of my beautiful home being built. I was happy. Excited. And you know it was just a dream. We were so happy – it's a new home, we can get the kids through school, and everything's gonna be alright." The neighbors moved in, and there was a big ribbon cutting ceremony with the mayor, some councilpersons, and some brass bands.

The first sign of trouble was when they tried to plant grass. Digging in the yard, Peggy and her husband turned over a lot of broken bottle glass. "Every shovel was filled with unbelievable things: tires, car parts, and bones. I mean bones!" Two friends gave them extraordinary house-warming presents: one donated six truckloads of dirt, the other St. Augustine sod.

But none of the trees would grow, and within a year, the house started to fall apart. The plumbing was rotting under the ground, the roof had problems, and the foundation was starting to crack. Then after a few years there, "boom, one of my neighbors died, another died. Cancer, tumors." She talked to someone at City Hall who mentioned that this had been a dump. She called some neighbors to meet in her house, and their concerns grew. "I started putting the pieces together, and finding out that a lot of people were sick back here."

Elodia's American Dream was turning into a nightmare. The neighborhood's struggle would take them to meet the mayor, representatives, congresspersons, and senators, and to travel to Washington, D.C., to meet with EPA and HUD and to protest in front of the White House. With activists from two other contaminated communities in Louisiana, Elodia would travel as the neighborhood's representative on a Greenpeace delegation to testify at the UN Commission on Human Rights in Geneva, Switzerland. On how she keeps going through this decade-long struggle, Elodia's bulldog determination comes through: "You have to continue to fight. You can't get complacent, or it won't get done." On why it has taken so long to be relocated, she believes that racism is part of it. "If this were a mixed community, we'd have been out. If we had some very influential white people living in this community, and if Press Park [the subsidized housing on part of the old dump] was not a low-income subsidized housing – I really believe we'd be out of here." When it's all over, would she continue with environmental justice activism? Elodia's response is immediate. "I can't stop fighting. I would help other communities. Oh, I gotta help other communities."

Elodia's neighbor Peggy GrandPre had a similar experience. Shocked to find out that her house was located on a landfill and that the area was actually toxic, she kept telling herself "this can't be happening."[2] When the neighborhood was put on the Superfund list of toxic sites, Peggy thought that "this is the federal government, and they're going to do what's right." However, the plan the EPA came up with was "ludicrous"; to her it seemed "almost like fiction." But after five years of leading the homeowners in a tormenting struggle against the city and federal government, Peggy knows that her experience at Agriculture Street is, in fact, "not a rarity."

At the beginning of the struggle against the EPA, Peggy did not take a major role. She describes herself as the type of person who went to work, came home, and didn't pay much attention to what was going on. She had never before been an activist. Yet she saw a lot of infighting in the community meetings with the EPA that she thought counterproductive, so she saw a need for new leadership. Her husband convinced her to become more active when the president of the protest group asked her to take over. Because the community was so sharply divided about what should be done, and because peoples' financial interests were at stake, Peggy began to receive threatening letters. She hired a private investigator to find out who was sending the letters, and the letters stopped.

"My role and mission is to find a solution, to find a way to get the residents off the site," said GrandPre. Being the president of the group of residents demanding relocation has changed her life, and not all for the good. "I now have a full-time job with a salary, a full-time job to the community, and a full-time job as a mother." She's exhausted: if the battle is resolved, she looks forward to not doing any more of this kind of work.

DIRT, POLITICAL DIRT, CONTAMINATED DIRT

The story of the Agriculture Street Landfill is important politically because it seems to show the level of power held by the environmental justice movement in Louisiana: able to move this difficult case part of the way, but not all the way, to resolution. The residents of the Agriculture Street community show plainly how uncertainty and worry about exposures to toxins creates an insidious stress on individuals and their communities. The case shows how the truly mixed results of scientific inquiry were used by the two sides in the struggle. Certainly most importantly, the case is important for the people in the neighborhood, who, most of all, feel trapped in a situation where they cannot sell the worthless homes in which they live.

At any one of the Wednesday night meetings that the Concerned Citizens of Agriculture Street Landfill hold each week, residents speak not of everyday neighborhood gossip but of what they consider the ongoing fight for their lives. Children play in the yard outside from where the residents gather. Across the street a six-foot chain-link fence topped with barbed wire surrounds an empty lot where more than 150 toxic substances and heavy metals have been detected. The entire neighborhood sits atop the old city dump – where New Orleans dumped its garbage for a half century from the 1910s to the 1960s. After an already long battle, citizens and environmental justice activists managed in 1994 to get the Agriculture Street Landfill neighborhood classified by the EPA as a Superfund site needing federal assistance for cleanup. After another half decade of struggle, however, the same agency would not meet their most fervent demand – to help the people be relocated to homes where they would feel safe.

The Agriculture Street Landfill saga began around 1910 when the City of New Orleans opened the site for operation as the city's municipal waste dump. The site continued to receive solid waste for fifty years, during which waste was incinerated on site and buried in the surrounding area. Nearby residents complained throughout the 1940s and 1950s of a terrible stench wafting from the landfill. "Household trash and mysterious sealed drums, day-old bread and canned goods, dead animals, medical waste, and, in the late 50s, ash from a nearby garbage incinerator, all of it went into the dump, unregulated and unrecorded . . . burning dead horses and cows."[3] To ease the worries of nearby residents about the dangers posed to them, city officials assured the residents that "the dump didn't pose a threat because it was sprayed weekly with the insecticide DDT." The Agriculture Street Landfill was reopened briefly in the 1960s to take in the mountains of waste from the devastating Hurricane Betsy. Upon closure, the landfill was seventeen feet deep and covered ninety-five acres downriver from New Orleans' famous French Quarter.

Ronald L. Brignac, then executive officer of the Housing Authority of New Orleans (HANO), wrote a memo in 1967 to his board of directors expressing that area civic groups were excited about possible construction of public housing units atop the old Agriculture Street Landfill. He recommended "trying to obtain the junkyard as a site for public housing."[4] HANO and the federal Department of Housing and Urban Development (HUD) first chose Agriculture Street as the site of the Press Park neighborhood, consisting of 167 public housing units. The neighborhood expanded in 1975 when a newly formed group called the Desire Community Housing Corporation (DCHC) submitted plans to construct sixty-seven single-family homes and an elderly care facility. The DCHC completed the construction of these properties, which they named Gordon Plaza, and the Gordon Plaza Elderly Housing Apartments, using $7 million in federal funds from HUD in 1981.[5]

Dutch Morial, the first black mayor of the city, and other city leaders billed the Gordon Plaza community and its respectable homes as a way for low- to middle-income African Americans to have a piece of the American Dream. Gordon Plaza attracted primarily first-time homeowners who were told that they were moving into the neighborhood as part of "a new wave of power in New Orleans' black community."[6] The multiple ironies of this statement would soon become apparent through the struggle that was to last for decades. It split residents against each other and tested their ability to fight a massive but unsatisfying cleanup plan pushed upon them by the EPA. That plan would cost $20 million – some three times the original development's budget.

Construction plans for the sixty-seven middle-income homes in Gordon Plaza included the removal of old landfill cover dirt and its replacement with eighteen inches of river sand. The river dirt was to cover the ground before any construction began. However, according to many reports, DCHC contractors never completed this cover-up component of the designs.[7] According to an editorial published in *The Gambit Weekly*, Mayor Dutch Morial, father of current Mayor Marc Morial, "worked closely on the project with a group of his friends and financial contributors, all of whom benefited financially from the deal." It continues, "In New Orleans' long tradition of ward-heeler politics [local political bosses and intermediaries], that would not have been so bad if things had turned out all right, for the new home buyers. Instead, it appears that the former landfill never was adequately covered – which cut costs and increased profits for the developers."[8] In addition to the lack of river sand fill, city officials, DCHC contractors, HUD representatives, and other responsible parties never tested the landfill soil for contaminants or warned residents that this possibility existed.

Once in their new homes, residents quickly noticed that their homes were a far cry from the American Dream they were promised. Shoddy construction of the houses and landfill debris in the yards foreshadowed impending problems related to living atop a landfill. One resident found the corpse of a cow in her front yard. Another resident found a rusted car door in her garden. In addition, almost all the ground surrounding the residents' homes contained broken glass and other debris.[9] Not only were they living on a landfill, they were living in faulty homes on an improperly capped landfill. Residents first complained to government officials about the conditions in which they lived in 1981.

In 1983, in spite of the complaints, the Orleans Parish School Board announced plans to build a $4.6 million elementary school, Robert R. Moton Elementary, on four acres of the landfill site. The school would serve 850 children (including those from the nearby Desire housing project), replacing the original aging Moton school, which had been demolished.[10] "Routine sampling" of the soil for construction of the school revealed high levels of lead and other toxins and prompted residents to request further testing.[11] Dr. Velma Campbell of the Ochsner Clinic expressed concern about the safety of the school site to the School Board, explaining that "long-term exposure to materials found at the site pose cancer and other health risks."

Other residents, however, sensing that their skin color and low income would force them to keep sending their children to far-away and crumbling schools in other parts of New Orleans, wanted Moton Elementary to be built on the dump site, despite possible risks. The local paper reported in early 1985 that "Some residents, believe the fuss over hazardous materials could be a sham to avoid building the school."[12]

Engineer Edgar Pavia of the Pavia-Byrne Engineering Corporation was brought in to consult on the problem. He stated that "under Environmental Protection Agency standards the site could not be classified as hazardous and can be made safe." On his word, the Orleans Parish School Board voted 3 to 2 to continue construction of the elementary school.[13]

After discovering that the land beneath and surrounding their homes contained dangerous contaminants, some of the most worried residents met with city officials and representatives from responsible parties on May 23, 1985, to discuss possible relocation of their community. State representative Johnny Jackson, Jr., who had been a driver of the project since the beginning as the head of the DCHC, told residents at that meeting that they "were lucky to have the good deals that got them into the subdivision in the first place."[14] Many residents did not feel that they were "lucky" to be living on a toxic landfill, feeling instead that they had been cheated. This initial failure was the beginning of Agriculture Street residents' disillusionment and battle with their government. They certainly cannot be said to lack an understanding of the importance of politics. In their struggle for relocation, the residents of Agriculture Street went on to enlist the support of numerous politicians, including New Orleans Mayor Marc Morial, Congressperson William Jefferson, and U.S. Senators John Breaux and Mary Landrieu. These politicians have written letters of support and verbally advocated on behalf of relocation of the community. However, residents believe that these politicians merely provide lip service to the relocation efforts and have failed to take any decisive action.

The EPA came to inspect the site on May 20 and 21, 1986, taking forty-five soil samples back to their labs. Some samples had lead concentrations greater than 1,000 parts per million (ppm), and three samples had lead concentrations of more than 4,000 ppm, all far above EPA "safe levels." Soil samples also contained lead, zinc, arsenic, mercury, and cadmium. There were polynuclear hydrocarbons, potentially dangerous oil products, in almost every sample.[15]

The EPA, however, determined that the site was not dangerous enough to secure Superfund status and the federal monies to relocate the residents and clean up the site that might come with such designation. The neighbors and their advocates continued to fight, with the assistance of the Gulf Coast Tenants Organization. The organization, led by civil rights veteran Pat Bryant, was taking up issues of environmental justice at the very start of the movement, and had become a national leader (see Chapter 2).[16] One resident recalled that Pat Bryant "first blew the whistle to the community that they were living on top of a landfill." From his work in civil rights and tenants' rights organizing, Bryant understood the power of sentiments of injustice for mobilizing people, he knew how to use the media, and he knew the importance of playing political hardball. Bryant put pressure on EPA to reconsider their methods of ranking sites. Congressperson William Jefferson brought his office's weight to bear with the help of the Congressional Black Caucus.

When the EPA originally assessed the Agriculture Street Landfill site in 1986, it gave the site a hazard ranking score of 3 out of 100, essentially saying the dangers were almost nonexistent. However, in 1986, the EPA addressed only air and water contamination as possible means of exposure, eliminating much of the contamination in the Agriculture Street area from consideration. Then, in 1990, EPA rules changed to include soil contamination in hazard ranking scores, changing the neighborhood's score to a 50 out of 100, much greater than the 28.5 needed for Superfund designation. So the same EPA scientists conducted both sets of tests in 1986 and 1990, yet came up with drastically different hazard rankings.[17]

The Agriculture Street residents were snared in the trap, which has ensnared dozens of Superfund sites around the country: their neighborhood was certified as hazardous enough to get listed, but it was not hazardous enough to get them relocated. According to EPA logic, for the Agriculture Street site to be considered dangerous enough for a buyout, the probability for chemically related deaths must be high. Local reporters characterized the EPA position on the issue this way:

For the contaminants to pose a significant health risk, residents would have to begin drawing their water from the ground, rather than the river; regularly eat the dirt in their yards; and move into the more hazardous sections of the old dump that have not been developed. Under this unlikely scenario, the EPA calculates, eight people in 10,000 would have died after 30 years of exposure to dump-linked contaminants.[18]

The Superfund program, meanwhile, was embroiled in politics between Democrats and the Reagan and Bush administrations. Many environmentalists feared that the Republican administrations were trying to subvert the program.[19]

Meanwhile, the science itself seemed to residents to be as murky as the politics behind ranking Superfund sites. The two may themselves be intertwined, as two jaded local journalists concluded: "What scientists say about Agriculture Street varies with their political stripe."[20] Concerns about living near or on top of landfills are supported in part by researchers who believe we should err on the side of caution with such things. Environmental researcher Peter Montague made the point clearly against landfills:

It should come as no surprise that living near a landfill is hazardous to your health and it doesn't matter whether the landfill holds solid waste or hazardous waste. Hazardous waste landfills hold unwanted toxic residues from manufacturing processes. On the other hand, municipal solid waste landfills hold discarded products, many of which were manufactured from toxic materials. The wastes go out the back door of the factory while the products go out the front door, but after they have been buried in the ground both wastes and products create very similar hazards for the environment, wildlife, and humans.[21]

Supporting this view, one New York State Department of Health report, which studied seven types of cancer, found elevated levels of all seven types, with statistically significant levels of bladder and leukemia cancers in women. The article concluded that "women living near solid waste landfills where gas is escaping have a four-fold increased chance of bladder cancer or leukemia."[22]

The neighbors pressured the state Office of Public Health to conduct a study of cancer rates in the neighborhood. The Environmental

Epidemiology section at the OPH used only existing government data, including tabulations from the Louisiana Tumor Registry and demographic information by census tract.[23] The OPH and the federal toxics agency ATSDR (the environmental arm of the Centers for Disease Control and Prevention) found that the undeveloped area of the site posed a public health hazard, but the residential areas and the Moton School areas posed "no apparent public health hazard." The OPH study found no differences on a series of cancers but did find a statistically significant increase of breast cancer (60 percent higher) for the period from 1988 to 1993. The study cautioned that the small numbers available for study make achieving statistical significance difficult and claimed that "clear environmental links to breast cancer are limited."[24] The OPH study cautioned that the chemicals found on the Agriculture Street site "have not been associated with breast cancer." In the matter of "adverse birth outcomes," the study claimed that the contaminant levels at Agriculture Street would not cause low birth weights, still births, and the like. These mixed results provided ammunition for both sides.

Two professors at Xavier, the historically black Catholic university in New Orleans, contributed to the scientific debate on Agriculture Street.[25] Sociologist and director of the Deep South Center for Environmental Justice, Beverly Wright, conducted a door-to-door survey of residents in the mid-1990s and submitted the results to EPA and the community.[26] A white chemistry professor named Howard Mielke did his own tests on lead and other heavy metals in the soils around the Agriculture Street neighborhood and the Moton Elementary School. Mielke found that the site was actually far *better* than most New Orleans black neighborhoods.

Mielke went on record in the *New Orleans Times-Picayune* as saying, "I'm glad the neighborhood is receiving help, but the science seems to be lost in all of this. Superfund sites are not driven by science, they're driven by the way the law was written. All they do is pit experts against experts." Dr. Mielke conducted several studies on lead-soil concentrations in other American cities, concluding that "proximity to a high-traffic route is a better predictor of soil-lead concentrations" than is any other factor.[27]

In a pointed memo to the city government's head of environmental affairs Jerald White, Mielke pled for reason to prevail.[28] "Major cities of the world have done this [siting communities on waste materials] to discard waste and then expand their land areas for developing new communities. New Orleans has several such sites. It is unfortunate and misleading that one such community has been singled out as hazardous." Mielke pointed out the danger of the solution the residents were so desperately seeking: "Relocation of the residents of the Agriculture Street Superfund site may in fact move them to more hazardous, not less hazardous locations. Relocating the children to other parts of the city may increase, not decrease their exposure to lead."[29]

Mielke said that he made maps available to Pat Bryant of the Gulf Coast Tenants Organization when Bryant originally looked at the site, and that he told Bryant that Agriculture Street was not a good community to include as a Superfund site. Mielke asserted that Bryant and others were "looking for a place to put EJ [environmental justice] on the front burner, and used Ag Street" to do so.[30] "I can't understand why EPA ever put Ag Street on Superfund. Politics drove everything."[31]

Also skeptical was Louisiana State University toxicologist Luann White, who went even further than Meilke in her statements of the politics of sampling: "Studying these people is doing nothing more than harassing them. We're not finding the Agriculture Street Landfill to be any different than any other part of the city. And the city is comparable to what we have found nationwide."[32]

On the other side, the distrust is such that some Agriculture Street residents fear that ATSDR and EPA are using the community as a unique opportunity to study the effects of a combination of chemicals on residents living on top of a Superfund site, a view that might strike outsiders as absurdly paranoid. "It takes 5 years to study the site, that's why they're leaving us on the site."[33] On EPA's cleanup plan, one resident said, "We are like lab rats, they're experimenting on us." The view seems less farfetched in light of the Tuskegee studies using black men as the unknowing subjects of research on the effects of untreated syphilis, to which some residents occasionally compare themselves.

TRAPPED IN THE AMERICAN DREAM[34]

While scientists debate the risks they fear, many Agriculture Street residents are terrified for their lives. They feel trapped in the homes they thought would bring them security and control over their finances by freeing them from being locked into rental apartments. As is common around the United States in contaminated communities, the studies conducted by health professionals at Agriculture Street failed to examine the role stress is playing in increasing the residents' misery. They are in a situation that virtually anyone would find intolerable, having to cope with several recurring emotions: uncertainty mixed with fear, the stigma of living on a dump, and the feeling of being trapped. This suggests that government agencies like the EPA, DEQ, OPH, and ATSDR must begin to examine stress in these communities to plan solutions to their problems.

This section gives space for the residents to express in their own terms what it's like to live in these conditions. It begins with a subtle terror, trying to perceive and understand toxic chemicals, which they know are invisible, sometimes odorless, and yet which they know lie under their feet all day and under their beds all night. The fear turns to anger as connections seem obvious between the exposures and what they believe are unusually frequent illnesses in their neighborhood and the lack of official response. What follows are excerpts from testimony where residents make these connections.

"I can't find what's making that smell. We don't have a trap in the sink and tub to catch the fumes, they come straight up the sink."

"You hear the dripping, see the dust. I can't ever seem to get this house clean."

"You've cleaned your house, you've mopped it clean and it still has this smell. I can't prove it, can't call people in the middle of the night about it or they'll think I'm crazy."

"Mentally you feel like you want to scream, become violent, you're angry."

"I am angry because I'm really sick."

"I have good days and bad days, with chest pains and high blood pressure."

"I've had several miscarriages, it's been very stressful."

"I take Zantac 150 three times a day for my ulcer. I can't sleep so I take a narcotic. The over-the-counter stuff doesn't work anymore, I need the prescription stuff now."

"I have ulcers, back spasms, heart palpitations."

"I feel like a zombie."

"You're spinning your wheels."

"I'm forty, I want to have a family, but my husband doesn't want to bring a child into this."

"It's this constant depressing thing, everything I do reflects back to where I live."

"It hurts."

With the fear of contamination has come a stigma; residents feel that they are damaged goods or were not worth much in the first place. Their neighborhood feels like a no-man's-land where others are afraid to go.

"It totally changed my life. Things that were important, I don't give a lot of shit about anymore. I don't feel good about myself being in this house anymore."

"You don't invite people in this neighborhood anymore."

"My daughter's friends' parents don't let their kids sleep over here."

"Holidays, I would not invite anyone to my home. I paid for my mother-in-law to stay in a hotel."

"We used to have family gatherings, parties for our nieces and nephews out in the backyard, that's gone now. No activities in the yard besides cutting grass."

"When people come to my house people say 'it looks like you're moving.' I've been here 18 years, but I'm ready to move at a moment's notice."

And regardless of the reality of the toxins or even of the stress, Superfund designation has rendered the Gordon Plaza subdivision homes "virtually worthless." EPA sources also admit to the financial devastation caused by Superfund designation at the site. One informed EPA source was reported in the Superfund Report as asserting that the community has been "'redlined' by the financial and real estate industry." Redlining refers to the practice of many banks to not lend in minority neighborhoods.[35] Residents feel, simply, trapped. They described the feeling of being trapped in one's own home this way:

"You need equity from this home to buy another, but you can't even rent elsewhere with this note to pay."

"I'm not putting money back into this house. The banks won't lend to us when they find out what area we're in."

"One man tried to take out a second mortgage on his house to buy a car. They only lent him $5,000. You can't even trade your house for a vehicle."

"Four people just walked away from their homes and mortgages after paying for 15 years."

"We're in prison."

"I wish I could walk away."

"I just want to live in a clean neighborhood."

"We just want to have a choice."

"To not live under restrictions."

"I want a similar home in a safe neighborhood."

"I just get so mad, baby, so mad. We live in America, we should not have to live this way."

"We aren't asking for punitive damages, just relocation expenses and home equity."

"Just don't give me another 30-year mortgage. Fifteen years would be fine."

"At our age, you're either going to move to your dream house, or you're going to fix up the one you're in."

"It's not the greatest neighborhood here and it's not the worst."

"I don't want to start over, but given the circumstances, I'm already packed up."

"You feel frozen, life is just a routine, you just exist."

"I feel trapped. Johnny Jackson doesn't want to break up the neighborhood. We're under his control."

"Even animals know when to run away from danger, but we can't run away."

"They [EPA, politicians, toxic polluters] don't have any respect for a human life, especially us, because we are black."[36]

A clear pattern of psychological and social effects is emerging from sites around the United States where hazardous facilities are located. Regardless of the level of direct effects of chemical exposures on their bodies, neighbors who fear the health effects of the plants on themselves and their children exhibit a series of stress-related physical and mental health disorders.

The pattern of hidden effects holds both at the individual and community levels. Sociologist Kai Erikson studied dozens of such cases and reported that "people in general find accidents involving toxins a good deal more threatening than both natural hazards of even the most dangerous kind and mechanical mishaps of considerable destructive power."[37] He identified a syndrome of trauma in individuals who fear toxins, whose initial symptoms include feelings of depression, helplessness, restlessness and agitation. Erikson likened the work of environmental sociologists studying these cases to that of clinical doctors – we are describing a disorder with symptoms that are not only at the level of the individual but also at the level of the community itself.

W. I. Thomas is often quoted in textbooks for having stated a profoundly basic law of human social behavior: that "situations defined as real become real in their consequences."[38] Another way to say this is that if people believe something is real, it might as well be real. The stressed condition of people fearing for their lives because of believed toxic exposures, therefore, has indirect but very real health effects. In research at Three Mile Island, for example, psychologists India Fleming and Andrew Baum discovered that people who feared exposures to radiation had higher blood pressure and "fight-or-flight" blood hormone levels (epinepherine) even seven years after the initial contamination scare.[39] These conditions can cause higher levels of heart and respiratory problems in people with elevated levels of stress. The immune system is directly connected to the condition of the brain, which emits the hormones, directing the body to be calm or to assume the fight-or-flight state of red alert. The health problems come from the alert never being turned off.

At the same time, Erikson reports that the trauma often "damages the texture of community."[40] As seen in the previous cases, sometimes individuals are pitted one against another as some expect benefits while others fear for its damages. As we have already seen and will discuss in Chapter 7, expected *benefits and risks* differ in important ways between different social groups. The ability to *control* the technology that causes the hazards also varies by social group, especially by race and gender. To study this, psychologist Paul Slovic and his colleagues asked people around the country how much they were worried about different types of hazards. He found that white males were the most unusual group, differing from women and minorities in far more strongly denying the dangers of technological risks.[41] This explains how "contaminated communities" can be "corrosive communities" along lines of race and gender: the men "minimize" the risks, whereas the women and minority populations refuse to trust the authorities who promise their protection. In the case of Agriculture Street, much of the division was along age and income lines, as we discuss later.

The pattern of toxic fears causing stress-related illness is not race- or class-specific, but it applies to people of all types who fear exposures in their homes or workplaces. However, the dimension of race is a critical one since African Americans in Louisiana (and the United States) face chemical hazards that are out of their control at a much higher rate than do white Americans. The January 1998 EPA draft demographic analysis prepared for the Shintech case (see Chapter 4) revealed that African Americans are more likely than non–African Americans in Louisiana to live near Toxic Release Inventory facilities .[42] And the effects of stress are real, regardless of the uncertain science of the risk analyzers.

ENTER THE LAWYERS

Faced with unsatisfying responses from government officials after a decade of pleas, some residents believed that only lawsuits could relocate them from atop the dump at Agriculture Street. For years the community had difficulty getting public interest lawyers to take up their case, and the private lawyers they found have been interested only in class-action lawsuits against the City of New Orleans, the Orleans Parish School Board, HANO, site developers, and the other parties involved in the construction of Press Park and Gordon Plaza. At the beginning, different lawyers came in and signed up different members of the community to different lawsuits with different terms and plans. The main suit still ongoing asserts that the City of New Orleans et al. caused the injuries and health problems of residents through "the pursuit of an abnormally dangerous activity" by operating the Agriculture Street Landfill from 1910 to 1965. Years later, the lawsuit remains under consideration by Seventh District Court Judge Nadine Ramsey.[43] There is virtually no movement on the suit because there is little chance of success and not much chance that even in winning the plaintiffs would be able to collect any penalty.

Without a guarantee of getting paid, even on a contingency basis, lawyers have not pushed the case. Many feel that the city is the sole responsible party for liability at Agriculture Street. According to Superfund law, the city's status as a responsible party means that, as owner of the landfill, it is responsible for the cost of cleaning up the site. Yet, the City of New Orleans, among the very poorest in the country, is broke. Recognizing this, EPA's director for Superfund reported in 1999 that "We have not exercised any enforcement actions against the city at this time, and have not yet made a decision on whether we will."[44] When EPA suggested that the City of New Orleans pay for the relocation of Agriculture Street, Mayor Marc Morial said, "For them to suggest that a city where one-third of its people live in poverty ought to bear a burden that the federal government ought to bear is just another example of their insensitivity. We think EPA's Superfund program ought to buy these people out like they've done in other cities."

Claiming a lack of funds available for the relocation of Agriculture

Street residents, Mayor Morial never signed the EPA Record of Decision (ROD). In signing the ROD, the Mayor would be admitting that the City of New Orleans is the official Possible Responsible Party. The City fears that if it admits responsibility for Ag Street, the EPA will force it to pay cleanup costs. However, according to Lois Gibbs, the EPA has never historically sued a Possible Responsible Party who cannot pay, making it unlikely that the City of New Orleans would be the first.[45] And still, the differences between the actual cleanup taking place at Agriculture Street and the remedies prescribed by the ROD are minimal. Because there is no signed ROD, the EPA activities must be classified as an "emergency removal," rather than an actual "cleanup," under Superfund law.

Residents of Agriculture Street have attempted several legal strategies in addition to their community activism. The Concerned Citizens of Agriculture Street Landfill (CCASL) filed a temporary restraining order against the EPA on January 15, 1998, to halt EPA cleanup activities set to begin in the community in October of that year. A U.S. District Court judge granted the restraining order and set a hearing for February 19, 1998. At that hearing, the judge heard arguments on EPA's motion to dismiss the restraining order, which was subsequently granted. This allowed the EPA to begin work on a cleanup that the homeowners' group CCASL didn't want.

A CLEANUP NOBODY WANTED

As already mentioned, the levels of contaminants at Agriculture Street registered high enough for the EPA to add the site to the National Priorities List of its Superfund Sites list in 1994. Agriculture Street received a hazard ranking score of 50; a score of only 28 is required to be placed on the Superfund list.[46] Local activists sought to get the site moved up to allow them to be relocated off the site, as had occurred at seventeen other Superfund sites. Even though relocation was the neighbors' ardent demand at Agriculture Street, the reality at EPA is that under Superfund the agency only has money for cleanups, not for relocation.

How different are the seventeen relocations completed by the EPA under Superfund and Agriculture Street? The EPA has relocated only one African-American community out of seventeen relocations under Superfund. The one that was relocated was in Pensacola, Florida, where a wood treating facility left an enormous heap of contaminated soil, known locally as "Mt. Dioxin."[47] There an activist community group pushed the EPA, which chose this site as its National Relocation Evaluation Pilot site.[48] The citizens' group there won partly by creating media pressure: the group purchased a full-page ad in the Florida edition of USA Today, addressed to President Clinton during his 1996 reelection campaign. The ad brought some national attention.

But EPA feared setting a precedent at Pensacola under which other communities would demand relocation.[49] EPA's project manager for Agriculture Street, Ursula Lennox, said "One thing we have to be careful of when we compare the records of decision is that we can almost feel there's a correlation between the two, but if memory serves me correctly, the difference between the two is in the contaminants." Residents at Agriculture Street argued that the EPA's own analyses showed both "contain lead, volatile organic compounds and polyaromatic hydrocarbons."[50] EPA spokesman David Bary responded that "All we can tell you is each site is evaluated individually. It's not possible to compare one set of RODs to another because each site is unique. The uniqueness of each site is what makes them different."[51]

Relocation requires a special emergency appropriations bill from the U.S. Congress. Congressperson William Jefferson from New Orleans has put up these appropriations bills, but never have they moved through the legislative process. In 1996, he and the Louisiana delegation worked to encourage the EPA to consider relocation of Agriculture Street through legislative action. An EPA appropriations bill passed in June 1996 encouraged the agency to relocate the community, but the appropriations bill's language was "non-binding" and failed to provide "actual authority to relocate the citizens."[52] The next year, a Senate/House Conference Committee issued report language on October 6, 1997, urging the EPA to "stay the remediation of the site . . . until this matter can be satisfactorily resolved."[53]

Another year later, on September 30, 1998, a letter from Senators Mary Landrieu and John Breaux to Barbara Mikulski, the ranking member of the Senate Subcommittee on Veterans Affairs, Housing and Urban Development, and Independent Agencies, asked for an appropriation of $11.9 million in fiscal year 1999 for congressional buyout of the community. The letter called Agriculture Street one of their "top priorities."[54] Jefferson attempted to add language to the House Appropriations Bill that would relocate the residents again in a letter to the Chair of the House Appropriations Committee in late April 1999.

This attempt, however, constituted the third time Jefferson tried to add language that would fund relocation of the community. The letter claimed that Agriculture Street was the only community in the United States living atop a Superfund site. Although Jefferson's request for relocation funds was welcomed, residents were correct in fearing that this attempt would have the same results as the first two: no relocation for the community.

The EPA did not, however, believe that Agriculture Street was dangerous enough to warrant relocation, and instead opted to remove two feet of contaminated soil from residents' yards, replacing it with a "geotextile" (a fine porous plastic mesh) barrier and two feet of "clean" soil, at a cost of approximately $20 million. With the two-foot barrier created by the EPA cleanup plan, all trees in the neighborhood were removed and residents were told which trees they could plant. The plans also restrict residents from making additions to their homes and from building in-ground swimming pools.[55]

Despite residents' protests and opposition from the City of New Orleans, the EPA began cleanup of the site in late 1998, starting with the undeveloped portion of the land surrounding the site and the Gordon Plaza Elderly Apartments, owned by the DCHC. When EPA finished cleanup of those areas in March 1999, they sought permission from HANO and HUD, who owned 124 of the Press Park public housing units. On March 5, 1999, HANO and HUD granted that permission to the EPA. The City of New Orleans then filed an injunction against the cleanup, but it was denied. EPA began excavation of the Press Park properties on April 29, 1999, and completed work in September.[56] EPA then sent "last chance" letters to owners of the single-family houses in Gordon Plaza, and one by one, many have accepted the cleanup. In this way, the EPA successfully divided the neighborhood and conquered it piece by piece.

Critics said that a major problem with this cleanup plan was the likely possibility that the "clean" soil will be recontaminated by surrounding "dirty" soil due to the low elevation of the site and its high water table, making the area extremely flood prone.[57] Cleanup efforts increased the danger of broken water lines and sewerage problems in the neighborhood, a serious concern of the neighbors who feared the toxics of the dump would seep into their drinking water. On January 29, 1999, a broken water main in Gordon Plaza caused a large portion of the street above it to cave in.[58] Several other water main breaks brought frothing brown water to the surface of the neighborhood streets, building fears among neighbors about the chemicals on which they stood.

During the cleanup actions, residents endured other inconveniences, and feared increased exposure to toxins due to the EPA's digging efforts. Dust covered everything in the neighborhood, from residents' cars to their dishes. The community experienced rodent problems due to the disruption of the decaying landfill beneath the community. Residents fear that the cleanup will not restore the values of their homes, which have been rendered virtually worthless since the fateful Superfund designation in 1994. Residents claim that the cleanup is inadequate in that it leaves residents with a huge liability: if a buyer of the homes (post-cleanup) became sick, previous homeowners could be held liable. Peggy GrandPre said, "We own a piece of liability, that's all we own."[59] She added, "We live on a landfill now, and we will live on a landfill $20 million later."[60]

EPA's Timothy Fields responded in a letter to GrandPre that "EPA does not believe that the removal action has compromised the health and safety of the families living at the site. Besides addressing the contamination, the removal action has provided the benefit of additional jobs to the community."[61]

Agriculture Street residents charge that rather than reviewing its decision on the subject of relocation, Timothy Fields and the EPA instead have issued "the third and biggest blow" against the community. Community leader Peggy GrandPre shot back a letter to Fields and the EPA, explaining that third blow came in the form of false hope. "You held a meeting with us in Washington, D.C., listened to our cries and gave the community hope. Now you send this letter only to justify your position and put us back in the same place. No action, just positive WORDS."[62]

IS THERE NO ESCAPE? LESSONS LEARNED
AND LASTING LEGACIES

"There always is a way out," said a philosopher. And the people of Gordon Plaza didn't give up, even as the EPA was pushing on them a $22 million cleanup they didn't want. They turned to free-market solutions, "brownfield initiatives," private buyouts, or anything else that could solve their problem.

In late October 1998, a private developer named Richard Blackmore, president of a Mississippi-based company known as Environmental Remediation Technology, Inc., offered to buy the Gordon Plaza homes for $59,000 to $62,000 each. Blackmore planned to "resell the homes at a profit after EPA removes and replaces 2-feet of topsoil contaminated with toxic chemicals and metals." It soon came out that Blackmore had been convicted of bank fraud just one week prior to offering to buy the Agriculture Street homes, and the deal fell through.[63]

"The onus is now on the Louisiana congressional delegation to take the lead in negotiating the buyout," said Mayor Morial in a statement to the New Orleans Times-Picayune.[64] Brow-beating the state's representatives in Washington didn't work. Meanwhile the city's own future landuse plan, released in 1999, suggested that the Agriculture Street site might be used for light industry, rather than as a residential area.[65] The new purchasers of this "brownfield" would be given a "comfort letter" from the city and EPA, protecting them from legal liability from lawsuits involving contamination in the future.[66] This effort is still in the planning stages and its future entirely uncertain. No purchaser has stepped forward to buy out the Gordon Plaza homeowners.

The maddening, alienating and surreal case of the Agriculture Street Landfill has pitted residents against a fragmented government that wouldn't respond. A city councilperson had a financial stake in the group that developed their neighborhood and, so, stonewalled their attempts to be relocated. The city claimed to be too poor to resolve the problem, but helped the residents by refusing to participate with the EPA in its attempts to undertake a cleanup many residents believed was absurdly inadequate. The EPA in turn fought HUD and other federal agencies to avoid paying for a relocation. The state government did almost nothing at all.

For the residents, months and years go by waiting for the results of health studies and soil tests; then, many prove inconclusive. The bulldozers and men in toxic waste suits finally come and tear up their yards and streets. With broken sewers and stirred up dust, the residents fear worse contamination. Finally the "cleanup" workers leave. In the end, the sadly absurd but fascinating case of Agriculture Street reflects the dysfunctions of our society's simultaneous denial of and obsession with racism, toxics, and psychological damage from worry, all of which boil to the surface again and again like poorly landfilled trash.

So the residents of Gordon Plaza and their supporters in the environmental justice movement seem to have mustered enough political momentum to get their neighborhood listed as a federal Superfund site, but they are still unable to get the relocation they so desperately sought. Why? Perhaps like Grand Bois, they initially turned to a private class-action lawsuit. However, there were no apparent "deep pockets" of a private corporation for the lawyers to target. There was territoriality between lawyers fighting over clients and bickering by residents divided by income and political ties. This was a poor way to start a movement: a lot of the effort in the neighborhood over the past decade has been spent in just keeping some unity and focus to move the protests forward. Although there was racial homogeneity, having three different sets of residents – low-income renters, middle-income homeowners, and retired people in an assisted-living facility – made the neighborhood nearly impossible to unify in its demands and strategy. The old people feared the change of moving out of their decent facility. Many low-income people were pleased to receive the new landscaping that came with the EPA cleanup. Having a group of people in the neighborhood (DCHC) who were against their relocation drive for apparently economic and political reasons proved a constant leg-iron for the protesting homeowners.

Some of these problems explain the difficulty the CCASL encountered in dealing with important outside supporters, politicians, and the EPA. There was some important help for the neighborhood from civil rights legal groups, environmentalists, and universities. But the support was not like that in the Shintech case. Some environmentalists and civil rights leaders said the neighborhood was "difficult to work with," "a black hole." There was important help from Greenpeace and some local press coverage, but their trips to Washington and Geneva were largely ignored by the national media. However, this doesn't explain it all. Different branches of government failed to agree on what should be done and who should pay. Each repeatedly ducked responsibility. In the end, the sense of frustration for the residents in dealing with the EPA was complete. "If you're talking about the head, they're talking about the tail. If you're talking about the tail, they're talking about the foot," said Elodia Blanco, the mother with whom this chapter began.[67] And some EPA workers expressed their own frustration at not being able to give the people what they wanted.

In spite of all the disadvantages this neighborhood faced, activists still applied tremendous pressure on the EPA and came tauntingly close to gaining relocation. One is led to wonder if Elodia Blanco was correct, that if their neighborhood was whiter and more influential, they would have gotten moved. The feeling is supported by the EPA's record on relocations. The Congressional delegation from Louisiana needed to flex some muscle in Washington, D.C., to get the appropriation, but they did not exert enough.

So those who were trapped remain so. The feelings have dangerous psychological effects, such as fatalism, anxiety, depression, alienation, and low self-esteem. Peggy GrandPre, president of the Concerned Citizens of Agriculture Street Landfill, explained a conversation she had with Ursula Lennox, site coordinator for EPA Region VI during an April 28, 1999, meeting of the CCASL. The topic of conversation between the two women centered around flowers that would be planted in the Agriculture Street neighborhood following EPA's cleanup. In discussing the proposed flowers, GrandPre said with exasperation, "What kind of plants are you gonna plant on a graveyard?"

7

The Empire Strikes Back

BACKLASH AND
IMPLICATIONS FOR
THE FUTURE

Earthjustice lawyer Monique Harden outside Shintech/LES solidarity rally in 1998.
[Photo by Timmons Roberts]

Given the extreme dominance of the oil and chemical industry with the state and federal governments, the ability of these four communities to gain any redress is fairly remarkable. Although not uniformly positive, the outcomes of the four cases detailed here show substantial gains for the environmental justice community in the 1990s. Others could be cited, such as the incinerators in Chester, Pennsylvania, or the refineries in South Los Angeles, but these Louisiana battles were among the most important cases in the nation for the period.

Having been surprised once, industry did not sit idly by. They fought back in several ways against the potential of environmental justice claims to create uncertainty in their planning. This backlash sought to change the game, making future struggles more difficult for communities. In this way, the Shintech struggle, especially, was like the Cuban Revolution: all later struggles will have to deal with its legacy – hardened positions on each side.

This chapter chronicles the backlash against environmental justice victories on the national and local levels in its first two sections. At its end, we survey the prospects for both sides and consider the future implications of the movement. There, we return to the three themes posed at the outset of the book. What is environmental justice? Who are they players, and what tools do they use to get their way? How do people experience environmental injustice? The first theme, what is environmental justice, has been addressed in each case study. Each group of residents fighting in the name of environmental justice has defined the concept in a way specific to them and their situation. In this chapter, we will see how the actors of the growth machine define the term or, at least, attempt to push policy and regulations to adopt their definition and way of handling it. One of the main points of this chapter is to emphasize that these struggles do not take place only at the local level; some of the most influential struggles do, in fact, occur at the state and national levels. Finally, we end the chapter by assessing the experience of individual residents in these battles and their role in the movement. There is a lot to sort out in these coming pages.

BACKLASH AT THE NATIONAL LEVEL: THE BATTLE OVER EPA'S
INTERIM GUIDELINES

Before it was issued and immediately thereafter, industry groups have been pressuring against President Clinton's 1994 Executive Order on environmental justice (see Chapter 1). They have claimed that the order, and especially EPA's February 1998 *Interim Guidelines* to institute the order, could hinder efforts to bring economic development to the very communities which the government was trying to help with programs such as enterprise and empowerment zones. U.S. Chamber of Commerce president, Thomas J. Donahue, claimed that the guidelines would have "significant adverse impact on economic growth and job opportunities in low-income and minority communities."[1] Ironically, in a speech on Earth Day 1998, Donahue claimed that the policy would "drive existing good-paying jobs out of those areas . . . this is not justice – it's economic, social and environmental insanity." Pointedly reminding him that he represented three million businesses, Donahue repeated these exact words in an open letter to President Clinton in the following weeks.[2]

The president of the Louisiana Association of Business and Industry (LABI), Louisiana's leading business lobby, editorialized that the *Guidelines* were the product of a misguided movement: "Environmental justice is largely the creation of activists who turned to civil rights when environmental doom-saying no longer yielded results."[3] To support their position, the U.S. Chamber enlisted African-American leaders from the business community and local government – the growth coalition we described in Chapter 1. They found Detroit mayor Dennis Archer and the president of the National Black Chamber of Commerce (NBCC) Harry Alford as important allies in the battle. Alford wrote for the NBCC:

Environmental racism is a claim that has been lingering around since the late '70's. As a strategy, Green Peace [sic], the Sierra Club and others have decided to fuel (fund) the concept and enlist newly recruited activists. These activists are quickly indoctrinated into thinking that this is a continuation of the successful Civil Rights Movement. The truth is it is a poor fake. . . . The recruited people scream and embellish their own resumes and their credentials do not

correlate to their alleged specialties. What we have, from my experience debating these "activists," are some "half-cocked nut cases" who cannot hold a
logical argument. . . . Their style is strictly to intimidate and disrupt.

Having laid waste environmental justice advocates, Alford went on to
blast Clinton and the EPA secretary Carol Browner:

The Clinton Administration has given these extremists and opportunists some
license via the official Environmental Justice Initiative. What the President
and EPA Administrator Browner have created is a "monster." These activists
don't fully appreciate the EPA although they gladly receive their grants. They
want nothing short of shutting down all business activity.[4]

Critiquing Detroit mayor Dennis Archer when he made a similar
point, Robert Bullard refuted the idea that the *Guidelines* would have
any impact on development in poor neighborhoods, which are the focus of empowerment and enterprise zone incentives for businesses.
"Archer is wrong because there are no Title VI complaints on brownfields [urban redevelopment of potentially contaminated sites] of all
the fifty-one which have been filed."[5] Facing critiques of business and
state regulators before the Oversight Subcommittee of the U.S. House
of Representatives just a week later, EPA's director of its Office of Civil
Rights Ann Goode made the same point in her testimony.[6]

Industry lobbyists and chief executives made their dissatisfaction
known. First, EPA was directly lobbied by industry through high-level
business organizations addressing the agency and its top administrator directly. Detailed comments were filed by industry group lawyers
with the EPA.[7] In them, the lawyers argued that EPA lacked the authority under the law to force states to undertake these new policies.[8]
State environmental officials perceived EPA's *Guidelines* as a heavy-
handed way of usurping their local authority: "It appears to be really
aimed at influencing, if not intimidating, the state permitting agencies," said Donald Welch from Pennsylvania's environment agency.[9] In
testimony before Congress, Robert E. Roberts, the executive director
of the Environmental Council of the States (ECOS),[10] pointed out
that states do three quarters of all enforcement on the environment:
"With all due respect of my friends in the Environmental Protection
Agency, and I am pleased to have many friends in that agency, environmental protection in America is done by States and local governments."[11] Roberts and his colleagues wrote that the entire conflict
over environmental justice had become "less about environmental pro-

tection and civil rights than it is about federal mandates, the rights of State and local governments to govern, and determining who is to decide environmental issues."[12] The issue, from their view, was a new battle over federalism, in essence, over "states' rights."

The battle riled the lower levels of governments, in a way that some saw as quite similar to civil rights intrusions of Bobby Kennedy and other Northerners in the 1960s.[13] The U.S. Conference of Mayors adopted a resolution late in June resisting the shift of "permit decision-making from local governments to the federal government."[14] The National Association of Counties sent a letter to EPA "strongly opposed" to the new *Interim Guidelines*. "Local governments cannot prevent residents from living in commercial or industrial areas or near an environmental facility, and invariably there are conflicts over mixed uses of property. These issues are properly issues of local concern, and should be dealt with locally."[15] They had concrete fears in mind: "a real possibility exists that nearly every new or expanded county landfill proposed to be located in an industrialized or rural area with a minority population will be subject to an additional set of citizen challenges and more litigation." They concluded by appealing to fairness. "It is patently unfair for EPA to ask local governments to solve the nation's long-standing difficulties in achieving racial equality through the permit process." The letter was penned by Joel McTopy, council member of St. John the Baptist Parish, which adjoins St. James, where Shintech proposed to build. But Robert Bullard pointed out, this issue was just like earlier rounds of the civil rights struggle: states claimed their sovereign rights were being trampled when the heavy-handed federal government rides into town. He argued, "The states just have to deal with it!"[16] Florence Robinson put it this way: "They said the same thing in the civil rights movement. 'Our darkies are happy. Why are they coming in, stirring things up?'"[17]

Second, when the next Environmental Justice Title VI case came up for a decision in front of the EPA, industries used it to beat back the LES precedent and EPA's attempt to handle the Shintech case. A company named Select Steel proposed to build a steel recycling mini-mill in Genesee Township, a poor minority community in Michigan. When Title VI environmental justice claims were made by Father Phil Schmitter and Sister Joanne Chiaverini of the St. Francis Prayer Center, EPA began to study the case.[18] The Select Steel Corporation presented EPA with an ultimatum, that if they were not given their permits in 90 days, they would move elsewhere. Under pressure, EPA hurried them through. EPA ruled in favor of Select Steel, saying that, if they were meeting legal limits on emissions and in compliance with the national ambient air standards (NAAS), they could not interfere with permitting.[19] This was a major step backward from the Shintech case, where "disproportionate impact" was considered regardless of whether the permitted discharges were within the letter of the law for single facilities. Select Steel decided to build in Ohio instead, but the specter of Shintech-style permitting analyses was apparently beaten back.

The legacies of Select Steel remain uncertain. "Ann Goode had to show that EPA was not 'anti-business,'" said Eunice Sullivan from Michigan's Sugar Law Center for Economic and Social Justice, about the Select Steel decision.[20] She argued that EPA chose Select Steel because it was a weak case with few lawyers involved. In terms of the outcome, the community group lost because they were not well prepared for that fight: "the difference is who got organized."

To beat back the *Interim Guidelines* more globally, however, another approach was required. Industry brought out its big guns in lining up influential congressional committee chairs to threaten the agency's blood supply – its congressional appropriation. Congressional Republicans placed into the massive VA-HUD Appropriations Bill in 1998 a one-year moratorium on the EPA's using any of its funds "to implement or administer the interim guidance" for Title VI complaints filed after October 21, 1998.[21] The moratorium was extended for another year in 1999. Proclaiming their victory upon its passage, William Kovacs, vice president for environmental policy of the U.S. Chamber of Commerce, said, "These appropriations provisions are central to our efforts to stop the worst excesses of the environmental movement. . . . This will block the worst kind of environmental lunacy masquerading as civil rights."[22]

Meanwhile, some environmental justice advocates argued that the *Guidelines* did not go *far enough*. For example, Luke Cole of the Center on Race, Poverty and the Environment said that minorities in polluted neighborhoods could be experiencing discrimination not only in terms of exposure to pollutants, but also by changes in land values, the stigma of living near toxins, and a lowered quality of life.[23] Shintech and Chester, Pennsylvania, were the two cases repeatedly cited by both sides in the debate over the *Guidelines*, but these broader criteria had never been used in Title VI hearings. Several of the cases we have studied (including the Agriculture Street landfill in New Orleans), and much of the environmental sociology literature, suggest that, in fact, this broader approach is necessary to redress the problems of toxic communities.

Seeing the handwriting on the wall, the EPA sought to bring legitimacy to its effort to clarify the *Interim Guidelines* by establishing a twenty-five-member committee to revise them. The committee included eight representatives from nongovernmental organizations (NGOs) and eight from state and local governments, five academics and four industry representatives.[24] If Logan and Molotch were correct that local governments tend to side with the businesses that fund their campaigns and pay their taxes, then the committee is weighted heavily for the growth coalition. If academics on the committee – such as environmental justice scholar-activist Robert Bullard of Clark Atlanta University – side with environmental activists in the NGOs, then the panel is almost exactly split down the middle with twelve or thirteen votes for each side. This split was confirmed by the committee's own statement after a series of long tough meetings that "Environmental justice advocates, including grassroots community representatives, and Committee members from the academy, are somewhat more satisfied with the *Interim Guidelines* than their industry and government colleagues."[25]

The group was planning to publish a revised version of the guidelines for comment in 1999; however, the process has been extremely contested.[26] The committee was forced to redefine its mission after it became clear that "the diverse constituencies represented by the Committee [were] unable to reach consensus on the most important of these issues." Instead, the committee decided to defer to EPA and present a report of diverging opinions and a structure for future decision making.[27]

Industry's bold opposition to the *Guidelines* placed the Clinton Administration in a delicate political situation.[28] State environmental agency heads from around the country met in New Orleans in March 1998 and drafted a blistering resolution to the EPA to annul the *Guidelines*.[29] In speaking on the same Earth Day as U.S. Chamber president Donahue, then–Vice President Al Gore said that federal agencies needed to reemphasize the administration's policy on environmental justice. "There have been strong expressions of concern from community leaders that our efforts to date have not been sufficient."[30] In this case, doing not enough was still doing too much.

After two years of intense pressure, committee meetings and internal machinations at EPA, the *Draft Revised Guidance for Investigating Title VI Administrative Complaints Challenging Permits* was finally released on June 16, 2000. The *Revised Guidance* ties civil rights violations to "an unjustified adverse disparate impact" on "a group of persons based on race, color, or national origin" (p. 9). This impact would have to be "sufficiently adverse to be considered significant" (p. 15). Much hinges upon that word: it would be up to the state environmental agencies like DEQ to decide what counts as a *significant* disparate impact. The *Revised Guidance* sets the bar very high: demographic disparity – that is, how many more African Americans would be affected by the pollutants than would be if the facility were sited in an "average" location – would have to be highly significant statistically: two to three standard deviations away from the mean (p. 19). Only the very worst cases would count under these criteria.

With a sixty-day public comment period, the *Revised Guidance* sought to walk the political tightrope between angered communities, industries, and state and local governments. The *Revised Guidance* included sections for those making complaints, a section suggesting ways for the states to run their environmental justice programs, and a long series of responses directly to the protests of the three angry parties. In these responses, EPA confronted industry by defending its constitutional right to enforce Title VI. It directed states that they have to do *something* to address these complaints. But it does so in a way that gives tremendous flexibility to state regulators. The language is vague, and not directive, with phrases such as "EPA believes you may wish to consider. . . . You are not required to adopt such activities or approaches."[31] The agency went on to warn states that their responses to complaints will determine how EPA rules on their efforts. After a tremendously lengthy process, EPA could eventually pull their federal funding and revoke their "delegated authority" to enforce environmental laws.

The *Revised Guidance* pushed *informal resolution* of environmental justice disputes, including "emission offsets," such as we saw with Dow reducing emissions to match Shintech's new pollutants in Plaquemine. EPA administrator Carol Browner repeatedly suggested informal resolution in statements to industry and the press before the *Revised Guidance* was released, suggesting that it is better for all sides in these disputes. Among the informal solutions are "emissions caps for areas of concern" (which have yet to be applied anywhere but which have been suggested for places like Louisiana's "Cancer Alley") and improved emergency response measures, a persistent demand of local groups (p. 22).

Nowhere in the *Revised Guidance* was the issue of broader effects of contamination, such as stigma, property values, and stress addressed. This suggests that the demands of community groups for the EPA and state agencies to deal with these issues has been entirely ignored.

Back in Louisiana, in a sneak attack at the very end of the fiscal-only state legislative session in late May 1998, state representative N. J. Damico introduced a "concurrent resolution," HCR 94, which called on the state to block any further environmental justice efforts. The resolution noted the Shintech case and blasted EPA for moving ahead on environmental justice issues. A similar resolution was passed earlier in the year by state environmental agency heads (ECOS) calling on the EPA to waive the *Interim Guidelines*. Louisiana's Department of Environmental Quality secretary Dale Givens testified for the resolution, believing the *Guidelines* were developed improperly, "without participation by co-regulators and the public."[32] The Louisiana resolution requested that the state's congressional delegation "take appropriate steps in Congress to declare that these 'Interim Guidance' standards [were unconstitutional, and] should be formally withdrawn by the EPA." It passed out of the House Environment Committee, the vote was called while two vocally opposed black committee members (Kip Holden and Avery Alexander) were out of the room.[33] It then was passed on the House floor 67 to 27, but representatives from eight predominantly black districts in the state had their districts "exempted from any sentiments in the resolution."[34]

This seemingly arcane parliamentary procedure was important because, when it got to the other side of the capitol building, the Senate Environment Committee passed the resolution and with a motion by Senator Max Malone, stripped off the House amendments exempting the eight minority districts. This action was considered dirty pool in the etiquette of the legislature, and after lobbying by LEAN, Sierra Club, the League of Women Voters, and Citizens For A Clean Environment (CFACE), the resolution was left to die on the Senate calendar without ever being voted.[35] This was one of only three legislative losses listed by business lobby LABI on their list of twenty-four bills on which they lobbied in the 1998 session.[36] Still, the EPA had been vilified in Baton Rouge and the effort had succeeded in educating lawmakers and galvanizing the business community on the perils of environmental justice and especially the *Interim Guidelines*.

Just three days later, citizens from Forest Grove and Center Springs (see Chapter 3) boarded a bus and traveled the five hours to get to the Pilgrims Baptist Church in Convent, to have a joint celebration of their victories with Shintech opponents. Citizens Against Nuclear Trash stood in the church's all-purpose room and told their story to the embattled members of Saint James Citizens for Jobs and the Environment (see Chapter 4). Greenpeace's Damu Smith, Monique Harden of Earthjustice Legal Defense Fund, and Albertha Hasten of LEAN brought the groups together as part of their emerging strategy: if communities expect help in their struggles, they must support other communities. As the meeting ended with prayers and songs, Harden packed the scorecard in the car: Formosa and LES were crossed out, Shintech was next.

BACKLASH AT THE STATE LEVEL: JUSTICE FOR SALE AND LEGAL REPRESENTATION DENIED

Industries in Louisiana have long been frustrated with the frequent successes that students from the Tulane Environmental Law Clinic have enjoyed in their battles with industry. In an attempt to disarm the clinic, several prominent firms and the chemical industry association had threatened to withhold donations to the university and encouraged alumni to do the same.[37] Since this approach was relatively unsuccessful, clinic opponents moved on to other approaches. The state's secretary of economic development Kevin Reilly ordered an investigation into the tax filings of the clinic and other environmental groups and sent a letter to the president of the university asking him to investigate the actions of the clinic. The governor publicly threatened the tax breaks for the university, and the state Board of Regents considered not providing millions in matching funds for the university's endowment (see Chapter 4).

But the breakthrough strategy came in May 1997 in a closed-door meeting between the New Orleans Business Council and Governor Foster. The new approach was reportedly suggested by the CEO of Entergy Corporation, the local utility which owned the land upon which the Shintech plant was proposed. Entergy also stood to make $70 million a year selling electricity to the plant. The idea was to have the area's business groups (the New Orleans Chamber of Commerce, the Louisiana Association of Business and Industry and the Business

Council of New Orleans) ask the State Supreme Court to investigate the "cases, positions, and stands" taken by law clinic faculty and students."[38] Subsequently, the three groups fired off letters to the chief justice of the State Supreme Court, Pascal Calagero. The letter written by the Louisiana Association of Business and Industry accused the clinics of activities bordering on soliciting, name calling, and intentionally trying to obstruct all industrial development. The letter also accused the clinics of representing clients who were not really indigent.[39]

The law clinics, which are overseen by the Louisiana Supreme Court, work in the areas of civil, criminal, juvenile, and immigration law. For approximately twenty years, clinics at three state schools (Tulane, Loyola, and Southern University) have provided services to low-income clients. Although the clinics employed federal poverty guidelines to determine eligibility, they also accepted hardship cases on behalf of individuals who earn more than the income level but still could not afford to pay for services.[40] The Tulane Environmental Law Clinic, founded in 1989, allows third-year law students to represent clients in state courts and before state agencies. The clinic typically has twenty-five students during the school year and four supervising attorneys (including the director). All cases are reviewed by an independent board of nine attorneys, who determine whether each case should be accepted. The major goal of the clinic is to train students through a hands-on program where the students serve as attorneys. In 1998, the clinic had 44 active cases.[41]

The Supreme Court responded to the business groups' request by ordering a review of all the law school clinics in the state. The court demanded that the clinics fill out detailed questionnaires regarding their activities, and two Supreme Court staff attorneys conducted on-site interviews with clinic administrators. Even though the court investigated all the law school clinics in the state, it was quite clear that the focus of the investigation was the Tulane Environmental Law Clinic (TELC). The court staff attorneys spent two and one-half days at Tulane as compared to one day each at the other law school clinics.[42] They found no violations at any of the Tulane clinics.

However, as in many states, judges are elected in Louisiana. Chief Justice Calogero was up for reelection, this time to his last possible ten-year term before his retirement. He faced an ambitious conservative who was a darling of the business community. As CBS's *Sixty Minutes 2* and PBS's *Frontline* would later describe it, the business community was beginning to wage a campaign to villainize Calogero as being too liberal for Louisiana. Both programs deduced that Calogero badly needed to throw the business community a bone.

In June of 1998, the Supreme Court announced a change for Rule XX, the rule that governs the activities of student lawyers, ordering three major changes that threatened to severely affect the operation of student law clinics. First, the Supreme Court prohibited law students from representing clients or groups affiliated with national organizations. Second, clinic clients would be required to meet the eligibility criteria used by the Legal Services Corporation. If a community group was to be represented by the clinic, at least 75 percent of its members had to meet the indigent eligibility criteria. Lastly, no students or staff of a law clinic could represent a community organization that they assisted in creating or incorporating. An editorial in the moderate *New Orleans Times-Picayune* was entitled "High Court Reins in Lower Class."[43] Local columnist James Gill said that the rule change amounted to class warfare.

These new rules caused an uproar among clinic advocates, national law organizations, and nonprofit groups throughout the state. A coalition of groups organized protest marches, one from a national law professors' convention to the Supreme Court building in the heart of New Orleans' business district, which drew 150 law professors from around the country and 50 community members.[44] On his weekly radio interview show, Governor Foster responded, "I still can't believe the picket bit . . . maybe they'll go out to the French Quarter and forget about picketing."[45] The Louisiana attorney general, the deans of Loyola and Tulane law schools, the executive director of the state American Civil Liberties Union chapter, the Association of American Law Schools, and the Louisiana State Bar Association all denounced the rules as substantially limiting access to the legal system for poor individuals and groups. In one of his last appearances in a long life of defying racist authority in Louisiana, civil rights leader and state representative Avery Alexander stated that the rule change "denies poor, working African Americans and people of color aggressive legal representation available to the rich and affluent in our society."[46] He likened the change to a rule passed during the Jim Crow era that required the NAACP to make public their membership lists. Harold Green, of the Southern Christian Leadership Conference said "they simply changed the rules of the game so that big business always wins."[47]

Also noting the NAACP ruling, Robert Kuehn, director of the TELC at the time, predicted that the income requirement would have a "chilling effect" on group formation, if individuals were required to make public their income level to receive clinic services.[48] He stated, "I don't think there's any question that the attack on the clinic through the court is an attempt to mute the voices of those who disagree with his [the governor's] environmental politics."[49] Kuehn recalled a hearing the year before that a student lawyer won against at least eight Shintech attorneys. He explained, "The sad commentary is that the governor and the court are trying to say that eight licensed attorneys against one student attorney are not good enough odds. They now want to make it 8 to 0."[50]

Members of the progrowth coalition were elated at the court's decision. Governor Foster stated that the court "is finally tightening up on that bunch of outlaws trying to shut everything down." The president of LABI stated, "The Supreme Court's ruling should not, in any way, impede TELC's mission of representing truly indigent individuals who have no other recourse for legal representation. But it will and should deter the faculty and staff from using the clinic as a soapbox to promote their anti-economic development agenda."[51]

After the protests and a request to rescind the rule change was filed by the deans of Tulane and Loyola law schools, the Supreme Court slightly modified the ruling. They lowered the level for the percentage of indigent members a community group must be required to have to be eligible for clinic services from 75 percent to 51 percent. Additionally, the court raised the income eligibility level for clients from 125 percent to 200 percent of the federal poverty level. This would be equivalent to $33,600 for a family of four. The clinic would also be able to represent groups that were affiliated with a national organization, but only if they met the income requirements. Very few of the clinic's previous clients could prove that they met these requirements.

According to clinic supporters, the rule changes did not go far enough. The very day these changes went into effect, they filed a suit in federal court accusing the state court of violating the U.S. constitution by imposing the changes to Rule XX. They stated that the rule changes violated the academic freedom of the professors, the rights of clients to representation, and the rights of students to an adequate education. The suit asked for the rule change to be declared unconstitutional. At least twenty-four organizations or persons signed on to the suit.[52]

In July 1999, federal judge Fallon threw out the lawsuit on the basis that the actions of the Louisiana Supreme Court were not illegal or unconstitutional. He stated that "Non lawyers have no constitutional or legal right to represent individuals or organizations in courts or before administrative tribunals." He went on, in a language so blunt as to be remarkable: "In Louisiana, where state judges are elected, one cannot claim complete surprise when political pressure somehow manifests itself within the judiciary." So he stated that law clinic's effort to overturn the rule "would more properly be focused on the political rather than the legal system."[53] He expanded, "The aim of the law clinics and the dedication of their staffs and students are indeed laudable. . . . However, unfairness does not always automatically rise to the level of unconstitutionality. Indeed, it rarely does."[54]

As this book goes to press, the Tulane Environmental Law Clinic and other law school clinics are functioning under the new rules and having to turn away clients that do not meet the income guidelines. At the end of 1998, the director of TELC stated that Tulane clinics turned away 148 of 236 applicants due to the rule changes. "So there's been a lot of legitimate fear about what the future holds for the clinic and for the students."[55] It must be noted, however, that the local and national media attention on the Louisiana Supreme Court for the Rule XX change has been almost uniformly critical. The business lobby has also suffered some bad public relations attention. Meanwhile, the Tulane Environmental Law Clinic has won national awards.

BLIPS OR PRECEDENTS? PROSPECTS FOR THE FUTURE

Between defusing the *Interim Guidelines* and declawing the Tulane Environmental Law Clinic, the empire has struck back decisively in response to the groundbreaking environmental justice cases chronicled in this book.[56] Business groups have put substantial energies behind turning back the tide, to keep these cases from becoming precedents. Why has the environmental justice movement drawn such intense resistance, seemingly beyond that faced by mainstream environmentalists a generation ago?

Several possible reasons need to be considered. First, mainstream environmentalism was mostly reformist and made compromises, and thereby worked with government agency personnel and corporate managers, who were at least of the same race and often the same economic class. Second, they and not-in-my-backyard (NIMBY) toxics activists often were mollified when firms simply went away to other backyards outside their realm of perception. That meant increased toxins and nuisances in "pollution havens," whether within their own states (but in poor or minority neighborhoods), in the lax states of the western U.S. Gulf Coast, or in poor nations overseas with weaker regulations and enforcement.[57] It is possible that environmental justice claims are so disturbing to industry precisely because they might take away that ability to use geographical mobility to avoid tough regulations; that is why they prefer to let states do the permitting of industrial sites. The words of many firms and industry groups are clear: they fear any precedent as sending us down a slippery slope where almost any siting of any unwanted facility could be questioned by community groups. This would be a new arrangement in the United States, one that they apparently want very much to avoid.

A third explanation must also be considered. That is, chemical and waste firms and their lobbyists have learned tough lessons since the wave of laws and regulations in the 1970s and 1980s saddled them with red tape and cleanup expenses (for example, the Clean Water Act, the Clean Air Act, and the solid waste bill – RCRA).[58] On the one hand, citizens of this nation and the world now respond differently to toxic contamination spills since the horrors of Love Canal in 1979 and Bhopal in 1984. On the other hand, firms have learned that they can stay ahead of regulators by being prepared when these disasters strike and by playing their cards very carefully. They established during the conservative decade of Reagan and Bush that "voluntary" standards can often be put forward to counter citizens clamoring for new or tightened regulations. They have also discovered the ability of environmental advertising to "green" their corporate image and thereby diffuse many attacks by environmentalists. Hundreds of millions of dollars a year are spent by firms on lobbyists and public relations firms to improve their position in the public mind.[59] Industry organizations like the Chemical Manufacturers of America (now the ACC, American Chemistry Council) and the U.S. Chamber of Commerce are working full-time to represent their interests and beat back new policy or regulations, such as those which environmental justice claims might impose.

These cases were important in strengthening people's movements and swaying public opinion toward the idea that something is indeed wrong and that something must be done about it. Recent polls indicate that attitudes about a jobs/environment tradeoff are shifting, and that even Louisianians don't want "development at any cost."[60] National polls have shown that the oil and chemical sector is held in the lowest regard of any industry, except tobacco.[61] As Florence Robinson was quoted in the industry magazine as saying, all industry skeptics have to do to oppose the public relations campaigns of the industries is bring a dozen people with signs and stand outside their factories.

The movement in the state has grown in important ways. At this writing in 2000, the Louisiana Environmental Action Network has several full-time staff in Baton Rouge, Labor Neighbor supports a large coalition of citizens' groups between New Orleans and Baton Rouge, and Louisiana Communities United provides day-to-day support for residents fighting against industrial facilities. In the academic arena, the Deep South Center for Environmental Justice at Xavier University in New Orleans continues to receive grants to support their research efforts. Over eighty local community groups are members of LEAN, several groups have web pages, and there are e-mail lists, phone trees, and other relatively new resources. The movement receives periodic support from national and international environmental groups like Greenpeace, the Sierra Club, Citizens for a Better Environment, and Earthjustice Legal Defense Fund; from civil rights groups like the Southern Christian Leadership Conference; and from environmental law groups in Dallas, Atlanta, Washington, and New York. Press coverage has also been important, sometimes intense, and generally favorable to their cause.

WHAT HAVE WE LEARNED ABOUT THE POLITICAL GAME?

So we are well on our way in discussing how chronicling these four cases and the backlash informs the questions we posed at the outset of this book. All four cases revealed how poor and minority communities can be invisible to planners because they lack representatives on local planning boards and chambers of commerce and in the mayor's and governor's office.[62] Some of these communities do not even appear on most maps. Existing policies, even some designed to help minority communities (for example, Enterprise Zones, Brownfields, and Superfund designations), can have unintended negative consequences for these communities. That is, decision makers assume that any development in these communities is good, but residents might feel otherwise. The needs of these local people are often ignored or misunderstood by decision makers and, many believe, by environmentalists. They are often used and ignored by outside agents on both sides to meet their political needs.

This last point raises two important issues for environmental justice activists. First, can government do its job of protecting the people from contamination? In all four cases, people turned initially to local and state governments for help, and all were bitterly disappointed by the responses they received. Once trust in government agencies was lost, it was difficult, if not impossible to regain. Local politicians such as the parish councils, the mayor's office, and the state departments of environment, development and health were widely considered traitorous and "in the pocket of industry" by environmental justice activists.[63] Sometimes the EPA and other federal agencies were considered more trustworthy and seen as the only ones who could deliver adequate protection for the community, but often their efforts failed to provide the outcomes residents desired. In both the Grand Bois and Agriculture Street Landfill cases, the EPA was bound by rules of how it could spend its money and, therefore, disappointed residents. However, in the Shintech case, the federal agency could do something – it was threatening to revoke the authority it delegated to the DEQ to enforce major national environmental laws, partly for its failure to address civil rights complaints. In fact, the state agency is still under investigation for its actions in other cases and could lose its federal funds if found guilty.[64]

Overall, then, most governmental agencies appear to residents as unwilling or unable to do their jobs as protectors, especially the local and state governments.[65] To return to the points of Chapters 1 and 2, local governments are extremely focused on growing the local economy; in fact, they are likely to have direct or indirect economic interests in the very siting cases they are deciding. If not, they are caught in the "fiscal trap," needing to boost tax revenues to fund their programs and the government offices they oversee. This suggests that decentralizing decision making to local governments risks supporting only the interests of elites, and not those of poor and minority residents.

The other side of this uncomfortable question is whether larger state, national, and international environmental and environmental justice organizations are using local groups to serve their own interests. Certainly this can be the case, even though they still provide some important services to those local groups. Should environmental justice groups seek to develop coalitions, or do they get led in the wrong direction by so doing? As Willy Fontenot said in Chapter 2, where the battles were fought and where they were really decided are often two different things. Different groups in the state have taken different approaches, and some groups have been far more successful in locating and sustaining the resources in the wider environmental and civil rights movements.

Without repeating the points made in those initial chapters, the four environmental battles described in this book showed that their cross-class, cross-race alliances were crucially important. In the case of LES, activists learned quickly that the struggle would be decided elsewhere, and their links to NIRS, the Sierra Club Legal Defense Fund, and Greenpeace proved crucial. The anti-Shintech group had dozens of coalition partners, most notably the Tulane Environmental Law Clinic and Greenpeace. The Concerned Citizens of Agriculture Street Landfill also got some help from The Deep South Center for Environmental Justice, Greenpeace, and Sierra Club, but each group was unable to exert enough pressure on the important pressure points: the city, the EPA, and HUD. It was Greenpeace's Damu Smith who organized their trips to Washington, D.C., and Geneva, Switzerland, to attempt to fight the bigger battles there, and these were the times that the residents seemed closest to moving the agency.

Finally, the Grand Bois families were successful in gaining some national and local press attention, but changing a prized law of the national oil industry (the exemption of oilfield wastes from the category hazardous) proved too difficult a mountain to move. The group got some support from state and national environmentalists, but nothing on the order of the Shintech case. National groups did not come through for them, perhaps because their campaign against oil companies did not link well with those of international groups. One could speculate that if they were fighting a firm targeted for major human rights abuses elsewhere, such as Texaco or Shell, then some international groups would have come forward. In the end, they were left relying heavily on their lawyer to move their case. As Nathalie Walker of Earthjustice said about the value of the legal approach, "Class action lawsuits, we have very few positive cases." Monique Harden continued, "Lawyers need protests and activism to keep the lawsuits moving. This is a classic mistake communities make — leaving it up to the lawyers. Litigation is not what drives things." She suggests that a crucial component in law school training is missing: "Communities don't know their rights. They don't work together, and lawyers don't have the skills on how to deal with communities." Finally, class-action lawsuits are often settled out of court, and these settlements are sealed, so future cases cannot build upon them.[66]

Why then are we stuck with a system where people so often sue, rather than taking their complaints to state agencies or to the legislature or Washington to solve these problems? In the heat of the battle over EPA's *Interim Guidelines,* three representatives for environmental officers in state governments across the country wrote in 1998, "If people do not like actions taken by their state agencies, their redress of grievances runs directly through their state legislative representative to the agency's budget and procedures and through the voting booth to the agency's ultimate boss, the governor."[67] This book shows just how badly this "pluralist" view – the one we were taught in junior high school civics class – ignores important realities. Specifically, with the current state of lobbying and campaign finance, this statement may be true for only millionaires in America today. In fact, even *they* would have trouble changing their representative over one issue and thus getting redress. So, when nothing else works for "common" people, there is an option available, as a lawyer for the NAACP Legal Defense Fund and environmental group NRDC pointed out. "You can lobby, you can have petitions, write letters and nothing happens, but file a 60-day notice of intent to sue," and things change.[68]

In Table 1, we attempt to determine the most influential factors in deciding the outcome of these cases. It is probably not just one factor that leads to success or failure for a protest group. Rather, a combination of factors serve to raise the group's power to levels that can challenge the growth coalitions they battle. The factors we consider range from characteristics of who the community group was fighting to their choice of legal strategy. Because they were seen in both victories and nonvictories, whether the protestors' opponent was a private company and whether the community was divided did not appear to be an important factor in their success or failure. However, the other factors might be related to case outcome.

One factor that perfectly corresponded to whether these cases were a victory or a loss for the environmental justice group was whether it was a new siting or an existing contamination. In the two siting cases, protestors successfully blocked the building of new facilities. Conversely, the results in the two cases in which there was existing contamination have been less than favorable for environmental justice advocates. This may simply be due to the political opportunity that the president's executive order afforded environmental justice activists fighting siting cases. Here was an executive order that was vague enough to require time-intensive efforts at interpretation and devel-

TABLE I. **What Factors Influenced the Outcomes of These Environmental Justice Struggles?**

Factor	LES	Shintech	Grand Bois	Agriculture Street	Deciding Factor?
Was opponent a private company?	+	+	+	−	−
Was it a new siting (Not an existing company)?	+	+	−	−	+
Was the community unified in their opposition?	−	−	+	−	−
Did they get strong support from national organizations?	+	++	−	+	+
Did they receive extensive national press coverage?	+	++	+	−	+
Were they represented by a private lawyer and enter into a class-action lawsuit?	−	−	+	+	+
Were they represented by public interest lawyers and appeal to federal government?	+	+	−	−	+
Was the case a victory for EJ group?	+	+	−	−	

opment of regulations on the part of the EPA and NRC, effectively delaying the siting of potentially offending plants. Protestors at existing contamination sites, on the other hand, did not have available legislation that was very favorable to their cause. And crucially, the delay strategy that proved so crucial in the LES and Shintech cases was not useful to those fighting existing contamination. So time is only on the side of those fighting new facilities.

Directly connected to this political opportunity was the strong support given to these local groups by outside organizations and the extensive national press coverage they received. National organizations benefit from working on causes that are "cutting edge," and, of course, the media is interested in reporting on such cases. The implications of the president's executive order were certainly breaking new ground in terms of civil rights and regulating private interests. Table 1 supports these findings. The protest groups in the siting cases that were successful received more outside aid and national press coverage than the protestors in the contamination cases.

Interestingly, the legal strategies chosen by the two groups were also consistent with failure or success. The protest groups in both the Shintech and LES cases tried to pressure federal agencies to develop environmental justice policy and regulations. The groups requested that state and federal agencies enforce existing regulations, the president's executive order, and Title VI. Although the government didn't directly decide in the residents' favor, this strategy resulted in substantial delays for the siting of the two plants that caused the companies to decide to not build or build elsewhere. The residents fighting battles related to existing contamination had little success in their attempts to get their state representatives to pressure the EPA or the state legislature to remedy their situation. In these cases, the protestors needed to change existing regulations or procedures to get relief. Finally, when this avenue yielded little success the residents in the Agriculture Street and Grand Bois struggles sought reparation and relief by hiring private lawyers to pursue a class-action lawsuit. This strategy got them only so far.

HOW WAS THE COMMUNITY DEFINED
AND WHO SPOKE FOR THEM?

To return to the question of what is community and who is its voice, we can see from each struggle that there is often no consensus on what "the community" consisted of, of who's in and who's out, and especially over who knows best or gets to decide whether they have a potentially polluting facility there. Only in one case was there a single voice of the community: Grand Bois, where every single one of the 301 residents in the tiny isolated town joined the class-action lawsuit. The literature out there on these contaminated communities suggests that this kind of unity is extremely rare.[69]

Far more common in these cases are "corrosive communities," where there is sharp disagreement on the nature of the risk and what should be done about it. The cases in this book suggest that factors like race, occupation, class, gender, and political power are all crucial in determining who believes the risk is acceptable or is outrageous. In the case of the LES uranium plant, people in the Claiborne parish seat town of Homer believed it was going to locate in their "community" and (probably unconsciously at first) ignored the wishes of the two communities that were the really closest: Forest Grove and Center Springs. The giant private consortium and Senator Johnston all believed that they had cleared the way with the important people: the "city fathers," those who ran the local chamber of commerce and made the political decisions around there. In the Shintech PVC factory case, the definition of community was even more complicated. One African-American neighborhood nearby had many people in favor of the project, but another opposed it. Parishwide, there was a slight majority of support for the project.

Finally, in the case of people living atop the old Agriculture Street Landfill, race was constant across the three groups, but they disagreed sharply about the EPA's proposed cleanup (instead of relocation). Although many of the homeowners were vehement in their cry for relocation, taking their demands to Washington and Geneva, a majority of those in the retirement home considered the risk worth taking, for the known comfort of their community. This is important but not surprising: psychologist Michael Edelstein found a similar difference in Legler, New Jersey, among suburban whites when confronted with the knowledge that their drinking water was contaminated.[70] At Agriculture Street, many of the low-income residents of the subsidized housing of Press Park were making comparisons of their current homes above the landfill with different risks in the Desire housing project, just six blocks away. So they were making complex decisions of costs and benefits and were not strong supporters of the protest group pressing for relocation.

Chemical plant owners and government officials have often called lawyers, students, and activists from environmental groups "outsiders" as they attempted to help these community protest groups. "Quite frankly, a lot of it is being fed by people who have a particular agenda," said Dale Givens, the head of Louisiana's DEQ.[71] However local groups don't like being told they are being manipulated. Convent activist Pat Melancon put it this way:

It wasn't outsiders coming in. It was us reaching out and saying come, can you help us with this, this and this. This is why any group is successful. They get together, network, and it's a coalition effort. There's no way we could have gone up against Shintech, all its allies and money, had we not had help from others, and we would have been fools not to take it.[72]

Damu Smith, now nine years fighting in Louisiana, says the "outsider" label is deceptive:

All one has to do is research the ownership of most of the big corporations in Louisiana, and you'll find most are foreign-owned: Taiwanese, Japanese, German. If you want to talk about outside interlopers, check out the chemical industry first. . . They are outside forces, and they work in collusion with DEQ, with the governor, and they do that unapologetically.[73]

Some in the movement believe that local groups have not used the national and international groups *enough*, and that they need to do so to establish long-term relationships with top-ranking federal agency personnel and their representatives in Washington.[74] But to do so, of course, often runs against the nature of grassroots groups.[75]

So who should get to decide? This is an extremely delicate question. It has often been said that, historically, in the United States wealthier communities exert much more control over their environment than poor communities. The novelty of the environmental justice movement is that it has been fairly successful in giving some control to communities that were previously ignored, railroaded, or cheaply bought off. We can see from these four cases some of the limitations of that control. For example, the only totally successful communities were those fighting *new sitings* as opposed to *existing facilities*.

There are probably a lot of reasons for this, but we see two things quickly happening after a facility's construction is begun. First, the economic knots grow increasingly complex and most people in the town are touched in one way or another, either from jobs, family members employed, donations to their schools or charities, sales in their stores, or tax revenues for their roads or police or ambulance.[76] In fact, this may be a way in which Louisiana's chemical industry has been short-sighted: the depth of its tax breaks and the shallowness of its efforts to employ locals has made opposition like that to Shintech's Convent plant more likely. The second thing that happens is more basic still: people simply get used to seeing the factory there, even smelling the fumes, and they begin to not notice it anymore.

BATTLES AFFECT INDIVIDUALS AND THE MOVEMENT

This familiarity leads us to the crucial topic of how people cope with hazards in their daily lives.[77] Most people seem to take passive coping strategies, such as minimizing or denying the risks, making comparisons with people who are worse off, focusing on other things (like the money from working in such places or the available jobs), or placing one's faith in God to protect them.[78] The question for social movement activists, critics, and scholars is why some people in some situations actively try to stop or avoid the exposures to these kinds of hazards. As some stress researchers have pointed out, people look around them and see if anyone else is doing anything to complain or try to change things. Seeing none, most will fall back to the passive types of coping styles.[79] However, those who believe that they might be able to do something to change things, for whatever reasons, will take up the cause. And as these four cases show, the battles are truly quixotic, pitting tiny volunteer community groups against powerful business interests with a lot to lose from their activism and a lot of influence to wield in the mayor's office, the state capital, or Washington, D.C. The sad truth is that when fighting seemingly endless battles against intransigent opponents, sometimes trying to change things can lead to depression, anxiety, and physical stress, as happened with people trying to shut down the Three Mile Island nuclear plant after the near meltdown there.[80] Kai Erikson's work with dozens of communities suggests that the people fearing for their lives and their children's health are experiencing *trauma,* and the effects of that trauma and chronic strain can last for decades.[81]

Even though the environmental justice movement appears irrational to some critics,[82] these people are exerting control where they can. As long as poor and minority people can only gain the leverage over new sitings, this is where they will exert it. Their demands, such as those for relocation or lifetime medical monitoring (in the case of Grand Bois) may appear extreme, but they are the product of fear, of disempowerment, of never being at the table where the decisions are made.

Christopher Foreman, in his 1998 Brookings Institute book *The Promise and Peril of Environmental Justice,* argued that the environmental justice movement is misguided, wasting energy and time on trivial risks to a community while ignoring important ones like those from smoking, eating, drinking, drugs, and crime.[83] There is certainly value for all communities to address the risks they face more broadly. But there are two problems with this argument. First, people of all types will object to imposed risks, while taking on seemingly huge amounts of voluntary risks. The core difference, of course, is *control*. Given more control over their own life course (such as their opportunities for a good education, jobs, not being singled out for discrimination by police or others, their physical safety), people will begin to take a closer look at the high-risk behaviors they are taking in their own lives. In this way, environmental justice is a logical product of social inequality and disempowerment: people will make what may seem unreasonable demands on the system when they are excluded from it.

Second, like governments or corporations, social movements have their own needs. That is, instead of profits, they need activists, members, a broad support group, and public attention. To gain these things, and to mobilize people, the environmental justice movement had to focus on race. As pointed out by Robert Bullard,[84] the issue of income and exposure to pollution had been made in the 1970s by the EPA and others, but it stirred little passion. But when the issue was tied to race, it took off because the issue of justice in this country has never been strongly linked to class and economic inequality. A race-based social movement found a way to get people energized. For awhile, it has even brought in some much-needed grants for these organizers. Now, around the end of its second decade, the movement continues to draw support from a wider base periodically. Its opposition appears far better organized in the wake of the Shintech and Chester, Pennsylvania, struggles, but they have also suffered some diffusion of attention and defections by companies not wishing to be associated with the extreme positions of the U.S. Chamber of Commerce and LABI in Louisiana.

Looking ahead, the environmental justice movement is showing positive and negative signs as it enters its third decade. From the movement side, there is an optimistic view that each struggle helps the next: "The grassroots get mowed down, then the roots get stronger, and they come back stronger each time."[85] Others see the movement diffusing and suffering devastating attrition as activists and supporters burn out, inevitably having to go back to their lives and jobs. Meanwhile, industry lobbyists and managers are always on the job, always there to attend to these issues. They are paid to attend long meetings, and they don't have to miss work to make it to a hearing or protest: it is part of their work. Some insiders complain that the movement lacks a national agenda, and that its leadership is exclusive. Even so, the movement has long suffered from divisive internal battles. Some of these battles are over who gets to claim credit for victories and use the cases for fund-raising.

Surveying these wrenching battles, and surveying this important movement, which has sought to bring social justice and environmental protection to people and places ignored by businesses, governments and environmentalists alike, we are reminded of an important fact. We cannot simply weigh their outcomes in "wins and losses," of sitings or no siting, of relocation or permits or enforcement events. These struggles changed these communities forever. Individuals on both sides bear invisible psychological scars, and in some cases there has been family tensions from disagreements over the issues or over the time and energy the struggles have drawn from their relations. Some friendships have been damaged or destroyed. But the positive impacts seem to outweigh those very real negatives. Some communities have emerged far stronger, tighter than most in our atomized nation. New social groups have been formed, and many of these have been friendships across class and race lines, changing the face of race relations in these communities forever. Certainly this is only the beginning of addressing the subtleties of racism here, but it may point to a broader trend. By participating in the protest groups, some people have learned tremendous amounts about the political system, and felt empowered to challenge authority on many other issues that came later.

Although we have recounted a backlash to the successful environmental justice cases, this may not be as detrimental to the movement as it appears on the surface. A social movement may actually be strengthened in the face of severe adversity. Events like the Rule XX change that are perceived as a gross injustice to activists can serve to energize and compel them to fight yet another round in their struggle. In fact, efforts by governments to compromise and concede small concessions to protestors may be more detrimental to movements than the construction of blatant roadblocks.

Of course, it is impossible to predict the future of any movement. One thing that can be said with certainty is that, in our highly technical and industrialized world, struggles over environmental injustice will not go away any time soon and are likely to grow more intense. Firms may change location, moving from the developed world to less challenging developing societies, but social movements are spreading across the world, and they may find no refuge from them there.[86] As community groups across the globe continue to fight these battles, no matter if they win or lose, they leave a lasting legacy, of public opinion and awareness, of citizens with experience as activists. A persistent change is that participants in environmental justice struggles continue to form networks among local, state, national and international groups, sharing their knowledge, energy, and organizational resources. As something of a counterbalance to the globalization being led by huge firms and international agencies, the work and networking of the environmental justice movement is spreading new visions for how they believe the world should work on several counts: equality, environment, and democracy.

Online Resources on Environmental Justice Struggles

WEB SITES OF ENVIRONMENTAL GOVERNMENT AGENCIES, GOVERNMENT SITES, AND KEY DOCUMENTS

First National People of Color Environmental Leadership Summit, Principles of Environmental Justice (1991)
http://gladstone.uoregon.edu/~caer/17principles.html
also at http://www.ejrc.cau.edu/

Environmental Council of the States, Environmental Justice
http://www.sso.org/ecos/projects/EJ/justice.htm

EPA's Envirofacts Warehouse [data and custom maps of toxics and poverty, race, etc.]
http://www.epa.gov/enviro

Louisiana Department of Environmental Quality (LDEQ)
http://www.deq.state.la.us/

Louisiana Department of Natural Resources
http://www.dnr.state.la.us/

President Clinton's Executive Order 12898 on Environmental Justice
http://www.epa.gov/civilrights/docs/eo12898.html
also at http://www.ejrc.cau.edu/
http://www.fs.fed.us/land/envjust.html

U.S. Environmental Protection Agency, Office of Civil Rights
http://www.epa.gov/civilrights/

INDUSTRY GROUPS

Louisiana Association of Business and Industry
http://www.labi.org/

Louisiana Chemical Association
http://www.lca.org/

American Chemistry Council (Chemical Manufacturers of America)
http://www.cmahq.com/

CITIZENS' GROUPS

The Environmental Justice Resource Center (EJRC)
at Clark Atlanta University
http://www.ejrc.cau.edu/

Community Coalition for Environmental Justice Links
on the World Wide Web
http://www.halcyon.com/ccej/EJlinks.html

Louisiana Environmental Action Network
http://www.leanweb.org

Coalition Against Environmental Racism
http://gladstone.uoregon.edu/~caer/home.html

Environmental Justice Database
http://www.msue.msu.edu/msue/imp/modej/masterej.html

Environmental Defense's "Scorecard" of Emissions
http://www.scorecard.org/

Facts on Louisiana Parishes (Government Information Sharing Project)
http://govinfo.library.orst.edu/cgi-bin/usaco-state?Louisiana

Witness to the Future: Interviews from "Cancer Alley" Louisiana
http://www.witnesstothefuture.com/meet/cancer.html

Environmental Research Foundation
http://www.rachel.org

Greenpeace, USA
http://www.greenpeaceusa.org/

The Good Neighbor Project
http://www.enviroweb.org/gnp/

Two Birds Films site on Environmental Justice
http://www.twobirdsfilm.com

Student Environmental Action Coalition
http://www.seac.org/

KEY LOUISIANA NEWSPAPERS

Baton Rouge Advocate
http://www.theadvocate.com/

The Gambit Weekly
http://www.bestofneworleans.com/frames/gwMain.html

L'Observateur (St. John The Baptist, St. Charles
and St. James Parishes, Louisiana)
http://www.lobservateur.com/

New Orleans Times-Picayune
http://www.nola.com/t-p/

Houma Courier
http://www.houmatoday.com/

Thibodaux Daily Comet
http://www.dailycomet.com/

Shreveport Times
http://news.shreveporttimes.com/

Suggested Places to Start:
A Few Worthwhile Next Readings

ENVIRONMENTAL JUSTICE PRIMERS

Books

Bryant, Bunyan, ed. 1995. *Environmental Justice, Issues, Policies, and Solutions.* Washington: Island Press.

Bullard, Robert. 1990. *Dumping in Dixie.* Boulder: Westview Press.

Bullard, Robert, ed. 1994. *Unequal Protection: Environmental Justice and Communities of Color.* San Francisco: Sierra Club.

Camacho, David, ed. 1998. *Environmental Injustices, Political Struggles, Race, Class, and the Environment.* Durham, NC: Duke University Press.

Faber, Daniel. 1998. *The Struggle for Ecological Democracy: Environmental Justice Movements in the United States.* New York: Guilford Press.

Foreman, Christopher. 1998. *The Promise and Peril of Environmental Justice.* Washington: The Brookings Institution Press.

Szasz, Andrew. 1994. *EcoPopulism, Toxic Waste and the Movement for Environmental Justice.* Minneapolis: The University of Minnesota Press.

Online Bibliographies

Neal, Ruth, and April Allen. 1996/1998. "Environmental Justice: An Annotated Bibliography." Report Series EJRC/CAU-1–96, Clark Atlanta University. http://www.ejrc.cau.edu/

Szasz, Andrew, and Michael Meuser. 1997. "Environmental Inequality Bibliography." http://www.mapcruzin.com/ejwww.html

TOXIC MOVEMENTS AND CONTAMINATED COMMUNITIES

Brown, Phil, and Edwin J. Mikkelsen. 1997. *No Safe Place: Toxic Waste, Leukemia, and Community Action.* Berkeley: University of California Press.

Dunlap, Riley E., and Angela G. Mertig, eds. 1992. *American Environmentalism: The U.S. Environmental Movement, 1970–1990.* New York: Taylor & Francis.

Edelstein, Michael R. 1988. *Contaminated Communities: The Social and Psychological Impacts of Residential Toxic Exposures.* Boulder: Westview.

Edward J. Walsh, Rex Warland, and D. Clayton Smith. 1997. *Don't Burn it Here: Grassroots Challenges to Trash Incinerators.* University Park: Pennsylvania State University Press.

Erikson, Kai. 1995. *A New Species of Trouble: The Human Experience of Modern Disasters.*

Gould, Kenneth A., Allan Schaiberg, and Adam S. Weinberg. 1996. *Local Environmental Struggles: Citizen Activism in the Treadmill of Production.* New York: Cambridge University Press.

Logan, John T., and Harvey Molotch. 1987. *Urban Fortunes: The Political Economy of Place.* Los Angeles: The University of Calforina Press.

Notes

NOTES FOR CHAPTER I

1. The need for the new lock has recently been thrown into question because the project was based on unreasonably high projections of commerce along the waterway, but commerce has dropped sharply from 1993 to 1999 (May 2000).
2. Rolwing 1997.
3. Baumbach and Borah 1981.
4. Wright 1997. From 119 businesses in 1966, North Claiborne dropped to just 58 businesses in 1983 (Raber 1990).
5. Warner 1999b; Rose 1974.
6. The siting of highways and rail transport through minority neighborhoods can have devastating effects indeed, as Beverly Wright (1997) and Bullard and Johnson (1997) argued. Done without due process, it can be argued that it is a form of institutional racism. A decade of research has shown that the road not only had a devastating impact on property values and community but also that lead from gasoline drifted off the elevated road into poor neighborhoods. Lead poisoning is subtle and often difficult to detect, but it has been linked to aggressiveness, juvenile delinquency rates, and depressed academic performance (Howard Mielke, memo to Jerald White, July 20, 1998). Dillard University Sociologist Daniel Thompson said that the exclusion of blacks in the 1950s made any protest extremely unlikely (Raber 1990). See ch. 2.
7. Authors' interview with Barry Kohl on June 29, 1999.
8. Certainly their hope is based on research and monitoring wells, but there is significant debate about the safety of the process. In Jefferson Parish, just up-river from New Orleans, Cytec injects nearly 20 million pounds of toxics into deep wells (LDEQ 2000). For othes who do the deep-well injecting, see EPA, DEQ, or EDF information at www.scorecard.org, www.epa.gov, or www.deq.state.la.us.
9. Ellis 1993. The quote is from Oliver Houck, professor of law at Tulane University.
10. The Navy tried to burn the Napalm in several other states but always met with protests, which were eventually successful. Students at Southern, an historically black university, wonder aloud why they are stuck with what no one else in the country wanted.
11. The Alsen case is discussed briefly in Chapter 2 and is documented elsewhere, such as in Bullard (1990) and Bullard and Wright (1992).
12. LDEQ 2000.

13. Environmental Defense Fund 1999.
14. Karl (1997) makes this point forcefully at the national level, comparing Venezuela and other oil-dependent nations around the world.
15. Koeppel 1999; Roberts and Thanos 2000.
16. Florence T. Robinson, North Baton Rouge Environmental Association, n.d., "Concepts of Environmental Justice," unpublished.
17. Lavelle and Coyle 1992.
18. Bullard 1999; Robert Washington, unpublished manuscript, "When Environmental Justice Confronts Risk Communication."
19. See the web sites section at the end of the book for several locations where the Principles of Environmental Justice are posted.
20. On these points, see also Bryant (1993).
21. People of Color Environmental Leadership Summit, 1991.
22. Schweizer 1999.
23. In Louisiana, *parish* is the term used to describe an area often referred to as a county in other areas of the country. See Chapters 2 and 4 for quotes from African-American leaders documenting these vote-buying practices.
24. Robinson, n.d.
25. Schweizer 1999.
26. McMahon 1997b.
27. The quote is from a Foster aide in the Shintech Tulane Environmental Law Clinic battle, see Chapters 4 and 7.
28. Sociologist James O'Connor (1973) termed this paradox, "the fiscal crisis of the state."
29. Molotch 1976; Logan and Molotch 1987.
30. Logan and Molotch 1987.
31. Stone 1989.
32. The state government's philosophy regarding development is reflected in the following statement from the web site: "Economic development is primarily a private sector phenomenon, the offspring of an active free enterprise system. Actions taken by government should be designed to foster private development not to supplant it." http://www.lded.state.la.us/new/topten.htm.
33. LDED web site. www.leded.state.la.us
34. Daugherty 1999.
35. Louisiana Coalition for Tax Justice 1995. The exemption is for five years, but is routinely extended another five years.
36. The state will provide an extra $2,500 for each position that is filled by a resident who was receiving state support through the Family Independence Temporary Assistance Program, a welfare-to-work initiative.
37. LDED, Business Incentives Division, 1999.
38. LDED, Office of Commerce and Industry, Business Incentives Division, 1997.
39. LDEQ web site.
40. Schleifstein 1998a.
41. Authors' interview with Gustave A. Von Bodungen, Assistant Secretary, Louisiana Department of Environmental Quality, June 1999.
42. LDEQ 2000, p. 25. Dunne 1999a; TRI definitions are shifting to include mining wastes.

43. LEAN 1998.
44. Myers 1998.
45. The average annual penalty assessed over the ten years of the study was $2,914,440 and the average amount collected annually was $1,184,595. In 1997, the amount of penalties assessed was $736,482 and the amount collected was $559,468 (LEAN 1998). These figures increased somewhat in 1999.
46. Lussier 2000.
47. See also Gould, Schnaiberg, and Weinberg, (1996).
48. Kuehn 1996.
49. Habermas 1970.
50. McQuaid 2000f.
51. E-mail posted on the internet from Marlene Ross, coordinator MEAN, to Bill Myers, May 4, 1999.
52. Of course, even if zoning existed, there is immense room for "variances" where nonzoned uses are allowed. The state environmental agency could in fact direct proposed development elsewhere using the IT (named for the International Tank case) questions (see Chapter 2) or other mechanisms (W. Fontenot, personal communication).
53. Authors' anonymous interview with Community Advisory Panel member of Dow Chemical Company CAP in June 2000.
54. See Roberts (1998), Freudenberg (1998), and Bandura (1997), among others.
55. Roberts 1993, 1998; see Karasek and Theorill (1990); Bandura (1997).
56. Roberts 1998.
57. Norton Tompkins told us this on May 25, 1999, at Elmira Wafir's house on May 25, 1999, while she smiled widely in agreement.
58. This point was made repeatedly and openly in the 2000 fiscal session of the state legislature, see *New Orleans Times-Picayune* and *The Gambit Weekly* reports and commentaries from May and June 2000. The tax structure of the state is a clear reflection of the relative power of the industry vs. the people: Louisiana is fourth in the nation in sales taxes, currently including 4 percent taxes on utilities and food. The corruption scandals often make entertaining bits on the national news: former Governor Edwin Edwards was investigated by fifteen different grand juries, and finally convicted at age 73 on seventeen racketeering charges (*New Orleans Times-Picayune* 2000).
59. Nationally syndicated columnist Cynthia Tucker was in New Orleans in the summer of 1998 for a conference of investigative journalists. Citing the case of the Clinton White House, she wrote about how the United States is becoming like Louisiana has long been: no level of scandal can raise significant outrage among the public. We argue that this reflects a weakening of civil society and its ability to restrain manipulation of laws and even the erosion of basic democratic institutions.
60. For an interesting comparison of an environmental justice case in Louisiana and a struggle of workers on a Costa Rican plantation, see Thanos (2000).
61. Lussier 2000a. Melancon was ruling on the case of the largest operator of private sewer systems in the state, which for years had gotten away with hundreds of violations and subjected residents to truly disgusting conditions. The

judge had called the secretary of the Louisiana Department of Environmental Quality Dale Givens from Baton Rouge for a special message.

62. This issue will surface many times in the book. For a broad-ranging investigation of DEQ, see Lussier (2000a, 2000b, 2000c, 2000d, 2000e, 2000f).
63. Bullard 1990.

NOTES FOR CHAPTER 2

1. Wilds, Dufour, and Cowan 1996; McQuaid 2000b.
2. Slaves numbered 533 in 1721, and Europeans numbered 1,082. By 1732, there were 3,600 slaves and 1,720 Europeans (McQuaid 2000e). Wilds et al. (1996) report that two ships brought 451 slaves in 1719.
3. Wilds et al. 1996.
4. McQuaid 2000b.
5. 1763: 4,598 slaves; 1788: 20,678 slaves.
6. McQuaid, 2000b; Wilds et al. 1996.
7. Another rebellion in 1811 of hundreds of slaves brandishing hoes and pitchforks began in what is now Norco, Louisiana, ending with the killing of sixty-six slaves and sixteen leaders, who were tried and executed, and their heads staked along the levee (Wilds et al. 1996, p. 62).
8. McQuaid 2000b, p. J-11; Schaefer 1994.
9. Fairclough 1995.
10. Wilds et al. 1996, p. 74.
11. July 25, 1899. Cited in Wilds et al. (1996), p. 50.
12. Wilds et al. 1996, p. 67.
13. Wilds et al. 1996, p. 74.
14. Wilds et al. 1996, p. 64.
15. Authors' interview with Bettsie Baker-Miller, Louisiana Chemical Association, in July 1999.
16. Authors' interview with Bettsie Baker-Miller, Louisiana Chemical Association, in July 1999.
17. Wright, Bryant, and Bullard 1994.
18. Louisiana Coalition for Tax Justice 1995.
19. LDED n.d.
20. Hirsh 1992.
21. Hirsh 1992.
22. Hirsh 1992.
23. U.S. Bureau of the Census 1999.
24. As many have argued before us, this poverty line is arbitrary and quite low (Delaker 1999).
25. Anderson 1986.
26. Authors' interview with Willie Fontenot in July 2000. Residents had complained about waste pits and dumping as early as the 1960s and 1970s in Tate Cove, Alsen, Sorrento, and Willow Springs.
27. Authors' interview with Willie Fontenot in July 2000.
28. *Times-Picayune* 1982a.

29. Authors' interview with William Guste in July 1999.
30. Authors' interview with Willie Fontenot in July 2000.
31. *Times-Picayune* 1982b.
32. Authors' interview with Willie Fontenot in May 1998.
33. See, for example, Bullard (1990).
34. Bryant 1993. Author's interview with Pat Bryant, May 1998.
35. Bullard and Wright 1992.
36. Authors' interview with Daryl Malek-Wiley in April, 1998.
37. Authors' interviews with Willie Fontenot in May 1998.
38. Authors' interview with Willie Fontenot in May 1998.
39. Louisiana Advisory Committee to the U.S. Commission on Civil Right 1993.
40. Authors' interview with Florence Robinson, April 2000.
41. Authors' interview with Florence Robinson, North Baton Rouge Environmental Association, in April 2000.
42. Authors' interview with Barry Kohl in June 1999.
43. German activist Bernhard Doenig's trial over the mailing list went on for a year before he was cleared (Leonard and Nauth 1993).
44. Leonard and Nauth 1993, p. 41.
45. Authors' interview with Dan Nicolai in July 1999.
46. Leonard and Nauth, 1993, p. 41.
47. Leonard and Nauth, 1993.
48. Reed 1991.
49. Collete 1997.
50. Leonard and Nauth 1993, p. 47.
51. Maraniss and Weiskopf 1987, cited in Schwab 1994.
52. Malek-Wiley 1998 interview, cited in Schwab 1994.
53. Tulane University School of Public Health and Tropical Medicine 1989.
54. Louisiana Advisory Committee to U.S. Commission on Civil Rights 1993.
55. Gaudet 1990, cited in Louisiana Advisory Committee to the U.S. Commission on Civil Rights 1993.
56. http://www.witnesstothefuture.com/meet/cancer/gaudet.html [Accessed July 9, 1999.]
57. LEAN 1996.
58. Authors' interview with Florence Robinson, North Baton Rouge Environmental Association, in April 2000.
59. Authors' interview with Mary Lee Orr, Executive Director of LEAN, in May 1998.
60. This is not hyperbole: The Tulane Environmental Law Clinic was given the top national prize by the American Bar Association in July 2000.
61. Dickerson and Ward 1995.
62. Authors' interview with Daryl Malek-Wiley in April 1998.
63. Frazier 1988.
64. Authors' interview with Daryl Malek-Wiley in April 1998.
65. Pope 1988.
66. Twenty-seven percent said that nothing good came out of the protest events, and thirty-six percent didn't have an opinion about the organization's impact.
67. Harris & Associates and Southern Media & Opinion Research, Inc. 1989.

68. Laborde 1988.
69. Kemp 1989.
70. Louisiana Advisory Committee to the U.S. Commission on Civil Rights 1993.
71. Louisiana Advisory Committee to the U.S. Commission on Civil Rights 1993.
72. Louisiana Advisory Committee to the U.S. Commission on Civil Rights 1993.
73. Angela Linsey report n.d., cited in Louisiana Advisory Committee to the U.S. Commission on Civil Rights 1993.
74. Kelly Alexander 1990, cited in Louisiana Advisory Committee to the U.S. Commission on Civil Rights 1993.
75. Foreman 1998.
76. Bullard 1994.
77. Commission for Racial Justice, United Church of Christ 1987.
78. There have been dozens of studies in the past fifteen years, with sometimes conflicting results. A substantial debate is over the unit of measurement one employs when looking at "proximity" to pollution sources. We refer readers to those references listed in the Reference section and to web sites listed. The most current studies are in academic journals, not in books. The debate is still open, but a majority of studies have shown race and income to be important predictors of proximity to hazardous facilities.
79. "Environmental Justice," 1995.
80. Daryl Malek-Wiley in an interview with the authors in April 1998, described the Summit Steering Committee tour as particularly effective because the members were able to have several hours of uninterrupted time, without phones or faxes, to get to know each other and discuss the reality of environmental justice.
81. Authors' interview with Pat Bryant, Gulf Coast Tenants Organization, in October 1998.
82. Authors' interview with Dr. Beverly Wright, Deep South Center for Environmental Justice, Xavier University, in July 2000.
83. Pitts 1989.
84. Ferstel 1998b; Tallie 1986.
85. McMahon 1997b.
86. Warren 1992.
87. Authors' interview with Willie Fontenot in July 2000. Later the parish president was convicted of extortion related to the Formosa selection process and the purchase of the Wallace property.
88. Schwab 1994.
89. Schwab 1994.
90. Authors' interview with Willie Fontenot in July 2000. A Texas activist named Diane Wilson had conducted three hunger strikes at the Point Comfort, Texas, location of Formosa Plastics vinyl chloride plant. As a result of her efforts, the EPA required the company to prepare an Environmental Impact Statement (EIS) for the plant's proposed expansion. The site in Louisiana was similar in size to that of the proposed Texas plant; therefore, the EPA was pressured to require an EIS for the Louisiana plant.
91. Warren and Broach 1992.
92. Broach 1992.

93. Ferstel 1998b.
94. Warren and Broach 1992.
95. Scallan 1992.
96. Louisiana Advisory Commission to the U.S. Commission on Civil Rights 1993.
97. Kucharski 1994.
98. Kucharski 1994.
99. Dickerson and Ward 1995.
100. Dickerson and Ward 1995.
101. Dickerson and Ward 1995.
102. www.epa.gov; see "Online Resources on Environmental Justice Struggles."
103. Title VI of the Civil Rights Act of 1964, states that "No person in the United States shall, on the grounds of race, color or national origin, be excluded from participation in, be denied the benefits of, or be subjected to discrimination under any program or activity receiving Federal financial assistance."
104. Authors' interview with Pat Bryant, Gulf Coast Tenants Organization, in October 1998.
105. Authors' interview with Pat Bryant, Gulf Coast Tenants Organization, in October 1998.
106. Bullard 1994.
107. Bullard 1990, p. 14.
108. Authors' interview with Florence Robinson, North Baton Rouge Environmental Association, in April 2000.
109. Authors' interview with Harold Green, Southern Christian Leadership Conference environmental justice coordinator, in October 1998.
110. Authors' interview with Mary Lee Orr, executive director of LEAN, in May 1998.
111. Authors' interview with Albertha Hasten, Louisiana Communities United, in March 2000.
112. Authors' interview with Albertha Hasten, Louisiana Communities United, in March 2000.
113. Authors' interview with Florence Robinson, North Baton Rouge Environmental Association, in April 2000.
114. Authors' interview with Mary Lee Orr, LEAN, in June 1999.

NOTES FOR CHAPTER 3

1. Authors' interview with Toney Johnson in May 1999.
2. "I mean I've had complaints that I hadn't brought things to North Louisiana." From an authors' interview with J. Bennett Johnston in June 1999.
3. Babcok and Morin 1990; Associated Press 1989. Johnston was a huge beneficiary of PAC (Political Action Committee) contributions in the period when LES was proposed. Between 1983 and 1989, Johnston had received more than $200,000 in campaign contributions and speaking honoraria from nuclear industry companies and electricity utilities.

4. Associated Press 1989.
5. Authors' interview with J. T. Taylor in May 1999.
6. Authors' interview with Essie Youngblood in May 1999.
7. Allen-Mills 1997.
8. Authors' interview with Juanita Hamilton in May 1999.
9. Lippman 1990.
10. Toney Johnson admitted he was angry at Senator Johnston because he led the derailing of the confirmation of Supreme Court nominee Robert Bork, one of the most polarizing political events of the mid-1980s.
11. Authors' interview with Toney Johnson in May 1999.
12. Fried 1993.
13. Mariotte 1998. Urenco's scandals in Europe and links to Iraq and other potential proliferation problems were largely unknown in the United States. Peter Jelinek was the Austrian president of Urenco. Urenco is a German nuclear fuel company with ties back to the Nazis through I. G. Farben, which made chemicals for Auswitz. Jelinek was managing director of Nukem, which was involved in bribery scandals in Belgium and West Germany and was forced to close a plant in Hanau, Germany (Mariotte 1990). Urenco may have leaked centrifuge technology to Saddam Hussein and Pakistanis. The Urenco scandal includes shadowy stories of seized records, a suicide in jail, and the buying of uranium from South Africa. In 1995, arms inspectors in Iraq uncovered 500,000 pages of secret documents on uranium enrichment, including hundreds of pages on Urenco's centrifuge technology. These included designs sold to Iraq by at least two German experts, especially Karl-Heinz Schaab, who was recently in a Rio de Janeiro jail fighting extradition to Germany (Shinkle 1998b, authors' telephone interview with Peter Shinkle in May 1998).
14. Mariotte 1990; authors' interview with J. Bennett Johnston in June 1999.
15. Authors' interview with J. Bennett Johnston in June 1999.
16. Shinkle 1997; authors' interview with Peter Shinkle in May 1998.
17. Authors' interview with Norton Tompkins in May 1999.
18. Ex-senator Johnston retorted, "I knew him, I didn't know the land would be his. . . . It angered me that the Ralph Nader crowd made those claims . . . they were just spreading lies, knowing they were lying, they were spreading ill will." JBJ continued, "I could not be involved in the siting of the plant – it was a technical decision. Wherever they would have put it in North Louisiana would have been equally good for me. . . . I mean I've had complaints that I hadn't brought things to North Louisiana." From authors' interview with J. Bennett Johnston in June 1999.
19. Authors' interview with Blake Hemphill in May 1999.
20. Shinkle 1997.
21. Personal communication with Jeanne Hand in January 2000.
22. Carson 1985.
23. Johnston 1985.
24. Authors' interview with Blake Hemphill in May 1999.
25. He later commented, "I wanted to bring them to LA, and get them what they needed from me [regulation change] and I didn't need to busy myself with

the details of their contracts and all that." From authors' interview with J. Bennett Johnston in June 1999.

26. Mariotte 1998.
27. Mariotte 1998.
28. Tompkins 1992.
29. Later, Johnston said, "I made the unfortunate mistake, I didn't know what Fiestaware was, it was not banned, you can still find it in flea markets. I was just trying to show people what radioactivity is, that it's not an explosive thing, what have you." From authors' interview with J. Bennett Johnston in June 1999.

   He continued, "People are just nuts about the hazards, when these hazards are not significant. The press, by and large, is anti-nuclear [even though we know that coal plants kill with respiratory illnesses]. The centrifuge technology, from the standpoint of safety, is a lot safer than a refinery . . . really safer than the corner filling station, certainly an LP gas plant, which they have all over rural Louisiana. People don't understand radioactivity. Your body is radioactive. You can get people very upset about it, even intelligent people. I think the majority of the people think space aliens landed at Roswell, New Mexico. . . . There's no impact. You've got this very nice plant, it looks nice . . . there's no negative impact of this."

30. Mariotte 1998.
31. Mariotte 1990.
32. Mariotte 1990.
33. Raber 1990.
34. Associated Press 1989.
34. Mariotte 1990.
35. Mariotte 1990.
36. Hechinger 1991.
37. Mariotte 1998.
38. Mariotte 1998.
39. Tompkins 1992.
40. Authors' interview with Toney Johnson in May 1999.
41. Authors' interview with Toney Johnson in May 1999.
42. Mitchell 1991a.
43. Mitchell 1991b.
44. Roy Martis and Willy Brooks were two of the only active black men, and they played important parts in the struggle.
45. Authors' interview with Essie Youngblood in May 1999.
46. Authors' interviews with Nathalie Walker in May 1999, and Monique Harden, Earthjustice Legal Defense Fund, formerly of Greenpeace, in July 1999.
47. Authors' interview with Essie Youngblood in May 1999.
48. Authors' interview with Elmira Wafir in May 1999.
49. The accounts of the founding meeting come from interviews with Essie Youngblood, Elmira Wafir, and Toney Johnson. No one could remember who the quoted speaker was.
50. Heyen 1991.
51. *Homer Guardian Journal*, n.d.
52. Authors' interview with Elmira Wafir in May 1999.

53. Norton Tompkins told us this at Elmira Wafir's house in May 1999, while she smiled widely in agreement.
54. Others also assisted. At the Institute for Energy and Environmental Research (EER) conference in Washington, D.C., on plutonium Argon Makajani, a physicist from an international group, told Dan Rather's producer about the LES proposal and got the issue on national news.
55. *Homer Guardian-Journal* 1991.
56. Claiborne Parish Industrial Development Foundation 1990.
57. NIRS 1991b.
58. Vicki Arroyo, assistant to the secretary, Louisiana DEQ, letter to Peter Loyson, NRC, dated August 14, 1991.
59. "As you are aware, the LDEQ is operating under a siting process mandated by Article IX of the Louisiana Constitution and a Louisiana Supreme Court Decision, *Save Ourselves Inc. et al. 5. The Louisiana Environmental Control Commission* (1984)." From Vicki Arroyo, Assistant to the Secretary, Louisiana DEQ, letter to Peter Loyson, NRC, dated August 14, 1991.
60. Louisiana Department of Environmental Quality, Division of Policy Analysis and Planning, 1991.
61. NIRS 1991a.
62. *Minden Press-Herald* 1992.
63. *Energy Daily* 1992.
64. Barrett 1993. Opponents also made much of a closer earthquake on the El Dorado fault (Heyen 1994).
65. *Homer Guardian-Journal* 1993b.
66. *Homer Guardian-Journal* 1993c.
67. Travis M. Tinsley, letter to Roy Mardis, CANT, dated January 4, 1993.
68. Heyen 1994.
69. *Environment Week* 1993.
70. The SCLDF quote is from Nathalie Walker. Both are from Reath 1993.
71. The DEIS was summarized for locals in the *Homer Guardian-Journal* 1994b. The reporting continued in *Homer Guardian-Journal* 1994c.
72. *News-Star* 1994.
73. The full text of the EPA letter was printed in the *Homer Guardian-Journal* March 3, 1994: "EPA Responds to Impact Statement for Planned Uranium Enrichment Plant."
74. Colwell 1993; *Homer Guardian-Journal* 1992.
75. *Homer Guardian-Journal* 1993a.
76. Heyen 1994b.
77. *Homer Guardian-Journal* 1994d.
78. Heyen 1995.
79. By having several issues moved back from a mid-1994 hearing to the 1995 hearing date, CANT and SCLDF won an important procedural issue by allowing them to delay the project and having only pay their expert witnesses to testify once, not twice (Heyen 1994b).
80. Authors' interviews with Nathalie Walker in May 1999, and Monique Harden, Earthjustice Legal Defense Fund, in July 1999.
81. Shinkle 1997.

82. Authors' interviews with Nathalie Walker in May 1999, and Monique Harden, Earth Justice Legal Defense fund, in July 1999.
83. Authors' interviews with Nathalie Walker in May 1999, and Monique Harden, Earth Justice Legal Defense fund, in July 1999.
84. Shinkle 1998a.
85. Ferstel 1998b.
86. Editor's note, *Homer Guardian Journal,* July 31, 1997.
87. Gray 1998.
88. Authors' interview with J. T. Taylor in May 1999. On the point of being against JBJ, this is a clear reference to Toney Johnson.
89. J. T. Taylor, president, Claiborne Economic Development Board, letter to Shirley Jackson, NRC chair, on July 25, 1997.
90. J. T. Taylor, president, Claiborne Economic Development Board, letter to Shirley Jackson, NRC chair, on August 20, 1997.
91. John Breaux letter to Dennis K. Rathbun, NRC, dated September 17, 1999.
92. LES 1998.
93. Roland Jensen, President of LES, letter to the three commissioners of the NRC dated April 1998.
94. Heyen 1998.
95. Earthjustice figures are estimated by Nathalie Walker, in interview with authors in May 1999. CANT figures are an estimate by Norton Tompkins, from interview with authors in June 1999.
96. Authors' interview with Toney Johnson in May 1999.
97. Authors' interview with Essie Youngblood in May 1999.
98. C. Gray 1998b.
99. Earthjustice Legal Defense Fund 1998.
100. Earthjustice Legal Defense Fund 1998.
101. Shinkel 1997.
102. June 2, 1997, letter from Michael Mariotte, urging sign-ons for his letter to NRC chair Shirley Jackson.
103. Shinkle 1998b.
104. Authors' interview with J. Bennett Johnston in June 1999.
105. *Minden Press-Herald* 1998.
106. Shinkle 1998a. More fully, Natalie Walker of SCLDF said, "If the process was slow, it was because LES made it slow. LES frequently had to amend their application papers. Frequently we had to fight with them over documents they should have turned over to us." LES president Roland Jensen disputes it, saying, "That is completely untrue. That is a bald-faced lie. We were completely responsive. We never withheld any documents."
107. This point was made by both Toney Johnson and Blake Hemphill in interviews on May 25 and 26, 1999.
108. Bullard discusses the case frequently in his lectures, and it is documented on the Clark Atlanta University Environmental Justice Resource Center web site; however, other authors rarely mention it. One paper that does discuss this case is by two philosophers, Wigley and Shrader-Frechette 1996.
109. Mariotte 1990. The other quotes are from confidential interviews.
110. Shinkle 1998a.

111. Mardis. Clark Atlantic University Environmental Justice Resource Center web site. [Accessed June 18, 2000]. http://www.ejrc.cau.edu.
112. C. Gray 1998b.
113. Coyle 2000.

NOTES FOR CHAPTER 4

1. Authors' interview with Dale Hymel, St. James Parish president, in July 1999.
2. Calsen 2000.
3. Authors' interview with Dale Hymel, St. James Parish president, in July 1999.
4. Authors' interview with Dale Hymel, St. James Parish president, in July 1999.
5. West n.d.
6. West n.d.
7. Authors' interview with SJCJE members Mary L. Green, Brenda Huguet, Gloria Roberts, Rose Ann Roussel, Dolores Simmons, and Emelda J. West in June 1999.
8. Authors' interview with Edie Michel, St. James Parish director of economic development, in March 1998.
9. Louisiana Advisory Committee to the U.S. Commission on Civil Rights 1993.
10. From 1959 to 1969, three chemical companies and two oil companies, all owned by firms headquartered elsewhere, set up processing plants in the parish. In the 1960s alone, this influx of industry created 1,017 permanent jobs. In the 1970s, three more large industrial companies located manufacturing sites in the parish. From 1972 to 1978, the parish received $445 million in new capital investments.
11. *St. James Parish News Examiner* 1973.
12. Authors' interview with Edie Michel, St. James Parish director of economic development, in March 1998.
13. Authors' interview with Carol Gaudin, vice president, St. James Citizen Coalition, in March 1999.
14. Authors' interview with Oliver Cooper, St. James Parish councilperson, in June 1999.
15. Parish services such as schools and the senior center still exhibit evidence of racial segregation. One black protest group member described segregation at the parish senior center. She stated, "Let me tell you something, you go there all the whites sitting on this end and all the people of color sitting on the other end." She went on to describe the segregated community response to a recent explosion at a nearby chemical plant. She said, "Now with the Kaiser explosion, the whites had their meetings [with lawyers] in one place and the blacks in another. It [racism] is just here with a big capital R."
16. Authors' interview with SJCJE members Mary L. Green, Brenda Huguet, Gloria Roberts, Rose Ann Roussel, Dolores Simmons, and Emelda J. West in June 1999.
17. Authors' interview with Carol Gaudin, vice president of St. James Citizen Coalition, in March 1999.

18. Authors' interview with Pat Melancon in March 1998.
19. Authors' interview with Gloria Roberts in June 1999.
20. The president of the group felt that the latter sentiment often got lost in the media's coverage of the case. She described this sentiment, "People, human-beings – it's about justice for all people. And that's what we're about. And we don't want anybody changing it to that [only focusing on minorities and poor people] – although some have done it and you can't stop people from doing what they're going to do." From authors' interview with Pat Melancon in March 1998.
21. Authors' interview with Pat Melancon, SJCJE, in March 1998.
22. Authors' interview with SJCJE members Mary L. Green, Brenda Huguet, Gloria Roberts, Rose Ann Roussel, Dolores Simmons, and Emelda J. West in June 1999.
23. Authors' interview with SJCJE members Mary L. Green, Brenda Huguet, Gloria Roberts, Rose Ann Roussel, Dolores Simmons, and Emelda J. West in June 1999.
24 Authors' interview with Monique Harden, Earthjustice Legal Defense Fund, formerly of Greenpeace, in July 1999.
25. Authors' interview with Monique Harden, Earthjustice Legal Defense Fund, in July 1999.
26. Authors' interview with Lisa Lavie, Supervising Attorney, Tulane Environ-mental Law Clinic, in June 1999.
27. Foster 1997.
28. Louisiana Public Broadcasting interview with Governor Foster in June 1997.
29. C. Gray 1997a.
30. Daugherty 1997b.
31. Kevin Reilley, DED, letter to Eamon Kelly, Tulane president, dated August 1997.
32. Authors' interview with Edie Michel, St. James Parish director of economic development, in March 1998.
33. Authors' interview with Carol Gaudin, vice president, St. James Citizen Coalition, in March 1999.
34. Payne 1997.
35. Authors' interview with David Wise, Shintech plant manager, in June 2000.
36. McMahon 1997a.
37. The loan provided matching funds up to $2.5 million for the Johnson-led Louisiana Community Development Capital Fund–Business Industrial De-velopment Corporation. The program aims to support minority and economi-cally disadvantaged business ventures by providing loans to eligible candidates.
38. Wardlaw 1997.
39. McMahon 1997a.
40. TELC 1998.
41. Herman Robinson, assistant secretary, Office of Legal Affairs and Enforce-ment, letter to Robert R. Kuehn, Director, Tulane Environmental Law Clinic, dated August 18, 1997.
42. Janice Dickerson, community industry relations coordinator, memo to Her-

man Robinson, assistant secretary, Office of Legal and Enforcement, re: Response to Bob Kuehn's August 18, 1997 accusation, dated August 8, 1997.

43. Authors' interview with SJCJE members Mary L. Green, Brenda Huguet, Gloria Roberts, Rose Ann Roussel, Dolores Simmons, and Emelda J. West in June 1999.

44. Southern Media & Opinion Research 1997. Survey was based on 300 randomly selected St. James Parish registered voters. The overall margin of error was plus or minus 5 percent at the 95 percent level of confidence.

45. C. Gray 1998a. Parishwide results were based on a telephone sample of 400 registered voters in St. James Parish. The results for the fourth district were based on a survey of every household with a phone that agreed to participate (137 voters). The survey had a margin of error of 5 percentage points.

46. Authors' interview with Dale Hymel, St. James Parish president, in July 1999.

47. Authors' interview with Gustave Von Bodungen, assistant secretary, LDEQ, in June 1999.

48. Von Bodungen 1998. Michael Meuser (personal communication 2000) points out that the Toxic Release Inventory data upon which these claims are made understate actual emissions (because many chemical facilities are excluded) and overstate reductions (since 1987 data was often grossly overreported).

49. Authors' interview with Dale Hymel, St. James Parish president, in July 1999.

50. Authors' interview with Gustave Von Bodungen, assistant secretary, LDEQ, in June 1999.

51. Brad Lambert, Harris, Deville, and Associates, Inc. memo to Dale Hymel, St. James Parish president, dated August 13, 1996.

52. Miculek 1996.

53. Miculek 1996.

54. Miculek 1996.

55. Miculek 1996.

56. Lisa Lavie, TELC, letter to Jack C. Caldwell, secretary, DNR, dated March 3, 1997.

57. Fax sent by Jody Chenier, St. James Parish director of operations, to David Tidholm, Shintech legal representative, on May 5, 1996.

58. Lisa Lavie, TELC, letter to Jack C. Caldwell, secretary, DNR, dated March 3, 1997.

59. Harris, Deville, and Associates, Inc. letter to Dale Hymel, parish president, dated August 13, 1996.

60. Harris, Deville, and Associates, Inc. letter to Dale Hymel, parish president, dated August 13, 1996.

61. Brad Lambert memo to Dale Hymmel and Edie Michel, dated December 18, 1996.

62. Authors' interview with David Wise, Shintech plant manager, in June 2000.

63. Authors' interview with Lisa Lavie Jordon, acting director, TELC, in June 1999.

64. Don Hays, international investment director, DED, dated July 22, 1997.

65. Anderson and Gray 1997.

66. Governor Mike Foster, letter to Chihiro Kanagawa, Shintech president, dated March 21, 1997.

67. Other nonlocal pro-Shintech speakers included thirteen industry consultants, lobbyists, or employees of contractors of Shintech and the Louisiana secretary of economic development, Kevin Reilly. The local pro-Shintech speakers included Dale Hymel, the president of the St. James Business Association, two district councilpersons, a representative from St. James Parish economic development board, the parish economic development coordinator, and the professor from the University of New Orleans who conducted an economic impact study. Additionally, at least five area businesspersons and two citizens spoke in support of the plant.

68. Robert Holden Liskow & Lewis letter to Gustave Von Bodungen, LDEQ, on behalf of Shintech, dated January 20, 1997.

69. Labor Neighbor, December 1996.

70. Christopher A. Ratcliff, attorney II, letter to EPA, Bill Luthans, associate director of air, pesticides, and toxics, dated Februray 24, 1997. He states, "According to unconfirmed calculations by Shintech, fourteen of forty-five-supporters exceeded the five-minute limit, with the extra speaking time totaling seventeen minutes and forty-five seconds. Fifteen of thirty-four opponents exceeded the five minute limit, with extra speaking time totaling thirty-two minutes and forty-two seconds."

71. Janice Dickerson, memo to Jim Friloux, dated December 11, 1996, re: Public Hearing – Romeville.

72. Giordano 1997d.

73. Giordano and Warren 1997.

74. Ferstel 1997a.

75. EPA 1997a.

76. EPA 1997a.

77. Giordano 1997c.

78. Giordano 1997c.

79. Orr 1997.

80. Authors' interview with Monique Harden, Earthjustice Legal Defense Fund, formerly of Greenpeace, in July 1999.

81. Authors' interview with Monique Harden, Earthjustice Legal Defense Fund, formerly of Greenpeace, in July 1999.

82. Ferstel 1997c.

83. Ember 1998.

84. Alpert 1998.

85. Authors' interview with representative from Air Quality Division, DEQ.

86. Authors' interview with Gustave Von Bodungen, assistant secretary, LDEQ, in June 1999.

87. EPA 1998.

88. J. Timmons Roberts, letter to Ann Goode, director OCR, dated February 29, 1988; Lisa Lavie, Robert Kuehn, and Jennifer Lewis letter to Ann Goode, director OCR, and Mary O'Lone, Office of General Council, EPA, dated February 18, 1998.

89. McQuaid 2000d.

90. Kriz 1998.

91. Ember 1998.

92. Schleifstein 1998b.
93. Authors' interview with Monique Harden, Earthjustice Legal Defense Fund, formerly Greenpeace, in July 1999.
94. Authors' interview with Monique Harden, Earthjustice Legal Defense Fund, formerly Greenpeace, in July 1999.
95. McKinney 1998b.
96. McKinney 1998a.
97. Chandler 1998.
98. Bourne and Hooker 1997.
99. Bourne and Hooker 1997.
100. Authors' interview with SJCJE members Mary L. Green, Brenda Huguet, Gloria Roberts, Rose Ann Roussel, Dolores Simmons, and Emelda J. West in June 1999.
101. Schleifstein 1998c.
102. Ferstel 1997b.
103. Authors' interview with David Wise, Shintech plant manager, in June 2000.
104. It is well known in Louisiana that Governor Foster is highly critical of trial lawyers and has been instrumental in promoting tort reform legislation that has had a negative impact on trial lawyers. Jerry McKernan is a past president of the Louisiana Trial Lawyers Association and is representing the group free of charge.
105. Authors' interview with David Wise, Shintech plant manager, in June 2000.
106. Authors' interview with Carol Gaudin, vice president, St. James Citizen Coalition, in March 1999.
107. Authors' interview with representative from Louisiana DEQ, Air Permit Division, June 1999.
108. Authors' interview with representative from DEQ, Community/Industry Relations office, June 1999.
109. Hymel 1999.
110. L. Gray 1998.
111. Cray 1998.
112. L. Gray 1998.
113. McQuaid 2000.
114. Authors' interview with Monique Harden, Earthjustice Legal Defense Fund, formerly Greenpeace, in July 1999.
115. Authors' interview with Lisa Lavie, supervising attorney, Tulane Environmental Law Clinic, in June 1999.
116. Authors' interview with Mary L. Green, Brenda Huguet, Gloria Roberts, Rose Ann Roussel, Dolores Simmons, and Emelda J. West in June 1999.

NOTES FOR CHAPTER 5

1. Snyder 1995; Jones 1998; Dunne and McMillan 1998. Other numbers are cited in the accounts, but the Alabama dumping prices are between 25 and 100 dollars, and the Louisiana prices are listed up to eight dollars.
2. Jones 1998.

3. Dunne 1998.
4. Dunne 1998c.
5. Dunne 1998c. There were manifests in the glove compartments detailing that they contained "Waste, environmentally hazardous," and notation that they contained benzene, Class III, 9. That 9 indicates "dangerous waste," Class III means flammable (McMillan 1997b).
6. McMillan 1997b.
7. McMillan 1997b.
8. Dunne 1998a.
9. Dunne 1998a.
10. Dunne 1998a.
11. Morris 1997b.
12. Morris 1997c.
13. Morris 1997c.
14. Morris 1997c, EPA 1997b. http://www.epa.gov/ngispgm3/iris/irisdat/0061.DAT.
15. EPA 1997b.
16. Morris 1997b. The quote is from a former EPA official, who asked not to be identified.
17. EPA 1997b.
18. EPA 1997b.
19. Morris 1997a.
20. Jones 1998.
21. Dunn 1998a.
22. Dunne 1998e.
23. McMillan 1997b; Dunne 1998c, 1998e.
24. Bradley 1998.
25. Daugherty 1997c.
26. McMillan 1997c.
27. Daugherty 1997c.
28. Daugherty 1997c.
29. Jones 1998.
30. Dunne 1998a.
31. Dunne 1998a. The rest of this paragraph is quoted from this article, which are from sworn testimony in the trial against Exxon and U.S. Liquids.
32. Dunne 1998b.
33. McMillan 1997c.
34. McMillan 1997a.
35. McMillan 1997a. As mentioned earlier, the loophole ended up with the obscure name Rule 29-B under Section 3001(b)(2)(A) of the Resource Conservation and Recovery Act.
36. McMillan 1997a.
37. Louisiana DNR, Office of Conservation, 1999b.
38. Louisiana DNR, Office of Conservation, 1999c.
39. McMillan 1997c.
40. Snyder n.d.
41. C. Gray 1997b.
42. Robichaux n.d.

43. DNR's Office of Conservation Mission Statement reads: "With recognition that exploration for and production of oil and gas and other natural resources are essential and beneficial economic activities in Louisiana, the mission of the Office of Conservation is to prevent and prohibit the waste of oil and gas and other natural resources, while providing protection of public health, safety and the environment through administration of programs of effective regulatory control regarding oil and gas and other natural resources, including the protection of underground sources of drinking water." [Revised on Friday, June 11, 1999 09:45:42 CDT by the DNR Web Team.]
44. McMahon 1997c.
45. C. Gray 1997b.
46. C. Gray 1997b.
47. Louisiana DNR, Office of Conservation, 1999a. The critic was chemist Wilma Subra, citing different positions the lid can be on the "sniffer" machine; from authors' interview in August 1999.
48. Louisiana Environmental Action Network, Sierra Club Delta Chapter, et al. 1997; McMahon 1997c.
49. McMahon 1997c.
50. *Gambit* 1998a.
51. Daugherty 1998a.
52. McMillan 1997c.
53. McMillan 1997c. But DEQ also put a shed by Acadian Shipyards, whose owner believed that they were becoming the scapegoat for the ExxonU.S. Liquids scandal. The owner sued the state for conspiracy between DEQ and U.S. Liquids.
54. McMillan 1997c.
55. Reible and Valsaraj 1999.
56. Reible and Valsaraj 1999, p. iv.
57. Reible and Valsaraj 1999, p. v.
58. Reible and Valsaraj 1999, p. v.
59. Authors' interview with Wilma Subra 1999; authors' analysis of raw data provided at http://www.dnr.state.la.us/cons/conserv.ssi [July 20, 1999]; Dunne 1999b.
60. Dunne 1999b.
61. Redman 1998b.
62. Ferstel and Shuler 1998.
63. Zganjar 1998b.
64. Ferstel and Shuler 1998.
65. Zganjar 1998b.
66. Ferstel and Shuler 1998.
67. McMillan 1998a.
68. Authors' interview with Dianne Dugas, director, Department of Environmental Epidemology, in May 1999.
69. McMillan 1998a; Ferstel 1998a; McQuaid 2000a.
70. Associated Press 1998.
71. *Baton Rouge Advocate* 1999.

72. *Baton Rouge Advocate* 1998. One critic pointed out that Brazzel owned 35,000 shares in the company, worth about $700,000. (*Baton Rouge Advocate* 1999).
73. Associated Press 1998.
74. Zganjar 1998a.
75. Authors' interview with Pat Williams in 2000.
76. McMillan 1997d.
77. *Thibodaux Daily Comet* 1999.
78. *Thibodaux Daily Comet* 1999.
79. In April, Williams said she didn't want to testify in the trial; she didn't want to take sides in the trial because it might influence her objectivity (McMillan 1998b).
80. McMillan 1998c.
81. Porteous 1998.
82. Dunne and McMillan 1998.
83. Dunne 1998d.
84. Dunne 1999.
85. Dunne 1998f.
86. Zganjar 1998c; Dunne 1998c.
87. Zganjar 1998c.
88. Dunne and McMillan 1998.
89. Dunne 1998g.
90. Dunne and McMillan 1998.
91. *Environment Watch* 1998.
92. Dunne 1998h.
93. Dunne and McMillan 1998.
94. Dunne 1998h.
95. Dunne and McMillan 1998.
96. Dunne and McMillan 1998.
97. This section draws heavily on Zganjar (1998d).
98. McMillan and Dunne 1998a.
99. McMillan and Dunne 1998b. Actually the award amounts were higher, but the jury only assigned Exxon 25 percent of the fault, and they were unaware of the settlement removing Campbell Wells and U.S. Liquids from the penalty.
100. Harold Jarvis, quoted in McMillan and Dunne (1998b).
101. Zganjar 1998e.
102. McMillan and Dunne 1998a.
103. McMillan and Dunne 1998a.
104. Zganjar 1998f.
105. *Gambit* 1998b.
106. Authors' interview with Wilma Subra in August 1999.
107. Daugherty 1997c.
108. Dunne 1998i.
109. To recall, DNR secretary Jack Caldwell said, "If you feel you are ever in a position where you have to shut a well because of the way you read the rules, give us a call. We will work something out" (*Gambit* 1998a).

110. McMillan 1998d.
111. McMillan 1998e.
112. Authors' interview with Pat Williams in 2000.
113. Daugherty 1997c.
114. *Thibodaux Daily Comet* 1999.
115. McMillan 1998d.
116. Wright 1999.

NOTES FOR CHAPTER 6

1. Authors' interview with Elodia Blanco in May 1999.
2. Authors' interview with Peggy GrandPre in March 1999.
3. Warner and Cooper 1995a.
4. Daugherty 1998d.
5. Daugherty 1998d.
6. *Gambit* 1986.
7. *Gambit* 1986.
8. *Gambit* n.d.
9. Daugherty 1998a.
10. McKendall 1985a.
11. Grissett-Welsh 1985.
12. McKendall 1985b.
13. McKendall 1985a.
14. Ridenhour 1986.
15. EPA, n.d. Further testing by the EPA in 1993 confirmed the 1986 tests indicating excessive levels of toxins such as lead, arsenic, chromium, and calcium. Tests also revealed the presence of "volatile organic compounds, polyaromatic hydrocarbons, metals" and other dangerous toxins. From Earthjustice Legal Defense Fund mimeograph, "Earthjustice comparison sheet," 1999.
16. See, for example, Bullard (1990).
17. Cooper and Warner 1995.
18. Cooper and Warner 1995.
19. See, for example, Szasz (1993).
20. Warner and Cooper 1995b.
21. Montague 1997.
22. New York State Department of Health. Undated report.
23. Authors' interviews with Dianne Dugas, director, Department of Environmental Epidemology, in May 1999, and with Kenneth Launier in May 1999.
24. One difficulty encountered by OPH in studying the area was that existing census tracts covered a far larger area than those sitting atop the landfill. Critics argued that this approach was akin to the joke about a drunk looking for his keys under a streetlight, when he dropped them somewhere else. When asked why he was searching under the light and not where he dropped them, the drunk replied "because there's better light over here."
25. "Health Consultation," 1997.

26. Authors' interview with Beverly Wright in July 2000.
27. Mielke studied lead concentrations in the soil around New Orleans. When applied to Ag Street, these results raise questions as to the source of the high lead-levels in the neighborhood, whether from car exhaust or from the land-fill beneath the homes. Agriculture Street lies near the foot of the I-10 high rise, just outside downtown New Orleans, in a high-volume traffic area. It is plausible to believe, with Mielke's studies in mind, that the source of lead in the soil at Agriculture Street is not caused by the landfill but rather by the car exhaust from I-10 traffic.

    Dr. Mielke does not believe that Agriculture Street is all that toxic, es-pecially as compared to the rest of New Orleans. Mielke explains that much of the City of New Orleans was built on landfills. For example, Bayou St. John has lead concentrations ten to twenty times greater than Agriculture Street, and Mielke says that this high lead concentration is "true all over the city." Agriculture Street, according to Mielke, has a median lead concentration of 200 parts per million (ppm) of lead, and has a good grass cover, making it less dangerous. Other communities have lead concentration at 2000 ppm. "The mayor's yard is more contaminated than Ag Street." From authors' interview with Howard Mielke in August 1999.
28. Howard Mielke, memo to Jerald White, New Orleans mayor's environment officer, dated July 20, 1998.
29. Mielke continued, "As I will argue, for the sake of the community and the whole city, actions to remove the community from Superfund status should be vigorously pursued." He put it bluntly: "I believe the problem is political, not scientific. . . . Without removal from the list, the members of the com-munity will continue to feel the effects financially, physically and emotion-ally." Of course, other cases around the nation have shown that even with re-moval from the Superfund lists, much of the stigma remains.
30. Authors' interview with Howard Mielke in August 1999.
31. He expressed frustration that Agriculture Street residents and those in the environmental justice movement, as well as the EPA, tended to ignore his re-search. He said that people have a "tendency to filter out what people want to hear," although he admitted that "I'd be terribly upset myself if I found out that what I fought bitterly for wasn't true." Mielke explained that attention of EJ is often focused on small communities. "It's easy to see smokestacks . . . hard to see exhaust pipes." This focus leads EJ movement to miss massive EJ problems. "If you really want to see EJ issues, go see the inner cities of every major city in U.S. Children are being poisoned." He was talking about lead poisoning. "The same kids who have lead poisoning today will be in prison to-morrow." A growing literature has shown that kids with lead poisoning are prone to violence, behavioral problems, and the like; see Mielke et al. (1999).
32. Cooper and Warner 1995. At the national level, a study published in the *Amer-ican Journal of Preventative Medicine* concluded that "no significant differ-ence" existed "in the prevalence of cancer, liver illnesses, and skin diseases between the exposed and comparison groups" living in or outside of Super-fund sites. The study did, however, find an increased prevalence of respira-tory diseases and seizures. This increased prevalence disappeared when con-

trolled for "cigarette smoking, consumption of homegrown vegetables, or source of water supply" (Najem, Strunck, and Fuererman, 1994). Many locals bristle at the implications that their lifestyle is responsible for diseases, a topic we discuss at length later. Others would argue that vegetables and water supply are obvious routes for toxic exposures and should not be controlled for. If smoking is a response to stress, there are questions about whether it should be controlled for (see, for example, Roberts 1993).

33. Concerned Citizens of the Agriculture Street Landfill 1999.
34. The quotes in this section are from Stephen Kroll-Smith and J. Timmons Roberts, "Stress and Fear of Toxic Exposures at the Agriculture Street Landfill Superfund Site," unpublished testimony of Agriculture Street landfill residents, collected February 12, 1998.
35. EPA 1996.
36. Stephen Kroll-Smith and J. Timmons Roberts, "Stress and Fear of Toxic Exposures at the Agriculture Street Landfill Superfund Site," unpublished testimony of Agriculture Street landfill residents, collected February 12, 1998.
37. Erikson 1995.
38. Macionis 1999.
39. Baum and Fleming 1993.
40. Erikson 1995, p. 232.
41. Flynn, Slovic, and Mertz 1994. Our own research on national sample of workers in dangerous workplaces revealed that women and minorities showed highest levels of psychological effects from fear of exposures (Roberts 1993; Roberts and Baugher 1995; Roberts 1998).
42. EPA 1998b, Table A1, among others.
43. *Theresa Berry and Phillis Smith vs. The City of New Orleans et al.* 1994.
44. *New Orleans Times Picayune* 1999.
45. Authors' personal communication with Lois Gibbs in July 1999.
46. Lois Gibbs. "Fact Sheet: Letter to Mr. Bob Martin." March 17, 1999.
47. According to the community's technical advisor Joel S. Hirschorn (1999), the community felt that "the removal action left highly contaminated surface soils as sources of continued releases into the environment and . . . caused preventable health threats."
48. The EPA's original plan included only sixty-six households for relocation. However, after a lengthy battle with EPA headquarters and Region IX, CATE and the Escambia community achieved relocation of all 358 households (Hirschorn 1999).
49. An Earthjustice Legal Defense Fund comparison of Agriculture Street and Forest Glen Subdivision in New York suggested that the similarities are striking but the approaches inconsistent: Forest Glen residents were relocated (Earthjustice flyer 1999).
50. *Gambit* 1999.
51. *Gambit* 1999.
52. An article in the Superfund Report continues, "When asked whether EPA could conceivably use remedial authority at this portion of the site, despite its earlier designation as a removal, the source says, "Is there a way? Of course there is, but we would not do that. . . . The answer is no." (EPA 1996).

53. According to a letter from William Jefferson et al. to Carol Browner on December 19, 1997, "the report reflects a consensus view among community residents and city and congressional representatives that the EPA should not begin its cleanup process at the Agriculture Street Landfill site until Congress has had an opportunity to fully review the matter and potentially secure an appropriation for a buyout and relocation of the residents." The letter further calls the remediation efforts "inadequate and inappropriate for the Agriculture Street Landfill Superfund site."

54. Mary Landrieu and John Breaux letter to the Honorable Barbara Mikulski, dated September 3, 1998; *Gambit* n.d.

55. Gibbs 1999.

56. Timothy Fields letter to Peggy GrandPre, dated July 7, 1999.

57. In a letter dated July 2, 1999, EPA acting assistant administrator Tim Fields explained that it removed "19,720 cubic yards of debris and 1,773 tires" on the forty-eight acres of undeveloped property. Residents and some experts expected the plan to affect only 10 percent of the Agriculture Street site, as the other 90 percent of the site is covered by roads, houses, sidewalks, and other obstructing structures. According to Lois Gibbs, who has served as a consultant and advocate for the Agriculture Street community, "they can't clean up under the school, homes or apartments. Once EPA is done with their scraping, putting down plastic and dirt, there will still be vertical and horizontal contaminants. When it rains, it's going to wash back and forth." This cleanup plan was to be voluntary for residents but has become a means for the EPA to pressure residents into a cleanup they do not want. Despite all the congressional language and action, EPA spokesman David Bary said, "Relocation is not part of our plan. We intend to do the work, with the residents' cooperation and agreement."

58. Schleifstein 1999b.

59. Schleifstein 1999c.

60. Daugherty 1998d. The EPA's "Brownfields" program is designed specifically to relieve property sellers and buyers from liability issues in the case of future contamination they did not cause.

61. Timoth Fields letter to Peggy GrandPre, dated July 7, 1999.

62. Peggy GrandPre letter to Timothy Fields, dated July 6, 1999 [emphasis in original].

63. Both the EPA and Gordon Plaza homeowners knew of Richard Blackmore's legal trouble, but when Blackmore requested a "prospective purchaser" agreement from the EPA asking that he not be required to pay for cleanup costs, EPA could not give such an agreement due to his conviction. It instead gave him a "comfort letter," a nonbinding agreement not to sue for cleanup costs. EPA's case manager Ursula Lennox said, "We don't want to interfere with any private negotiations or business dealings. To interfere would be stepping on people's toes, and that's not our role as a government agency. Our role is to protect the public health and the environment" (Schleifstein 1998e). *The Gambit Weekly* editorialized that "The sense of hopelessness and desperation felt by Gordon Plaza residents over their predicament – and the continued squabbling among governmental agencies that are supposed to help them –

leaves them vulnerable to questionable propositions such as the one offered by Richard Blackmore" (*Gambit* n.d.).

64. Schleifstein 1999e.
65. "Although the land-use plan, a replacement for a city blueprint adopted in 1980, would have no legal authority, it would heavily influence an effort under way to requite the city's fragmented zoning code and would serve as the centerpiece of a master plan for city development." (Warner 1999a). In an attempt to attract light industry to the Agriculture Street site, Mayor Morial asked the Washington, D.C.–based Smith-Free Group consulting firm to prepare a plan that would "figure out how to bring some economic development opportunities to the Agriculture Street area and provide resources to buy out the residents." This was according to Robert Hickmott, former EPA and HUD senior appointee (Schleifstein 1999e).
66. Authors' interview with Linda Calvert in March 2000.
67. Authors' interview with Elodia Blanco in May 1999.

NOTES FOR CHAPTER 7

1. U.S. Chamber of Commerce 1998a.
2. Juneau 1998.
3. Juneau 1998.
4. NBCC 2000.
5. Authors' interview with Robert Bullard in July 1998.
6. Goode 1998b.
7. Cushman 1998.
8. U.S. Chamber of Commerce 1998a.
9. Cushman 1998.
10. The Environmental Council of the States (ECOS) is a group of state environmental agency directors.
11. Roberts 1998.
12. Roberts, Conrecode, and Leftwich 1998.
13. McQuaid makes this point in his May 2000 special series in the *Times-Picayune*, citing several activists.
14. U.S. Conference of Mayors 1998.
15. McTopy 1998.
16. Authors' interview with Robert Bullard in July 1998.
17. McQuaid 2000e.
18. Goode 1998a.
19. Goode 1998a, 1998b.
20. Sullivan 1999.
21. EPA 2000a.
22. U.S. Chamber of Commerce 1998b.
23. Cushman 1998.
24. EPA 2000b.
25. EPA 1999, p. 3.
26. EPA 1999.

27. Sissell 1999.
28. Cushman 1998.
29. ECOS 1998.
30. Cushman 1998.
31. EPA 2000, p. 6.
32. Authors' interview with Dale Givens in June 1998.
33. Briesacher 1998, personal communication.
34. Redman 1998a.
35. Burgin 1998, personal communication.
36. LABI 1998.
37. Reportedly this group included American Cyanamid, DuPont, Chevron, and the Port of South Louisiana.
38. Kramer 1998.
39. Hanson 1998.
40. Daugherty 1998c.
41. Authors' interview with Audrey Evans, outreach coordinator, TELC, in March 1998.
42. Kramer 1998.
43. Gill 1998.
44. Schleifstein 1999a.
45. Anderson 1999a.
46. Wardlaw 1998.
47. Fairley 1999.
48. *Baton Rouge Advocate* 1998.
49. Daugherty 1998b.
50. Ellie 1998.
51. Gyan 1998.
52. Schleifstein 1999d.
53. The director of Loyola's Poverty Law Clinic, Bill Quigley, decided to do exactly that. He ran against Calogero for the Supreme Court because he was so angry about the Rule XX changes, with a campaign slogan of "Justice for ALL." He lost, but received just over 14,000 votes. The election was covered in major pieces on CBS's *60 Minutes* and PBS's *Frontline*.
54. Gyan 1999. The intevening segment of this quote is the following: "They should be commended for their enthusiasm, hard work, and willingness to devote time and effort toward altruistic endeavors. The court recognizes the pronounced degree of anger, angst, and frustration they are experiencing as a result of this alteration in the practice rules. To them such a change appears unfair."
55. Authors' interview with Lisa Lavie, supervising attorney, TELC, in June 1999. She stated that an attorney in the Civil Clinic has had one of her clients challenged under the new rules: "She [the client] is going to be deposed now about that specific topic, that's bad news, you know that's bad news. Not many people want to go through that and then, of course, [if] somehow we've made a mistake and accepted a client who actually doesn't need the representation, we're open for sanction."
56. And, of course, there are many others like them across the country.

57. The debate over pollution havens is a complex and important one. It is not necessary to prove that firms fled only to avoid environmental regulations (labor costs are usually much more important: see, for example, Low and Yeats [1993]). Rather, once in a location with a weak government, firms often backslide in their pollution control spending. This is apparently true in both Louisiana and the so-called Third World.

58. See, for example, Szasz (1993).

59. Greer and Bruno 1996.

60. A majority of East Baton Rouge voters, for example, said that they favored limiting industrial expansion to control pollution (57 percent versus 34 percent). There was important variation in who held this opinion: three out of four African Americans agreed, compared with 49 percent of whites. And importantly, people's concern was related to their distance from the facilities. Still, both the governor and DEQ secretary Dale Givens saw no reason to limit industrial expansion (Dunne 1999c). Of course, we must consider that this study was done at a time of near record-low unemployment.

61. Hunter 2000a, 2000b.

62. The *National Law Journal* study showed that nationally, minority communities are less likely to get cleaned up, and when they do, the cleanups take longer to occur. This study was conducted before the wave of activism in the mid- and late-1990s (Laelle and Coyle 1992).

63. Scientists and university doctors often ended up on both sides of these battles; either hired up by polluting companies or the state government on the one hand or consulting or volunteering for environmental groups on the other.

64. DEQ is still under investigation by the EPA from prior environmental justice complaints (Shintech, GTX, Alsen landfill, Industrial Pipe–Oakville, Supplemental Fuels–St. Gabriel) (Ferstel 1999). The source for the statement "The agency could lose its federal funds if found guilty" of civil rights violations is a confidential interview with an EPA employee in July 1999.

65. The one exception in some people's minds is the unit in the Louisiana Attorney General's Office headed by Willie Fontenot that provides information and support to residents who feel that their health and safety is being threatened by industrial facilities and other polluters.

66. Fox 1991.

67. Roberts et al. 1998.

68. The quote is from Deborah Van Dyken, quoted in Fried (1993).

69. See, for example Erikson (1995), Brown and Mikkelson (1997), Roberts (1998), Couch and Kroll-Smith (1991), and Arnoff and Gunther (1997).

70. Edelstein 1988.

71. McQuaid 2000e.

72. Authors' interview with Pat Melancon, SJCJE, in March 1998.

73. McQuaid 2000e.

74. Authors' interview with Jerald White in October 1999.

75. E.g. Freudenberg and Steinsapir 1992; Bullard and Wright 1992.

76. There is a substantial literature debating these points. Some of our points can be found in Roberts (1998).

77. Some of the key writings in the field of coping are those of Pearlin and Schooler (1978), Lazarus and Folkman (1984), and Taylor, Repetti, and Seeman (1997).
78. See Brody (1988); J. Timmons Roberts and John E. Baugher unpublished manuscript, "Coping with Hazards at Work: The Impact of Coping Styles on Stress."
79. Bachrach and Zautra 1985; Baum, Fleming, and Singer 1983; Unger et al. 1992.
80. Baum, Fleming, and Singer 1983; Collins, Baum, and Singer 1983.
81. Erikson 1995. See also Aldwin, Sutton and Lachman (1996).
82. See, for example, Foreman (1998).
83. Foreman 1998.
84. Bullard 1998.
85. Authors' interview with Audrey Evans, outreach coordinator, TELC, in March 1998.
86. We are currently completing a book entitled *Trouble In Paradise,* which examines these transnational social movements.

References

Aldwin, Carolyn M., Karen J. Sutton, and Margie Lachman. 1996. "The Development of Coping Resources in Adulthood." *Journal o f Personality* 64: 837–71.

Allen-Mills, Tony. 1997. "Louisiana Blacks Win Nuclear War." *London Sunday Times.* May 11.

Alpert, Bruce. 1998. "Shintech Review Weighs on EPA." *New Orleans Times-Picayune.* June 15.

American Tort Reform Association. n.d. 2000 Tort Reform Record. [Accessed August 11, 2000] http://www.atra.org/record/

Anderson, Bob. 1986. "Run Silent, Run Deep: A Story on the Condition of Louisiana's Environment." *Louisiana State University Magazine.* June.
    1994. "Environmental Justice leads gripes to DEQ." *Baton Rouge Advocate.* October 2.

Anderson, Ed. 1999. "Foster slams law professors' protest." *The New Orleans Times-Picayune.* January 7.

Anderson, Ed, and Chris Gray. 1997. "Foster Endorses Probes of Shintech Adversaries." *New Orleans Times-Picayune.* November 7.

Aronoff, Marilyn, and Valerie Gunter. 1992. "It's Hard to Keep a Good Town Down: Local Recovery Efforts in the Aftermath of Toxic Contamination." *Industrial Crisis Quarterly* 6: 83–97.

Associated Press (AP). 1989. "Johnston campaign funds questioned." *Lake Charles American Press.* July 3.
    1998. "State must wait for Grand Bois research." *New Orleans Times-Picayune.* May 5.
    1998. "Grand Bois Residents Prepare for Trial." AP wire. July 12.
    1999. "More Research on Environmental Justice Urged." *New Orleans Times-Picayune.* March 23.

Babcock, Charles R., and Richard Morin. 1990. "Following the Path of Self-Interest: Do PACs find the candidates, or vice versa?" *Washington Post Weekly Edition.* June 25–July 1.

Bachrach, Kenneth M., and Alex J. Zantra. 1985. "Coping with a Community Stressor: The Threat of a Hazardous Waste Facility." *Journal of Health and Social Behavior* 26: 127–41.

Bandura, Albert. 1997. *Self-Efficacy: The Exercise of Control.* New York: W. H. Freeman and Company.

Barrett, Mary L. 1993. "New Madrid fault imperils enrichment plant site," Letter to the Editor. *Shreveport Times.* June 29.

Baton Rouge Advocate. 1998. "Law Clinics Say Rules Hurt Poor." June 18.

Baugher, John E., and J. Timmons Roberts. 1999. "Perceptions and Worry About Hazards at Work: Unions, Contract Maintenance, and Job Control in the U.S. Petrochemical Industry." *Industrial Relations* 38 (4): 522–41.

Baum, Andrew, and India Fleming. 1993. "Implications of Psychological Research on Stress and Technological Accidents." *American Psychologist* 48 (6): 665–72.

Baum, Andrew, Raymond Fleming, and Jerome E. Singer. 1983. "Coping With Victimization by Technological Disaster." *Journal of Social Issues* 39 (2): 117–38.

Baumbach, Richard O., Jr., and William E. Borah. 1981. *The Second Battle of New Orleans: A History of the Vieux Carre Riverfront-Expressway Controversy.* Tuscaloosa: University of Alabama.

Theresa Berry and Phillis Smith vs. The City of New Orleans et al. 1994. Court document.

Bourne, Gregory, and David A. Hooker, 1997. "Convening Assessment, Issues Involved with the Shintech Facility Siting Process in St. James Parish, Louisiana." Draft Convening Assessment Report. Southeast Negotiating Network. October 27.

Bradley, Ed. 1998. "Investigative Reports: Town Under Siege." Aired December 23, 1997.

Broach, Drew. 1992. "In the Wake of Formosa's Exit." *New Orleans Times-Picayune.* October 17.

Brody, Julia G. 1988. "Responses to Collective Risk: Appraisal and Coping Among Workers Exposed to Occupational Health Hazards." *American Journal of Community Psychology* 16 (5): 645–63.

Brown, Phil, and Edwin J. Mikkelson. 1997. *No Safe Place: Toxic Waste, Leukemia, and Community Action.* Berkeley: University of California Press.

Brumfield, Les. 1976. "Louisiana's Disappearing Land." *New Orleans States-Item.* May 11.

Bryant, Pat. 1993. "Tenants and Toxics: New Orleans, LA." *Southern Exposure* 21 (4): 22–9.

Bullard, Robert. 1990. *Dumping in Dixie.* Boulder: Westview Press.

——— ed. 1994. *Unequal Protection: Environmental Justice and Communities of Color.* San Francisco: Sierra Club.

——— 1998. Comments as Presider in session "Environmental Issues from a Race, Gender, Class Perspective." American Sociological Association's 93rd annual meeting. San Francisco. August 21–25.

——— 1999. "EJ 101: An Outline Presentation." EJ Resource Center. http://www.ejrc.cau.edu/ej101.html

Bullard, Robert, and Glenn S. Johnson, eds. 1997. *Just Transportation: Dismantling Race and Class Barriers to Mobility.* Gabriola Island, B.C., Canada: New Society Publishers.

Bullard, Robert, and Beverly Wright. 1992. "The Quest for Environmental Equity: Mobilizing the African-American Community for Social Change." In *American Environmentalism: The U.S. Environmental Movement, 1970–1990.* Riley E. Dunlap and Angela G. Mertig, eds. New York: Taylor & Francis.

Calsen, Frances, ed. 2000. Directory of Louisiana Manufacturers 2001. Published in cooperation with the State of Louisiana DED: Harris InfoSource.

Carrier, Cornelia. 1977. "West Bank should save, use wetlands." *New Orleans Times-Picayune,* October 9.

Carson, Michele, 1985. "No Dump in Our Back Yard, says Claiborne Parish." *Shreveport Times,* March 25.

Chandler, Adam. 1998. "Another Delay at EPA." *PVC Activism Update.* July 1.

Claiborne Parish Industrial Development Foundation. 1990. "An open letter to the citizens of Claiborne Parish." *Homer Guardian-Journal.* January 11.

Collete, Will. 1997. Coal group, presentation at the Louisiana Environmental Action Network annual conference. Baton Rouge, Louisiana. November.

Collins, D. M., A. Baum, and J. E. Singer. 1983. "Coping With Chronic Stress at Three Mile Island: Psychological and Biochemical Evidence." *Health Psychology* 2: 149–66.

Colwell, Steve. 1993."Uranium Enrichment Plant still four years away from production." *Claiborne Advertiser.* July 13.

Commission for Racial Justice, United Church of Christ. 1987. *Toxic Wastes and Race in the United States.* New York: United Church of Christ.

Concerned Citizens of the Agriculture Street Landfill. 1999. Community meeting. May 15.

Cooper, Christopher, and Coleman Warner. 1995. "Is old dump site toxic? Not very, EPA says." *New Orleans Times-Picayune.* April 4.

Couch, Stephen R., and Stephen Kroll-Smith, eds. 1991. *Communities at Risk: Collective Responses to Technological Hazards.* New York: Peter Lang.

Coyle, Pamela. 2000. "N.O.'s Landfill Appeal Rejected." *New Orleans Times-Picayune.* February 12, p. B3.

Cray, Charlie. 1998. "Shintech Pull-out is Major Civil Rights Victory; Greenpeace Pledges to Oppose Any Expansion." Greenpeace press release. September 17.

Cushman, John H. 1998. "Pollution policy is unfair burden, states tell EPA." *New York Times on the Web.* May 10.
www.nytimes.com/yr/mo/day/early/051098states-epa-dispute.html

Daugherty, Christi. 1997a. "Polluter, Heal Thyself." *The Gambit Weekly* (New Orleans). May 20.

1997b. "Not Easy Being Green." *The Gambit Weekly* (New Orleans). July 22.

1997c. "Legal Poison: Grand Bois Residents Want the State to Shut Down the Oil Waste Pit Next Door." *The Gambit Weekly* (New Orleans). November 25.

1998a. "Toxic Town." *The Gambit Weekly* (New Orleans). June 23.

1998b. "In a Filthy State." *The Gambit Weekly* (New Orleans). July 14.

1998c. "Clinic Cut-off." *The Gambit Weekly* (New Orleans). September 8.

1998d. "Digging In." *The Gambit Weekly* (New Orleans). November 3.

1999. "Pay Up or Else." *The Gambit Weekly* (New Orleans). May 18.

Delaker, Joseph. U.S. Bureau of the Census. 1999. *Poverty in the United States: 1998.* Washington, D.C.: U.S. Government Printing Office.

Dickerson, Janice, and Roger Ward. 1995. *Environmental Justice In Louisiana.* Baton Rouge: The Louisiana Department of Environmental Quality, Environmental Justice Program.

Dunne, Mike. 1998a. "Grand Bois Plaintiffs Tell of Illnesses." *Baton Rouge Advocate.* July 24.

1998b. "Grand Bois Man Describes Fear, Tells of Videotaping Trucks, Burning Eyes." *Baton Rouge Advocate.* July 21.

1998c. "Exxon Engineer Testifies in Lawsuit; Records on Waste Showed Toxic Content." *Baton Rouge Advocate.* July 22.

1998d. "Engineer Testifies in Lawsuit: Records on Waste Showed Toxic Content." *Baton Rouge Advocate.* August 4.

1998e. "Pair Unaffected by Oilfield Waste." *Baton Rouge Advocate.* August 4.

1998f. "Expert Testifies No Illness Found; Grand Bois Case Continues." *Baton Rouge Advocate.* August 6.

1998g. "Witness Raises Credibility Questions." *Baton Rouge Advocate.* August 7.

1998h. "Grand Bois Defendant Settles with Plaintiffs: Exxon Now Stands Alone Against Allegations." *Baton Rouge Advocate.* August 8.

1998i. "Grant to Help State Study Grand Bois Waste Facility." *Baton Rouge Advocate.* August 18.

1999a. "TRI Emissions Inch Up in Louisiana for 1997." *Baton Rouge Advocate.* May 27.

1999b. "Analyst Says Oilfield Waste Tested Under New Program Could Be Hazardous." *Baton Rouge Advocate.* June 11.

1999c. "Voters: Limit Industry to Control Pollution." *Baton Rouge Advocate.* January 13.

Dunne, Mike, and John McMillan. 1998. "Grand Bois Deliberations Resume Today." *Baton Rouge Advocate.* August 9.

Earthjustice Legal Defense Fund. 1998. "Earth Day Environmental Justice Victory." Press release. April 23.

Edelstein, Michael R. 1988. *Contaminated Communities: The Social and Psychological Impacts of Residential Toxic Exposures.* Boulder: Westview.

Ellie, Lolie Eric. 1998. "Clinic's Odds Even Worse." *New Orleans Times-Picayune.* June 19.

Ellis, William S. 1993. "The Mississippi: River Under Siege." *National Geographic* special issue on Water. November/December.

Ember, Lois. 1998. "Environmental Justice as Issue." C&EN. July 13.

Environment Watch. 1998. "Grand Bois residents settle with U.S. Liquids." September 10.

Environment Week. 1993. "NAACP throws support behind enrichment plant opponents." December 16.

Environmental Council on the States (ECOS). 1998. "Resolution 98–2. Environmental Protection Agency's Interim Guidance for Investigating Environmental Permit Challenges." Approved March 26, New Orleans, LA. http://www.sso.org/ecos/policy/resolutions/98–2.htm

"Environmental Justice and the States." [Accessed April 23, 2000.] http://www.sso.org/ecos/projects/EJ/justice.htm

Environmental Defense Fund. 1999. "Environmental Release Report: Entire United States." [Accessed June 10 1999.] http://www.scorecard.org/env-releases/us.tcl

"Environmental Justice: A Matter of Perspective." A report for the National Council of State Legislators by the Environmental Justice group. September 1995.

REFERENCES

Environmental Protection Agency (EPA). 1996. "EPA Unlikely to Relocate Citizens at Agriculture Street Landfill Site." Superfund Report. July 8. Mimeograph.

——. 1997a. "Order Partially Granting and Partially Denying Petitions for Objection to Permits." September 10.

——. 1997b. "Hydrogen sulfide; CASRN 7783–06–4 (03/01/97)." [Accessed June 25, 2000.] http://www.epa.gov/ngispgm3/iris/irisdat/0061.DAT

——. 1998a. "Title VI Administrative Complaint, re: Louisiana Department of Environmental Quality/Shintech Permit." Draft Demographic Information. January. Mimeograph.

——. 1999. "Report of the Title VI Implementation Advisory Committee: Next Steps for EPA, State, and Local Environmental Justice Programs." March 1. http://www.epa.gov/ocem/nacept/titleVI/titlerpt.html

——. 2000a. "Title VI Implementation Advisory Committee." http://www.epa.gov/ocrpage1/t6faca.htm

——. 2000b. "Title VI Implementation Advisory Committee." [Accessed April 10, 2000.] http://www.epa.gov/ocem/nacept/titleVI/titlemem.html

——. 2000c. 1996 Toxic Release Inventory. [Accessed June 12, 2000.] www.epa.gov/envirofactrs

——. n.d. "Record of Decision (ROD) Abstracts: Agriculture Street Landfill." [Accessed July 27, 1999. EPA Record of Decision.] www.epa.gov/oerrpage/superfund/sites/rodsites/ 0600646.htm

Epstein, Barbara. 1995. "Grassroots Environmentalism and Strategies for Social Change." *New Political Science* 32: 1–24.

Erikson, Kai. 1995. *A New Species of Trouble: The Human Experience of Modern Disasters.* New York: Norton.

Fagin, Dan. 1996. *Toxic Deception: How the Chemical Industry Manipulates Science, Bends the Law, and Endangers Your Health.* Secaucus, NJ: Carol Pub. Group.

Fairclough, Adam. 1995. *Race and Democracy, The Civil Rights Struggle in Louisiana, 1915–1972.* Athens: University of Georgia Press.

Fairley, Peter. 1999. "Tables Turn on Louisiana's Supreme Court." *Chemical Week.* May 19.

Feeney, Susan. 1987. "Plan to Save Wetlands Proposed." *New Orleans Times-Picayune/States-Item.* March 4.

Ferstel, Vicki. 1997a. "EPA Reopens Shintech Permit Hearing." *New Orleans Times-Picayune.* September 11.

——. 1997b. "Shintech Inc. Offered Help on Jobs, Businesses." *Baton Rouge Advocate.* December 16.

——. 1997c. "Shintech Becomes Test Case EPA Trying to Apply New, Vague Order." *Baton Rouge Advocate.* September 12.

——. 1998a. "Tests reveal abnormal levels of lead in Grand Bois residents." *Baton Rouge Advocate.* December 22.

——. 1998b. "Court Ruling Alters Site Evaluation Methods." *Baton Rouge Advocate.* June 21.

——. 1999. "State DEQ Still Under Federal Investigation." *Baton Rouge Advocate.* January 16.

Ferstel, Vicki, and Marsha Shuler. 1998. "Grand Bois Blood Report Spurs Foster to Order Tests." *Baton Rouge Advocate*. April 18.

Fleming, Raymond, Andrew Baum, Martha M. Gisriel, and Robert J. Gatchel. 1982. "Mediating Influences of Social Support on Stress at Three Mile Island." *Journal of Human Stress* 8: 14–22.

Flynn, J., P. Slovic, and C. K. Mertz. 1994. "Gender, Race, and Perception of Environmental Health Risks." *Risk Analysis* 14 (6): 1101–8.

Folkman, Susan, and Richard S. Lazarus. 1980. "An Analysis of Coping in a Middle-Aged Community Sample." *Journal of Health and Social Behavior* 21: 219–39.

Foreman, Christopher H., Jr. 1998. *The Promise and Peril of Environmental Justice*. Washington, DC: Brookings Institute Press.

Foster, Mike. 1997. Interview by Louisiana Public Broadcasting. June.

Fox, Steve. 1991. *Toxic Work: Women Workers at GTE Lenkurt*. Philadelphia: Temple University Press.

Frazier, Lisa. 1988. "Parish, Marchers, Reach Agreement." *New Orleans Times-Picayune*. November 10.

Freudenberg, William R. 1993. "Risk and Recreancy: Weber, the Division of Labor, and the Rationality of Risk Perception." *Social Forces* 71: 909–32.

Freudenberg, Nicholas, and Carol Steinsapir. 1992. "Not in Our Backyards: The Grassroots Environmental Movement," pp. 27–38. In *American Environmentalism: The U.S. Environmental Movement 1970–1990*. Riley E. Dunlap and Angela G. Mertig, eds. Philadelphia: Taylor & Francis.

Fried, John J. 1993. "Pollution as Racial Insult." *Philadelphia Inquirer*. June 27.

The Gambit Weekly. 1986. "Gordon Plaza." February 22.

——— 1998a. "Local Pearl Harbor." Editorial. June 30.

——— 1998b. "Change the Law." Editorial. September 1.

——— 1999. "Press-ed to Action." Editorial. February 9.

——— n.d. "Clean Up This Mess." Editorial.

Gill, James. 1998. "High Court Reins in Lower Class." *New Orleans Times-Picayune*. June 21.

Giordano, Maria. 1997a. "Shintech Assesses Loss of Permit." *New Orleans Times-Picayune*. September 12.

——— 1997b. "DEQ Clears Way for PVC Plant." *New Orleans Times-Picayune*. May 28.

Giordano, Maria, and Bob Warren. 1997. "EPA Rejects Permit for Shintech Plant." *New Orleans Times-Picayune*. September 11.

Goode, Ann E. 1998a. Director, EPA Office of Civil Rights. Letter to Father Phil Schmitter, Co-Director, Sister Joanne Chiaverini, Co-Director, St. Francis Prayer Center; and Russell Harding, Director, Michigan Department of Environmental Quality. October 30, 1998. http://www.epa.gov/region5/steel-cvr.htm

——— 1998b. "Testimony of Ann E. Goode, Director, Office of Civil Rights, U.S. Environmental Protection Agency, Before the Subcommittee on Oversight and Investigations, of the Committee on Commerce, U.S. House of Representatives." August 6.

Gould, Kenneth, Allen Schnaiberg, and Adam Weinberg. 1996. *Local Environmental Struggles*. New York: Cambridge University Press.

Gray, Chris. 1997a. "Law Clinic Under Fire." *New Orleans Times-Picayune*. August 3.

1997b. "Town Claims Toxic Victory: CBS Set to Air Oil Waste Expose." *New Orleans Times-Picayune*. December 22.

1998a. "Shintech foes live closest to the site, poll says." *New Orleans Times-Picayune*. January 18.

1998b. "Louisiana uranium project is scrapped." *New Orleans Times-Picayune*. April 23.

Gray, Leonard. 1998. "Shintech Leaving St. James, Heading to Plaquemine." *L'Observateur*. September 21.

Greer, Jed, and Kenny Bruno. 1996. *Greenwash: The Reality Behind Corporate Environmentalism*. Penang, Malaysia: Third World Network.

Grissett-Welsh, Sheila. 1985. "Under Houses." *New Orleans Times-Picayune/States-Item*. September 19.

Gyan, Joe. 1998. "Group Demonstrates in Front of LA Supreme Court Against Law Clinic Restrictions." *Baton Rouge Advocate*. June 27.

1999. "Judge Tosses Challenges to Law Clinic Restrictions." *Baton Rouge Advocate*. July 28.

Habermas, Jürgen. 1990. *Towards a Rational Society: Student Protest, Science, and Politics*. Boston: Beacon Press.

Hanson, Susan. 1998. "Backlash on the Bayou." *American Lawyer*. Jan/Feb: 50.

Harris & Associates and Southern Media & Opinion Research, Inc. 1989. "A Public Opinion Survey Concerning Greenpeace Activities in the State of Louisiana." February. Baton Rouge.

Harris DeVille & Associates, Inc. 1998. "NAACP Environmental Justice Summit." Memo. Southern University, Baton Rouge, Louisiana. June 18.

"Health Consultation: Review of Health Outcome Data for the Agriculture Street Landfill Site, New Orleans, Louisiana, Cerclis No. LAD981056997. 10–22–97." October 22, 1997.

Hechinger, John. 1991. "Duke Power Customers Start Paying 4% Rate Hike after 9.2% Increase Denied." *Charlotte Observer*. November 13.

Heyen, Curtis D. 1991. "Churches Reject Gift from 'Enemy.'" *Shreveport Times*. April 12.

1994a. "Earthquakes Jar Some to Attention." *Shreveport Times*. April.

1994b. "NAACP Voices Opposition to Plant: Chapter's President Had Approved Plan for Uranium Plant in Claiborne Parish." *Shreveport Times*. May 11.

1994c. "Homer Dodges Uranium." *Shreveport Times*. June 8.

1995. "Opponents Cry 'Take it!' As Some Welcome Uranium Plant." *Shreveport Times*.

1998. "Firm kills plans for uranium facility." *Shreveport Times*. April 23.

Hirsh, Arnold. R. 1992. *Creole New Orleans: Race and Americanization*. Baton Rouge: Louisiana State University Press.

Hirschorn, Joel S. 1999. "Two Superfund Environmental Justice Case Studies." [Accessed July 11, 1999.] www.igc.org/envjustice/hirschorn.html

Homer Guardian-Journal. 1991. "Citizens Against Nuclear Trash – Fact Sheet." July 18.

1992. "LES President Addresses Homer Lions." April 2.

1993a. "LES issues coloring book." April 1.

1993b. "CANT Schedules Meeting, Dinner"; "CANT to Host Environmental Group." September 23.

1993c. "LES Sends Letter to Parish Residents." December 23.

1994b. "Environmental Study on Uranium Plant Discusses Earthquakes . . . Chemicals." January 27.

1994c. "CEC's Impact Statement Includes Information on Jobs, Decommissioning." February 3.

1994d. "NRC Officials Meet With CANT Members; Tour Proposed Plant Site." June 16.

Hunter, David. 2000a. "CMA Becomes American Chemistry Council [Editorial]." *Chemical Week,* June 14, p. 3.

2000b. "Negative and Positive [Editorial]." *Chemical Week,* June 14, p. 3.

Johnston, J. Bennett. 1985. Letter to the Editor. *Homer Guardian-Journal.*

Jones, Gladstone N., III. 1998. "Lessons for the Plaintiff: Clarice Friloux, et al. vs. Campbell Wells Corporation and Exxon Corp.: The Grand Bois Litigation." Conference Presentation, LSBA (Louisiana State Bar Association) Environmental Law Section, Annual Seminar. November 20. New Orleans, LA.

Juneau, Dan. 1998. "Government by Oxymoron." Louisiana Association of Business and Industry. [Posted June 22, 1998.] http://www.labi.org/default.html

Karasek, Robert A., and T. Theorell. 1990. *Healthy Work: Stress, Productivity, and the Reconstruction of Working Life.* New York: Basic Books.

Karl, Terry Lynn. 1997. *The Paradox of Plenty: Oil Booms and Petro-States.* Berkeley: University of California Press.

Kemp, Robin. 1989. "The Brief and Strange History of Revilletown, Louisiana." *The Gambit Weekly* (New Orleans). November 8.

Koeppel, Barbara. 1999. "Cancer's Playground." *The Gambit Weekly* (New Orleans). November 16.

Kramer, John. 1998. "LA Supreme Court Rule XX – The Ethical Rights and Limitations Upon Student Practice before LA State Courts and Agencies." Louisiana State Bar Association Annual Seminar. November 20.

Kriz, Margaret. 1998. "The Color of Poison." *National Journal.* September 11.

Kuehn, Robert. 1996. "The Environmental Justice Implications of Quantitative Risk Assessment." *University of Illinois Law Review.*

Kucharski, William A. 1994. "Final Report of the Louisiana Legislature on Environmental Justice, Louisiana Department of Environmental Quality." August 24. Mimeograph.

Labor Neighbor. 1996. "LDEQ Public Hearing on Shintech Permit Summary." December.

Laborde, Errol. 1988. "Dying for a Drink of Water." *The Gambit Weekly* (New Orleans). November 8.

Lavelle, Marianne, and Marcia Coyle. 1992. "A Special Investigation, Unequal Protection, the Racial Divide in Environmental Law." *National Law Journal.* September 21, p. 51.

Lazarus, Richard S., and Susan Folkman. 1984. *Stress, Appraisal, and Coping.* New York: Spring Publishing Company.

Leonard, Richard, and Zack Nauth. 1993. "Beating BASF: OCAW Busts Union-Buster." *Labor Research Review* 16: 35–49.

Lippman, Thomas. 1990. "Uranium Plant Poses Test for Industry, Senator." *Washington Post*. March 5, p. A4.

Logan, John T., and Harvey Molotch. 1987. *Urban Fortunes: The Political Economy of Place.* Los Angeles: The University of Calfornia Press.

Louisiana Advisory Committee to the U.S. Commission on Civil Rights. 1993. "The Battle for Environmental Justice in Louisiana. . . . Government, Industry, and the People." U.S. Commission on Civil Rights.

Louisiana Association for Business and Industry (LABI). 1998. "1998 Regular Session of the Louisiana Legislature." [Posted June 15, 1998.] www.labi.org

Louisiana Coalition for Tax Justice. 1995. "People's Report on the 10 Year Industrial Property Tax Exemption Program: A System of Checks and No Balances." Mimeograph.

Louisiana Department of Economic Development (LDED). 1999. "Louisiana Business Incentives, The Facts." Baton Rouge: LA DED, Office of Commerce and Industry – Business Incentives.

——— 2000. "Top Ten Reasons to Locate in Louisiana." [Accessed April 23, 2000.] www.lded.state.la.us/new/topten.htm

Louisiana Department of Economic Development (LDED), Office of Commerce and Industry, Business Incentives Division. 1999. "Enterprise Zone Program: The Facts." February 3. Mimeograph.

——— n.d. "Louisiana Overview." [Accessed June 9, 2000.] www.leded.state.la.us

Louisiana Department of Environmental Quality, Division of Policy Analysis and Planning. 1991. "Key Issues Recommended for Inclusion in the EIS for the Proposed Uranium Enrichment Facility of Louisiana Energy Services, Claiborne Parish." Submitted to Nuclear Regulatory Commission August 14.

Louisiana Department of Environmental Quality (LDEQ). 1994. Untitled document. Mimeograph.

——— 2000. *Toxics Release Inventory 1998,* 10th ed. Baton Rouge: LDEQ.

Louisiana Department of Natural Resources (DNR), Office of Conservation. 1999a. "Declaration of Emergency, Amendment to Statewide Order No. 29-B (Emergency Rule)." May 29. [Accessed July 20, 1999.] http://www.dnr.state.la.us/SEC/EXECDIV/PUBINFO/NEWSR/emer_rule5.pdf

——— 1999b. "Permitted Commercial Facilities, as of September 17, 1997." Accessed July 20, 1999.] http://www.dnr.state.la.us/cons/conserin/commfac.pdf

Louisiana Energy Services (LES). 1998. "Louisiana Energy Applauds NRC Reversal of Licensing Board's Decision on Environmental Justice." Press release. April.

Louisiana Environmental Action Network (LEAN). 1996. *LEAN News.* Spring/Summer.

——— 1998. "Study Finds DEQ Enforcement at Historic Low, State Fails to Penalize Violators, Foster's DEQ Worse than Edwards." Press release. June 12.

Louisiana Environmental Action Network, Sierra Club Delta Chapter. 1997. *Louisiana Legislature Environment and Health Report Card.* Pamphlet.

Low, Patrick, and Alexander Yeats. 1993. "Do 'Dirty' Industries Migrate?," pp. 89–104. In *International Trade and the Environment.* Patrick Low, ed. World Bank Discussion Papers. Washington, D.C.: International Bank for Reconstruction and Development.

Lussier, Charles. 2000a. "State Habitually Tolerates Pollution for Years." *Houma Courier.* February 25.

——— 2000b. "Lacking its own spin." *Houma Courier.* February 24.

——— 2000c. "DEQ fines far from ironclad, study shows." *Houma Courier.* February 22.

——— 2000d. "Critics assail agency charged with protecting Louisiana's environment." *Thibodaux Daily Comet.* February 22.

——— 2000e. "Replacing Fines with Projects." *Thibodaux Daily Comet.* February 23.

——— 2000f. "DEQ works to break down barriers." *Thibodaux Daily Comet.* February 24, 2000.

Macionis, John. 1999. *Sociology,* 6th ed. Upper Saddle River, NJ: Prentice-Hall.

Mardis, Roy. n.d. "CANT Defeats Uranium Enrichment Plant." Clark Atlantic University Environmental Justice Resource Center web site. [Accessed June 18, 2000.] http://www.ejrc.cau.edu

Mariotte, Michael. 1990. "Uranium Enrichment Plant Battle is First of Second Nuclear Generation." *Groundswell.* Nuclear Information and Resource Service. Undated newsletter.

——— 1998. "Earth Day Victory! Louisiana Energy Services Drops Bid for License to Build Uranium Enrichment Plant." [Accessed May 11, 1999.] http://www.nirs.org/mononline/ LESEarthDayVictory.htm

McKendall, Rhonda. 1985a. "N.O. elementary school to be built on dump site." *New Orleans Times-Picayune/States-Item.* April 10.

McKendall, Rhonda. 1985b. "Desire Residents want Moton school despite dump site." *New Orleans Times-Picayune/States-Item.* February 2.

McKinney, Joan. 1998a. "Shintech Solution Problem." *Baton Rouge Advocate.* July 26.

——— 1998b. "Jefferson Joins Fight Opposing Shintech." *Baton Rouge Advocate.* September 17.

McMahon, Bill. 1997a. "President says NAACP Mulling Shintech Issue." *Baton Rouge Advocate.* August 13.

——— 1997b. "Panel Trying to Weight Industry Benefit, Risks." *Baton Rouge Advocate.* September 26.

——— 1997c. "DNR Chief Offers Oil-Well Waste Regulations." *Baton Rouge Advocate.* November 5.

McMillan, John. 1997a. "Grand Bois Catalyst for Change in Environmental Regulations." *Baton Rouge Advocate.* November 2.

——— 1997b. "Records: Exxon Told to Clean Up Act, Then Used La. As Dump Site for Waste." *Baton Rouge Advocate.* November 3.

——— 1997c. "Complaints, Publicity Led to Test Order." *Baton Rouge Advocate.* November 4.

——— 1997d. "Toxicologist Grilled About Study Results." *Baton Rouge Advocate.* November 5.

1998a. "Grand Bois Blood Study Starts – Officials Using Grant to Monitor Chemicals." *Baton Rouge Advocate.* March 19.

1998b. "EPA Heeds Request on Grand Bois." *Baton Rouge Advocate.* April 29.

1998c. "No Jurors Picked in Grand Bois Suit." *Baton Rouge Advocate.* July 15.

1998d. "Grand Bois Ruling Angers Attorney." *Baton Rouge Advocate.* July 29.

1998e. "Judge Halts Grand Bois Testimony." *Baton Rouge Advocate.* July 30, p. A1.

McMillan, John, and Mike Dunne. 1998a. "Grand Bois Plaintiffs Shocked Jury Didn't See Harm." *Baton Rouge Advocate Online.* August 10.

1998b. "Exxon Cleared of Most Claims." *Baton Rouge Advocate Online.* August 10.

McQuaid, John. 2000a. "EPA Caught in Crossfire over Civil Rights." *New Orleans Times-Picayune.* May 22.

2000b. "Uneasy Proximity." *New Orleans Times-Picayune.* May 23.

2000c. "Transforming the Land." *New Orleans Times-Picayune.* May 21.

2000d. "From Swamp to Cane to Chemicals." *New Orleans Times-Picayune.* May 21.

2000e. "Racial Statistics Open Doors, Cloud Issues." *New Orleans Times-Picayune.* May 21.

2000f. "Calling in Help Risks 'Outsider' Label." *New Orleans Times-Picayune.* May 22.

2000g. "A Health Risk." *New Orleans Times-Picayune.* May 23.

McTopy, John. 1998. National Association of Counties. "Title VI Guidance Letter to EPA." [Accessed April 23, 2000.] ww.sso.org/ecos/projects/EJ/justice.htm

Miculek, Lisa W. 1996. "Minutes from St. James Parish Coastal Zone Management Committee Public Hearing." November 13.

Mielke, Howard W. 1999a. "Lead in the Inner Cities." *American Scientist* 87 (1). Available at http://www.amsci.org/amsci/articles/99articles/Mielke.html

1999b. *The Urban Environment and Children's Health: Soils as an Integrator of Lead, Zinc, and Cadmium in New Orleans, Louisiana, U.S.A.* San Diego: Academic Press.

Miller, Branda. 1997. "Witness to the Future" (Video and web production). [Accessed July 9, 1999.] http://www.witnesstothefuture.com/meet/cancer.html

Minden Press-Herald. 1992. "CANT Coalition Moves LES Fight to New Ground." July 10.

1998. "North Louisiana Loses Big." Published in *The Claiborne Parish Advertiser.* May 4.

Mitchell, Marilyn. 1991a. "Proposed Plant Produces Concern." *Shreveport Times.* July 28.

1991b. "Plan to Build Plant Challenged." *Shreveport Times.* July 28.

Molotch, Harvey. 1976. "The City As a Growth Machine: Toward a Political Economy of Place." *American Journal of Sociology.* 82 (2): 309–33.

Montague, Peter. 1997. "The Right to Know Nothing." *Rachel's Environment and Health Weekly* #552. June 26.

1998."Landfills are Dangerous." *Rachel's Environment and Health Weekly* #617. September 24.

Morris, Jim. 1997a. "New alarm over hydrogen sulfide: Researchers document lasting damage to human nervous system." *Houston Chronicle*. November 12.

1997b. "Lost Opportunity: EPA Had Its Chance to Regulate Hydrogen Sulfide." *Houston Chronicle*. December 14.

1997c. "The Brimstone Battles." *Houston Chronicle*. December 14.

Myers, Doug. 1998. "EPA Says DEQ Action to Resolve Problems." *Baton Rouge Advocate*. August 4.

Najem, G. Reza, Terry Strunck, and Martin Fuererman. 1994. "Health Effects of a Superfund Hazardous Chemical Waste Disposal Site." *American Journal of Preventative Medicine*. 10 (3): 151–5.

National Black Chamber of Commerce (NBCC). 2000. "Environmental Justice: Another Major Distraction." [Accessed April 10, 2000.] http://www.nationalbcc.org/issues/environm.htm

New Orleans Times-Picayune. 1982a. "Environmental Help Offered in Office Created by Guste." January 21.

1982b."Still Guste vs. Simoneaux." November 27.

1986. "Wetlands Still Washing Away." September 21.

2000. "The Life and Times of Edwin W. Edwards." May 10, p. A8.

News-Star. 1994. "Agencies Do Battle Over Plant." February 5.

Nuclear Information and Resource Service (NIRS). 1991a. *Nuclear Monitor* 6 (20), June 17.

1991b. *Nuclear Monitor* 6 (2), September 23.

O'Connor, James. 1973. *Fiscal Crisis of the State*. New York: St. Martin's Press.

Orr, Marylee. 1997. "Louisiana Citizens Declare Partial Victory in PVC Plastics Fight." Louisiana Environmental Action Network. Press release. July 15.

Payne, Henry. 1997. "Environmental Justice Kills Jobs for the Poor." *Wall Street Journal*. September 16.

Pearlin, Leonard I., and Carmi Schooler. 1978. "The Structure of Coping." *Journal of Health and Social Behavior*. 19:2–21.

People of Color Environmental Leadership Summit. 1991. "Principle of Environmental Justice." October. Washington, D.C.

Pitts, Stella. 1989. "Persistence Won the War for Waste Plant Opponents." *New Orleans Times-Picayune*. July 9.

Pope, John. 1988. "Police Escort Toxics March then Arrest 8." *New Orleans Times-Picayune*. November 20.

Porteous, William A., III. 1998. "Defendants' Perspective, Counsel for Landowners in the Grand Bois Case." LSBA Environmental Law Section Annual Seminar. November 20.

Raber, Rick. 1986. "Louisiana coastal areas may benefit from bill to protect wetlands." *New Orleans Times-Picayune/States-Item*. August 13.

1990. "Johnston trying to wash egg off radioactive plate." *New Orleans Times-Picayune*.

Reath, Viki. 1993. "NAACP Throws Support Behind Enrichment Plant Opponents." *Environment Week* 6 (49).

Redman, Carl. 1998a. "EPA Needs Sensible Policies on Complaints, House Urges." *Baton Rouge Advocate*. June 5.

1998b. "DNR Stops On-Site Oilfield Waste Tests." *Baton Rouge Advocate.* October 8.

Reed, Susan. 1991. "His family ravaged by cancer, an angry Louisiana man wages war on the very air that he breathes." *People.* March 25, pp. 42–8.

Reible, Danny D., and K. T. Valsaraj. 1999. "TCLP Characterization of exploration and production wastes in Louisiana." Final Report to Louisiana Department of Natural Resources." [March 29, 1999; revised April 7, 1999. Accessed July 20, 1999.]
http://www.dnr.state.la.us/cons/CONSERIN /Wastrule/lsufinalreport.pdf

Ridenhour, Ron. 1986. "Time Bomb? The Saga of Gordon Plaza." *The Gambit Weekly* (New Orleans). February 22.

Roberts, J. Timmons. 1993. "Psychosocial Effects of Workplace Hazardous Exposures: Theoretical Synthesis and Preliminary Findings." *Social Problems* 40: 74–89.

——— 1998. "Negotiating Both Sides of the Plant Gate: Gender, Hazardous Facility Workers and Community Responses to Technological Hazards." *Current Sociology* 45 (3): 157–77.

Roberts, J. Timmons, and John E. Baugher. 1995. "Perceived Work Hazards and Job Strain in Eleven Nations." *International Journal of Contemporary Sociology* 32 (2): 235–49.

Roberts, J. Timmons, and Nikki Thanos. 2000. "We Need to Understand the New Louisiana to Help It Grow." *Delta Sierran* (New Orleans). May/June.

Roberts, Robert E. 1998. "Statement Before the Committee on Commerce, Subcommitee on oversight and Investigations, United States House of Representatives on EPA's Title VI Interim Guidance and Alternative State Approaches." August 6.

Roberts, Robert E., Molly Conrecode, and Carol Leftwich. 1998. "Environmental Justice and EPA's Title VI Guidance: What Must Be Done." [Accessed April 25, 2000.] http://www.sso.org/ecos/publications/oldECOStates.htm

Robichaux, Michael R. n.d. Letter to the editor. *New Orleans Times-Picayune.*

Rolwing, Rebecca. 1997. "Jury Awards $3.4 billion to victims of train fire." AP wire. September 9.

Rose, Al. 1974. Storyville, New Orleans. University, AL: U. Alabama Press.

Scallan, Matt. 1992. "St. John Looks to the Future Formosa Pullout Shows It's Hard to Attract Heavy Industry." *New Orleans Times-Picayune.* November 3.

Schaefer, Judith Kelleher. 1994. *Slavery, the Civil Law, and the Supreme Court of Louisiana.* Baton Rouge: Louisiana State University Press.

Schleifstein, Mark. 1998a. "Foster, Clinics, Face Off on Rules." *New Orleans Times-Picayune.* August 2.

——— 1998b. "Congressman: EPA Reneging in Shintech Case." *New Orleans Times-Picayune.* August 28.

——— 1998c. "Shintech Opponents Win Round, Judge Supports Hearing on Claims of Bias by State Officials." *New Orleans Times-Picayune.* September 1.

——— 1998d. "EPA Spurns Pleas for Home Buyout." *New Orleans Times-Picayune.* September 8.

——— 1998e. "Felon offered to buy landfill homes." *New Orleans Times-Picayune.* November 9.

1999a. "Professors protest law clinic rules." *New Orleans Times-Picayune*. January 8.

1999b. "Water Main Renews Toxic Fears." *New Orleans Times-Picayune*. January 30.

1999c. "EPA Vows to Begin Landfill Cleanup." *New Orleans Times-Picayune*. February 26.

1999d. "Groups file suit to challenge limits on law clinics." April 17.

1999e. "Ag [sic] Street Residents Livid over EPA Ruling." *New Orleans Times-Picayune*. July 10, p. A1.

Schwab, Jim. 1994. *Deeper Shades of Green: The Rise of Blue-Collar and Minority Environmentalism*. San Francisco: Sierra Club.

Schwan, J. V. 2000. "The Trial Lawyer Class Action Scam." Citizens for a Better Economy web site. [Accessed May 15, 2000.] http://www.cse.org/informed/670.html

Schweizer, Errol. 1999. "Interview with Robert Bullard." *Earth First Journal*. July 6. [E-mail version.]

Shinkle, Peter. 1997. "Race Factor in Denial of Uranium Plant." *Baton Rouge Advocate*. May 13.

Shinkle, Peter. 1998a. "Uranium Plant Plan Dropped." *Baton Rouge Advocate*. April 23.

Shinkle, Peter. 1998b. "92 Deal Helps Uranium Plant." *Baton Rouge Advocate*. May 4.

Shuler, Marsha. 1997. "LA Economic Development Council Made Promise to Johnson." *New Orleans Times-Picayune*. September 14.

Sissell, Kara. 1999. "Equity Programs Strain State Resources." *Chemical Week*. July 28, p. 36.

Snyder, David. 1995. "Grand Bois: Small Town Refuses to Hold Nose Any More." *New Orleans Times-Picayune*. November 23.

n.d. "Whistleblower Takes on Lafourche." *New Orleans Times-Picayune*.

Southern Media & Opinion Research, Inc. 1997. Public opinion survey. St. James Parish Louisiana. Executive summary (report).

St. James Parish News Examiner. 1973. "Parish Industrial Growth in Top Ten." August 4.

Stauber, John C. 1995. *Toxic Sludge Is Good For You: Lies, Damn Lies, and the Public Relations Industry*. Monroe, ME: Common Courage Press.

Steinberg, Mary Ann. 1996. *Past and Present on Louisiana Historic Byway*. Baton Rouge: Louisiana State University Press.

Stone, Clarence. 1989. "Urban Regimes and the Capacity to Govern. A Political Economy Approach." *Journal of Urban Affairs*. 13 (3): 289–97.

Sullivan, Eunice Q. 1999. Presentation in the session "Environmental Justice in the Wake of Shintech." Tulane Environmental Law Conference, February 27. New Orleans, Louisiana.

Szasz, Andrew. 1993. *Ecopopulism: Toxic Waste and the Movement for Environmental Justice*. Minneapolis: University of Minnesota Press.

Tallie, Tim. 1986. "Group Examines Record on IT Application: Environmentalists Still Fight Proposed Waste Treatment Plant." *Baton Rouge Advocate*. April 10.

Taylor, Shelley E., Rena L. Repetti, and Teresa Seeman. 1997. "Health Psychology: What Is an Unhealthy Environment and How Does It Get Under the Skin?" *Annual Review of Psychology* 48: 411–47.

Thanos, Nikki Demetria. 2000. "Economic Development, Corporate Accountability and the Environment: Comparative Case Studies from Costa Rica and Louisiana." Tulane University Honors Thesis.

Thibodaux Daily Comet. 1999. "Residents Disgruntled." Editorial. June 8.

Tompkins, Norton. 1992. Letter to the Editor. *Homer Guardian-Journal.* April 9.

Tulane Environmental Law Clinic (TELC). 1998. Application for Supervisory Writs of Review and Relief from the LA DEQ and Request for Expedited Consideration and Stay of Proceedings, SJCJE, LEAN, SCLC – Applicants. April 13.

Tulane University School of Public Health and Tropical Medicine. 1989. "St. Gabriel Miscarriage Investigation East Bank of Iberville Parish, Louisiana." Report. September 27.

Unger, Donald G., Abraham Wandersman, and William Hallman. 1992. "Living Near a Hazardous Waste Facility: Coping with Individual and Family Distress." *American Journal of Orthopsychiatry* 62 (1): 55–7.

U.S. Bureau of the Census. 1999. "How the Census Bureau Measures Poverty." Created October 15, 1999. [Accessed December 12, 1999.] http://www.census.gov/hhes/poverty/povdef.html

U.S. Chamber of Commerce. 1998a. "U.S. Chamber Urges President to Withdraw EPA Environmental Justice Policy." Press release. May 5.

U.S. Chamber of Commerce. 1998b. "VA-HUD Appropriations Bill: Key U.S. Chamber-Backed Environmental Riders Block Kyoto Climate Treaty and 'Environmental Justice.'" Press release. October 5.

U.S. Conference of Mayors. 1998. "Resolution No. 32 *U.S. EPA's Interim Guidance for Investigating Title VI Administrative Complaints.*" [Accessed April 23, 2000.] http://www.sso.org/ecos/projects/EJ/justice.htm

Von Bodungen, Gustave. 1998. "Enclosure B Comments by the Louisiana Department of Environmental Quality." Draft Revised Demographic Information prepared by the Office of Civil Rights, EPA. May 26. Mimeograph.

Wardlaw, Jack. 1997. "Foster: Shintech, Loan Not Tied." *New Orleans Times-Picayune.* September 16.

——— 1998. "Alexander Knocks Court Law Clinic Curb." *New Orleans Times-Picayune.* July 3.

Warner, Coleman. 1999a. "Planners to unveil land-use proposal for N.O." *New Orleans Times-Picayune.* March 2.

——— 1999. "Iberville work stops for archaeological survey." *New Orleans Times-Picayune.* June 10.

Warner, Coleman, and Christopher Cooper. 1995a. "In past, dump's neighbors plagued by stench, smoke." *New Orleans Times-Picayune.* April 23.

——— 1995b. "Scientists Dispute Dangers of Pollution." *New Orleans Times-Picayune.* April 23.

Warren, Bob. 1992. "Giant Rayon Plant in St. John is Cancelled, Permit Troubles, Lawsuits Blamed." *New Orleans Times-Picayune.* October 8.

Warren, Bob, and Drew Broach. 1992. "Little Guy Won Formosa Battle, Foes Say." *New Orleans Times-Picayune.* October 9.

West, Emelda. n.d. "Ms. West's Story: Economic Development and Prosperity for Whom?" Preamble Center volume.

Wilds, John, Charles L. Dufour, and Walter G. Cowan. 1996. *Louisiana Yesterday and Today: A Historical Guide to the State.* Baton Rouge: Louisiana State University Press.

Wigley, Daniel C., and Kristin Shrader-Frechette. 1996. "Environmental Justice: A Louisiana Case Study." *Journal of Agricultural and Environmental Ethics* 9 (1): 61–82.

Witness to the Future CD and web site. [Accessed July 9, 1999.] http://www.witnesstothefuture.com/meet/cancer/amos.html

Wright, Beverly. 1997. "New Orleans Neighborhoods Under Siege." In *Just Transportation: Dismantling Race and Class Barriers to Mobility.* Robert Bullard and Glenn S. Johnson, eds. Gabriola Island, B.C., Canada: New Society Publishers.

——— 1999. Comments at the Tulane Environmental Law Conference, February.

Wright, Beverly H., Pat Bryant, and Robert D. Bullard. 1994. "Coping with Poisons in Cancer Alley." In *Unequal Protection: Environmental Justice and Communities of Color.* Robert D. Bullard, ed. San Francisco: Sierra Club.

Zganjar, Leslie. 1998a. "Foster: Grand Bois Residents Not Cooperating." *New Orleans Times-Picayune.* May 16.

——— 1998b. "Louisiana Again Seeks Help in Grand Bois." *Baton Rouge Advocate.* May 31.

——— 1998c. "Exxon Knew Waste Was Potentially Hazardous, Engineer Testifies." *New Orleans Times-Picayune.* July 21.

——— 1998d. "Most Receive Nothing from Dump; Grand Bois Suits Aren't Over Yet." *New Orleans Times-Picayune.* August 10.

——— 1998e. "Health Hazards to Be Assessed; Officials Probe Grand Bois Risks." *New Orleans Times-Picayune.* August 11.

——— 1998f. "Grand Bois Shows Need for Change; Oil Field Waste Is Presumed Safe by Law, but Not by Science." *New Orleans Times-Picayune.* August 22.

Index